INTRODUCTION
TO
THE LITURGY

INTRODUCTION TO THE LITURGY

By

I. H. Dalmais, O.P.

Translated by Roger Capel

With a Preface by Frederick R. McManus

1961

HELICON PRESS

BALTIMORE, MARYLAND

TABLE OF CONTENTS

PREFACE BY FREDERICK R. McMANUS J.C.D. . . . ix

CHAPTER ONE—LITURGICAL REALITY   1

LITURGY AND COMMUNITY 3
LITURGY AND HUMAN ACTIONS 5
THE FOREST OF SYMBOLS 8
LITURGY AND THE SACRED 12
LITURGY AND TRANSCENDENCE 17
LITURGICAL ACTION : CELEBRATION AND FEAST . . 21

PART ONE
THE THEOLOGY OF THE LITURGY

CHAPTER TWO—THE CHRISTIAN LITURGICAL
ASSEMBLY: THE CHURCH   27

THE PARABLES OF THE CHURCH 28
THE LITURGICAL ASSEMBLY, EXPRESSION OF THE
    MYSTERY OF THE CHURCH 34

CHAPTER THREE—
THE LITURGY, 'ACTION' OF THE CHURCH   38

THE ACTION CONSTITUTING THE CHURCH . . . 41
THE ACTION EXPRESSING THE CHURCH 44
THE COMMUNAL NATURE OF THE CHRISTIAN LITURGY . 46
THE ONE LITURGY OF EARTH AND HEAVEN . . . 49
AN HIERARCHICAL ACTION 50

CHAPTER FOUR—
THE LITURGY: MYSTERY OF WORSHIP   56

THE TERM 'MYSTERY' 60
MYSTERY AND SACRAMENT 64

MYSTERY AND TIME IN THE CHURCH 69
THE PASCHAL MYSTERY 74
THE DIMENSIONS OF THE MYSTERY 83
    The Sacramental Order 83
    The liturgy of the saints and the 'mystery' . . 87
    The liturgy of the season 91

PART TWO

THE FORM OF THE LITURGY

INTRODUCTION 99

CHAPTER FIVE—THE CONSTITUENT ELEMENTS
          OF THE LITURGY . . . 101

HOLY SCRIPTURE 101
PSALMODY AND HYMNS 105
LITURGICAL PRAYER 110
RITES 114
THE LITURGY AND THINGS 119
    Water, Ashes and Dust 120
    Bread, Wine and Oil 121
    Lights and Incense 122
    Buildings and Images 123

CHAPTER SIX—THE PRINCIPAL KINDS OF
          LITURGICAL CELEBRATION . . 125

THE SACRAMENTAL LITURGY 125
    Baptism 126
    Confirmation 128
    The Sacrament of Penance and Penitential
      Ceremonies 129
    The Liturgy of the Sick and the Dead . . . 131
    The Rites of Marriage and of Religious Consecration 133
    The Liturgy of Order 135
    Rites of Consecration and Blessing of
      Persons and Things 137
THE EUCHARISTIC LITURGY 138
THE DIVINE OFFICE 143

CHAPTER SEVEN—LITURGY AND HISTORY:
THE DEVELOPMENT OF WESTERN LITURGY 148

THE PERIOD OF ORIGINS 149
THE GOLDEN AGE OF ROMAN LITURGY 153
THE ACCEPTANCE BY ROME OF FRANCO-GERMANIC
    PRACTICES (950-1200) 158
THE LITURGICAL REFORM OF THE ROMAN CURIA AND
    LOCAL PECULIARITIES (1260-1564) . . . 162
FROM THE VICTORY OF RUBRICISM TO THE LITURGICAL
    REVIVAL (1563-1903) 167
STAGES OF THE LITURGICAL REVIVAL 171

CHAPTER EIGHT—
LITURGY AND HUMAN SOCIETIES:
THE VARIOUS LITURGICAL FAMILIES 174

THE WESTERN RITES 175
    The Liturgy of Visigothic Spain 176
    The Ambrosian Liturgy of Milan 177
    The Gallican Liturgies 178
    The Romano-Frankish Liturgies 178
THE SYRO-ARAMEAN LITURGIES 179
    The Edessene liturgy 180
    The liturgy of the Patriarchate of Antioch . . 184
THE LITURGY OF THE BYZANTINE WORLD . . . 188
THE ARMENIAN RITE 193
THE EGYPTIAN LITURGY: COPTIC AND ETHIOPIAN
    RITES 194

It is a great mystery
we worship.
Revelation made in human nature,
justification won in the realm of the Spirit;
a vision seen by angels,
a mystery preached to the Gentiles;
Christ in this world, accepted by faith,
Christ, on high, taken up into glory.

1 Tim. 3, 16

PREFACE

THE liturgical movement is many things, but above all it is an attempt to strengthen and to deepen the faith and piety of the Christian people.

It is a movement of study and prayer, of education and participation. It seeks the honour of God and the holiness of men. And if it is a movement of change, the change is from formalism to sincerity, so that every word of public piety may be genuine.

In his excellent explanation of the liturgy, Father Dalmais shows the depths of the liturgical movement and of the sacred services of worship. If the Christian liturgy is, on our side, prayer and praise and sacrifice presented to the Father by Christ and his people, and if it is, on God's side, the work of re-creating and revivifying a holy people, then the depths to be studied are profound indeed.

This book appears in English at an opportune juncture in the development of the sacramental or liturgical apostolate. There is, at the moment, a sudden and almost embarrassing success of congregational participation in some parts of the English-speaking world. It is of critical importance that the singing and the recitation, characteristic of parish programmes, should not degenerate into mechanical regimentation for the sake of mere activity.

Not that Father Dalmais' study of the liturgy is presented as a kind of antidote to shallow externalism. It is an original and creative contribution to a serious appreciation of things liturgical with a theological soundness that does not inhibit the warmth and enthusiasm of the author. It is the doctrine of the liturgy with a thorough, if brief, application to the history, the forms, and the rites which have shaped our Christian worship.

The circumstances which make this translation particularly opportune deserve recounting. Only in 1958, at the death of Pius XII, did the liturgical movement—already sound, substantial, and flourishing on the continent—catch fire in any widespread or popular fashion among the pastors and people in English-speaking lands.

The limited interest shown among us in the liturgical renewal until 1958 is curious in view of the Roman teaching for half a century of papal statements and in view of the eloquent and brilliant promoters of the movement in our midst.

In 1956, for example, Pius XII restored the rites of the great Week of Redemption. The surprised reaction in clerical and lay circles was almost incredible in its ignorance of the past decades of liturgical progress. The story is even told of an editor who questioned the legitimacy of the congregation's responding "Et cum spiritu tuo" on an occasion not specifically and explicitly mentioned in the rubrics, although he could tolerate the response when the pontifical documents spelled it out. Another editor substituted the rubric "choir" where the Holy See had said "all". And, in general, there was little thought of extending the norms of popular participation to all the Church's year and to all the Church's rites.

The same reaction, or lack of reaction, had followed the encyclical on Christian worship issued by Pius XII in 1947. Clearly and forcefully the pontiff explained the people's part in the liturgy, especially in the Eucharist. He blessed and encouraged dialogue Masses and all that would make the Eucharist manifest the unity of Christ's Mystical Body more vitally. But neither the doctrine nor the practice proposed in the Encyclical *Mediator Dei* created any universal or widespread response.

The story might be traced further back to Pius XI in the 1920's, to St. Pius X at the beginning of the century. The principles were enunciated by these pontiffs but, in many countries, the conclusions were not drawn or applied and the liturgical movement grew slowly, if soundly. In the last days of the life of Pius XII, however, an instruction appeared "on sacred music and the sacred liturgy". This lengthy document summed up in juridic form the papal exhortations to liturgical renewal which had appeared during six decades.

The now celebrated instruction of September 3, 1958, had little that was new. It was unprepossessing in its detailed treatment of sacred music. It seemed meagre and even dated in countries where liturgical study and experience had developed more rapidly. It revealed the pressing need for further radical liturgical reform.

Yet in the English-speaking world the instruction, dealing with principles and norms for popular participation in the liturgy, was a revelation. Overlooked was the fact that the document only confirmed what the promoters of the movement had preached and urged for years; and happily, providentially, parochial and diocesan plans for sung and recited Masses were initiated—not universally, of course, but widely enough to be considered common and general.

The details of this extraordinary and rather sudden development need not be recited here. They include the establishment of diocesan liturgical commissions (first urged by the Holy See in 1947), the publication of booklets, leaflets, prayer and hymn cards, the issuance of pastoral directives and letters, and in very many parishes the introduction of congregationally sung Masses and dialogue Masses with or without sacred song.

All this, desirable in itself and indeed demanded by the nature of the Church and of the Church's sacrifice, was accompanied, it would seem, by only a minimum of doctrinal explanation and instruction. This is the problem and almost the crisis : that the doctrine and the sense of liturgical participation have not been preached and proclaimed at the same time that the forms of external song and prayer have been introduced.

It is a truism that before, during, and after these programmes of liturgical participation there must be study of the *theology of the liturgy* and the *form of the liturgy,* to employ Father Dalmais' titles for the two parts of his book. The chapters of this volume

from 'Liturgical Reality' and 'The Christian Liturgical Assembly'
to 'Liturgy and Human Societies' are the substance of what must
be known by teachers and preachers if the active participation of
the faithful in sacred rites is to be genuine and meaningful.

Comparatively speaking, it is easy to rehearse the words of
unison recitation or the brief responses of holy Mass. It is even
easier for congregations of the faithful to sing the simple chants
and hymns. The difficult task is the comprehension and the pro-
pagation of underlying doctrine.

For this purpose Father Dalmais' introductory study is admirable. It is not the stuff of a Sunday sermon or a catechetical instruction. It is a serious reflection upon the profound questions of
Christian worship, addressed to all the worshippers who are themselves willing and able to be serious students of things sacred, but
above all addressed to those who teach and preach, those who
write and publicize, those whose concern with our common
liturgy goes beyond the ordinary and the superficial.

Let there be no mistake. We have a desperate need to celebrate
the holy liturgy more fruitfully and more worthily, that it may be
worship in spirit and in truth. Our need is equally desperate to
understand what it is we do when we assemble as the people of
God in our response to his call. We dare not worship God with
our lips only; true faith and piety require an ever deeper appreciation of the Mass, the sacraments, and the Church's prayer.

To the venerable promoters of the liturgical movement of the
1920s and 1930s it must seem patronizing indeed to hear the
suggestion in the 1960s that the liturgical movement needs depth
and doctrine. In the United States, the pioneers still living—
Busch, Reinhold, Ducie, Hellriegel, Ellard, and the rest—have
from their first writings and teachings insisted on the primacy of
the interior element in the liturgy. Their consistent and constant
anxiety has been for doctrinal content and genuine devotion.
From the first volume of *Orate Fratres* under the editorship of
the great Virgil Michel to the most recent copy of *Worship* under
his brilliant successor, Godfrey Diekmann, from the first Liturgical
Week in 1940 at Chicago to the most recent meeting on 'The
Liturgy and Unity in Christ' at Pittsburgh in 1960, the liturgical

movement has represented a theological and doctrinal approach to all the outward manifestations of public prayer and sacrifice.

At the same time the task is only beginning and the very breadth of current interest in liturgical participation has created the fresh problem mentioned above—the need to deepen the understanding of priest and people who join Christ in his worship of the Father in heaven.

Father Dalmais' book is an important step, as this fruit of European scholarship and study is made available in English. That his thorough and profound description of the holy liturgy is done with eloquence and clarity recommends his book all the more. It will add breadth and lustre to the liturgical movement which is a modern 'sign of the working of the Holy Spirit in the Church'.

FREDERICK R. McMANUS

Chapter 1

Liturgical Reality

What is the Liturgy?

THE question is easy enough to ask, but are we capable of understanding the answer? Don't we need for that certain human presuppositions, a certain attitude to reality and to ourselves which we no longer possess? Before analysing our Christian mystery we must regain that intimate understanding of being and of things without which our insight can scarcely be profound.

We must apply ourselves to this first of all. The preliminary remarks of the next few paragraphs are simply a brief invitation to discover what man really is, to explore the mystery of man as a social being, forming a community with other men. In practice, a bias towards individualism, our lack of what is called the social sense of civic spirit, prevent us even from beginning to understand the liturgy, just as much as does totalitarianism, which denies the absolute rights of the individual. There is a balance between the Person and society, which is a mystery. It will exist and continue to exist only if the individual and society are both referred to him who gives them their meaning, to God in all his transcendence. And this reference, expressed and experienced, is the liturgy in the widest meaning of the word.

Liturgy belongs, then, to the inmost nature of human society: that is why it makes use of human means of expression and contact—gestures, natural at the outset, then ritualized, are the normal means by which men express and effect their mutual cohesion and their relationship with God. Here again we have a rediscovery to make; it is that of the irreplaceable value of primitive manifestations of the human spirit through the *body*. We can feel something of it easily enough in the case of poetry, music, sculpture—art, in short. Why then should it be absent from human relationships in our humdrum daily existence or, at the other end of the scale, in their highest form which is the adherence of the community to God in worship? It is possible that we shall be led to perceive, experimentally and compulsively, not only the high spiritual value of our bodies and the wonderful mission of our controlled feelings but also the great riches of meaning, of expression, of the true import in those human manifestations to which men devote themselves together body and soul—of which games are the commonest form and liturgy the loftiest. In this light we see also the real face of the world of things. We are body and spirit and so, to some extent, is everything in the world. Our privilege as men is to discover the latent significance of things. It is not necessary to be a mystic to hear forest or mountain say something beyond themselves. Those who have rediscovered their full humanity in union with their brothers and the worship of God can hear the canticle of created things; they hear everything speak, find in everything a symbol.

Then creation as a whole resumes its sacred character and in it man takes naturally the place and attitude belonging to him. In the community to which he belongs feasts and celebrations occur which sustain and renew the general balance of people and of things, and strive effectively by their provision of new life and enthusiasm against the forces of death and decay. And what will happen if God himself comes, in Christ, to restore all things to unity, coming among men whose harmony with God, with others, with themselves and with creation has been broken by sin?

To shape ourselves again to this forgotten outlook, we need only to become concretely aware of what we might call the 'phenomenon of liturgy'. Man acts liturgically by nature and it is not possible to drive out beyond recall this part of his nature. In this introduction to the liturgy it is right, then, that we should first look at liturgical manifestations, many and varied in form, but with common roots in the need from which they spring. In this way certain constant factors will emerge, those that we have just mentioned, of which we must come to a deeper understanding; namely the communal, ritual and symbolic aspects of liturgy: its sacred character and its relationship with the Transcendent: and, lastly, the actual framework of its celebration.

LITURGY AND COMMUNITY

Liturgy means the 'work of the people' ($\lambda\epsilon\iota\tau o\upsilon\rho\gamma\iota\alpha = \H{\epsilon}\rho\gamma o\nu$ $\tau o\tilde{\upsilon}$ $\lambda\alpha o\tilde{\upsilon}$). By borrowing from the political language of the Greek cities a word of no special religious significance, the Greek translators of the Bible endowed it with implications which we must explore. First, we confine ourselves to etymology, without over-emphasizing the historical significance of the word. A people and an activity: in these there is enough to open broad horizons to us—horizons we must never lose sight of when the liturgy of Christians brings us to the verge of perspectives hitherto un-suspected.

A people means an organized community, a human group whose unity is forged by a common destiny, a group conscious of its unity, tending always to strengthen this unity by institutions and laws, by stocking its collective memory with 'myths'. Whether based on strict historical fact or not, men cling to them because of their meaning and it is these myths, as we shall see below, which in the liturgy take on form and life for the present-day community.[1]

[1] As it is the aim of this introduction to describe the characteristic marks of liturgy in the widest sense, it should not cause surprise if we occasionally use the vocabulary of comparative religion although to do so is, it is true, not usual in dealing with the Christian liturgy alone.

Until recently, a 'myth' was by definition whatever is contrary to reality (in particular to historical reality). But historians of religion have gradually discovered the importance and value of myths as the foundation of social life and culture in societies of archaic type. Here, for example is how Mircéa Eliade defined the role of myth in his recent work *Myths, Dreams and Mysteries*, (London, 1961). 'One fact strikes us instantly : for such societies, myth is deemed to express *absolute truth*, because it recounts a *sacred event*, that is a trans-human revelation which occurred at the dawn of the Great Time, at the holy time of beginnings (*in illo tempore*). Being *real* and *sacred*, the myth becomes *exemplary* and consequently

3

A common destiny, a social organisation, a collective memory: these elements are all-important for the celebration of the liturgy; and conversely, without a people there could be no liturgy in any real sense of the word. Let it be added at once, without a people gathered together and taking an active part; the liturgy is 'the work of the people', their most typical action, the action, which, as we shall see, more than any other, gives them the ability to realise themselves and express themselves in their deepest reality, beyond all contingencies of politics and history. And, in passing, that is why there is no more certain way of getting at the essential nature of a human community than by studying its celebrations and festivals.

By recognising that there is no liturgy that is not the act of an organised community we do not cease to be aware of the dangers involved in bringing into play the powers of the collective psyche. We must also say in what sense the liturgy is a game—which it certainly is not in the sense that it distracts man from his real obligations. Rather, it is the most serious thing that it is possible to do, in which human companionship reaches a profundity not found elsewhere. It is one of the few means by which a community can reach union, that is, the intimacy of exchange, that transparency

repeatable, for it serves as a model for and, at the same time, a justification of, all human actions. In other words, a myth is a *true story*, something which happened at the beginning of time and serves as a model for human behaviour. By imitating the exemplary acts of a god or a mythical hero, or simply by narrating their adventures, man in archaic societies cuts himself off from profane time (the time in which he lives) and magically returns to the Great Time, the sacred time.'

The Christian liturgy is based entirely on a similar scheme: by narrating the institution of the Eucharist at the Last Supper, we are reunited with the primordial happening (the 'myth') of the Passion and Resurrection of the Saviour, really present under the appearances of consecrated bread and wine. Of course, in the case of this liturgy instituted by Christ himself, it is our belief that the primordial event of which the Mass is the memorial is an *historical* event, of known and verifiable date, in contrast to the 'mythical' happenings celebrated by other liturgies. On the other hand, the miracle of the Real Presence of the Lord permits our union with him to be not merely 'magical' but sacramental, that is, effective and bilateral: Christ is active in and through the sacrament; it is not only we who make contact with him in a magical rite. These differences and this fundamental superiority of the Christian liturgy in no way prevents us from acknowledging similarities with a way of thinking which has become only too foreign to us, so making more difficult our real participation in the liturgical action.

4

which brings to an end 'I' and 'you' and leaves only a unanimous 'we'. The peril is great when that communion is replaced by social monolithicism or affective exaltation which is wholly sensual, for both are equally destructive of the inalienable value of the individual. It would be presumptuous to think that the Christian liturgy avoids these dangers absolutely. But at least whilst it remains true to its own nature it is on the way to surmounting them.

LITURGY AND HUMAN ACTIONS

There is no authentically human activity which does not find expression in gesture. We ought to be ashamed to state such a truism, but everywhere we have arrived at such a degree of abstraction, wrongly sheltering under the name of spirituality, that the time is not long past when the liturgy was, and perhaps in some places still is, regarded with contempt, merely because it could not be conceived without rites, that is without gestures, as stylised and impoverished as it is possible to imagine them.

So we must first recover a lively sense of the wholeness of man. Man is that spiritual being who, in order to make contact with other beings and to express himself to himself and to others—which is the twofold vocation of a spiritual being—is woven into the material of a body which enables him to give himself, to express himself. It is thus that he attains to the dignity of the person, the autonomous centre of an infinity of relationships and exchanges.

Human gesture is the conveyor of this immeasurable richness; through and in gesture man becomes involved with others of his kind; through them he gives significance to his connections with a world not immediately accessible to his senses. Not only does all social life rest on gesture: access to the supra-human requires it, as does encounter with the sub-human, which is humanized only by being made significant by gesture. Thus we see that liturgy, the complete expression of the involvement of man in all his dimensions, must be pre-eminently a matter of gesture, refining human gestures in order to reveal their ultimate significance, making them ritual so that, purged of their profane function (which still implies something of the sub-human), they become tangible signs of spiritual realities.

To do this, liturgies base themselves on the most elementary, the most primitive, it is tempting to say the most biological gestures—those in which man reveals the most deep-seated needs of his nature and betrays the inmost longing of his vocation.

Of all the great archetypes the communal meal is the most universal. Man sustains his life by food, and can there be imagined a more appropriate sign of the union attained by a group of men with invisible powers, than the eating in common of the same food, of which the divinity, in one way or another also receives his share? Yet it is a somewhat rare privilege for so profoundly biological an action to assume transcendent significance without losing its nature and being perverted. We have only to remember the sexual aberrations so common in nature religions.

Certain attitudes and postures, though they vary according to custom and place, are shared by all men. There are attitudes of repose and of tension; attitudes of welcome and joy, of introspection, of servility, of concentration and recollection: these are the fundamental attitudes of a being which expresses itself in gesture.

Through the way in which he behaves with things man gives meaning to them, he lays hold of the cosmos in its totality and through him it yields to a human, even to a superhuman, order. Sacramentalism, the sacred use of elements and of things, occurs, more or less richly developed, in every liturgy. The higher kinds of sensory phenomena—light and colour, sounds and scents— become an integral part of the liturgical action. The great rhythms of nature have their place in it—day and night, the succession of seasons, with all the changes they involve in the sky and on the earth, and, finally, things—the elements first of all, those realities which appear to the still childlike gaze of man to constitute the very stuff of the universe, fire and above all water, for they are less ponderously material, and yet amenable to human hands. Contemporary psychology has only begun to explore the vast field of reactions which these archetypes linked with the elements and natural phenomena may arouse in the deepest parts of our being.[2] The great actions and rhythms of life are involved in the same way with the material order—the emphasis may be on this or that animal or flower or fruit but will be determined by the particular, and often apparently quite arbitrary, customs of each separate human group.

Research into these matters is not the purpose of our study, but no one could make claim to any understanding of Christian rites, even in their most specific characteristics, without first recovering this awareness of the sacredness of nature. Children feel it spontaneously, but we let it atrophy even if we do not deliberately destroy it by preventing the child from looking beyond the function of things to their real meaning.

Yet a liturgy confined to such actions has not solved the ambiguity of the holy. This is often the case, as could be verified without difficulty in some typical liturgies. The danger of naturalism will never be completely eliminated—it is the price we must pay because cosmic realities can disclose perspectives greater than themselves. They bear witness to the Divine by their very existence, yet they are not great enough to reveal it in its transcendence. For this reason a liturgy which respects the true order and hierarchy of being gives a place to gestures and rites which have significance only in human relationships, to arbitrary gestures, as diverse as languages and, like them, the tools of communication and regulators of human relationships. They are linked with what it is customary to call etiquette, a word full of meaning, expressive of the essential characteristic of ritual acts such as these. Etiquette concerns those gestures which are most closely bound up with the customs of a given society. It is natural that society should carry over those attitudes governing the relationship of its members into its highest and most expressive activity. Thus our kissing and kneeling, carrying lights in procession and offering incense are all acts acquired from the etiquette of the imperial court of the successors of Diocletian, who themselves borrowed from the eastern monarchies.

[2] See the works of G. Bachelard: *Psychanalyse du feu* (Gallimard), *L'eau et les rêves*, *L'air et les songes*, *La terre et les rêveries de la volonté et du repos* (J. Corti) and, the last to appear, *La poètique de l'espace* (P.U.F.).

By such rites, a liturgy becomes human; likewise, it takes on a special form, and the danger of its growing fossilized arises when these actions no longer have a meaning but become their own justification and are all the more stubbornly immutable because of it.

THE FOREST OF SYMBOLS

Gestures ritualized by the liturgy take their value less from what they are than from what they evoke. They bring into the sphere of the visual and the sensible realities and values which in themselves are foreign to it. In other words the liturgy, the act of a community using its every means of expression, continually appeals to the symbolic value of these means, actions or words, and it is chiefly in this way that it functions in the manner of a game.

In a game,[3] man goes beyond the immediate and utilitarian purpose of his actions. He rises to a level at which what in everyday life is not more than a means takes on its own reality and reveals a significance which enthralls not only its author but also those who, watching and listening, make their own the game at which they are present. There is a twofold danger in play: the overstepping of the ordinary bounds of life which it makes possible may turn either to escape or to satiety.

But the liturgy stands out from all other play because it relates to situations utterly beyond our human condition, at least as it is in the present historical order of duration. Liturgies appeal to a different order of time—*in illo tempore*—which, according to the circumstances and particular form of each religion, may be a primordial time (or duration) anterior to history (e.g., myths of origin in nature religions), an eschatological time towards which history is moving, an atemporal and abstract duration as in Islam or, finally, in the unique case of religions founded on biblical revelation, to historical events which are signs of God's intervention in human history. The limited range of ritual expression

[3] Huizinga: *Homo Ludens*, Gallimard, Paris.

often obscures this basic attitude to different kinds of time, so that it is always absolutely necessary to see the rites within the framework of the religion to which they belong and the conceptions of the world underlying them.

This variety of references is expressed in the words which accompany the rites and define their meaning. Explicitly or by allusion, they refer to a narrative or, to use the technical term, to a 'myth'. Once again[4] it must be made quite clear that this word is used without prejudice to the reality or otherwise of the events described; it merely shows that these events, whatever their historical reality, are endowed with a permanent significance and power through which they are made actual whenever they are ritually recalled. There is no liturgy which does not claim, more or less explicitly, to effect what it signifies and it is this claim which distinguishes liturgical action from every other mode of representation; it is also because of this that liturgy always runs the risk of degenerating into magic by losing touch with a transcendent reality which, left to itself, human action is unable to grasp. So it is wrong to think that the material performance of the rite is enough for the expected spiritual effect to be automatically released. Although nothing is further removed from the characteristic liberty of the Spirit than magic pure and simple, it is none the less impossible to conceive of a liturgy that does not in one way or another imply belief in some correspondence between the performance of the ceremony and the re-presentation of the myth.

While it is quite futile to claim to establish a general theory of the relationship between rite and myth, and to desire to set up one or the other as of prime importance in every instance, on the other hand it is of the greatest interest to endeavour in each separate case to determine whether the 'myth' gave rise to the ritual expression or whether a rite, primitively simple and utilitarian in function, whose real purpose has been forgotten, has given birth to the 'myth', which then seems to reveal its inmost significance through the rite[5]. But such historical research is far

[4] See footnote 1, page 3.
[5] Cf. Van der Leeuw: *La religion dans son essence et ses manifestations*, Payot, Paris.

from being always possible; very rarely can we go to the root of the matter and discover the purely liturgical value of a rite or a narrative. This value is measured by the response that the celebration as a whole provokes in the congregation, that is, the way in which the symbolic significance of the word and gesture can be recognized.

We must pause therefore to consider the nature of symbolic expression.[6] The symbol cannot be reduced to a mere sign. It is not confined to reference to something else through association based on proximity, coincidence, dependence, resemblance, analogy or any other manner or relationship. Objects, words or actions are symbols only in so far as they can be immediately recognised as bearers of a significance surpassing their own reality, or, more precisely, as being in some way something different from and greater than they seem to be. It is this materiality, this concrete value attaching to a 'thing', which constitutes the realism and solidity of a symbol and makes it fit to convey the realities of the spiritual world which overflow and prolong it. Furthermore, it is not possible to diminish the material things a liturgy uses—the water of Baptism, the bread and wine of the Eucharist—without at the same time lessening their powers of suggestion. Unfortunately, after several centuries of dualist thinking (in which the spirit is seen only in opposition to the body), the part played by material things in our liturgy has too often become purely formal. And so they are no longer able to sustain the process of thought which, in normal circumstances, should grasp the implications of the rite *in* and *through* the material means by which it is performed. Up to a certain point this perception may be universal and it is for psychology to identify the archetypes to which it refers and to study the various ways in which it can be expressed. This is a vast field of research in which exploration has hardly begun, and in which the liturgist has the greatest possible interest. He can himself provide excellent material by carefully setting the rites he describes in the perspective proper to every celebration and by discerning, through apparent similarities and differences, the meaning they acquire in each case.

[6] See Mircéa Eliade: *Myths, Dreams and Mysteries*, (London 1961).

Of its nature the symbol is polyvalent and ambiguous : in this lies its richness, but also its dangers. While reason is satisfied only with clear and distinct ideas, symbolic thought delights in the ceaseless mobility of the ideas evoked by a symbolic theme: water which cleanses, quenches thirst and quickens, water transparent, liquid and cool, which also swamps, stifles and dissolves, the wave which roars and crushes, the treacherous, elusive, insinuating element, the opposite of everything firm and stable. It is only the part it plays in the celebration, and the 'myth' accompanying its use, which allow us to disentangle its present significance without, however, destroying the polyvalence of the symbol.

This polyvalence may be lost to sight and the symbol itself turned into allegory. An intuitive and all-embracing perception is replaced by an analysis appealing to the processes of logical thought. Only too frequently has the liturgy been the victim of this confusion. The myth then becomes the material for intellectual speculation or moral teaching; the rite is dissected into its component parts, for each of which justification is sought. Far from entailing any simplification of practices whose meaning is no longer perceived, allegorism generally leads to complication, to over-refinement in secondary details, which burgeon and proliferate like suckers and finally stifle those essential elements in the rite, which convey the richest symbolic values.

Sometimes, however, symbols at first unrecognised will gain in reality through this process. A good example is to be found in the history of the 'blessing' of the Paschal candle. Originally this was a utilitarian rite, but inherent in it is the symbolism of fire and light, evoking the eschatological parables and the true light of Christ shining forth through the world in his Easter glory. The chant of the *praeconium paschale* orchestrates this theme by evoking the pillar of fire at the first passover. But at this point allegory is introduced in regard to the material of the candle, the wax made by the bee whose fruitful virginity is hymned; the commentators take the opportunity to elaborate further by drawing a distinction between the wax, the wick and the flame, comparing them to the flesh, soul and divinity of Christ. A wrong interpretation of the word *incensum* led to the intrusion of five grains of incense connected with the five wounds of Christ. The new rite for Easter night restores the text's original meaning but keeps the grains of incense, very briefly indicating the significance they have come to have in the symbolism of the candle as standing for Christ. So fortunate a result is in fact very rare; as a rule, allegorism leads to irremediable 'fossilizing' of the rites.

LITURGY AND THE SACRED

If we are to be in a position to discuss liturgy it is not enough to think of it as a communal action performed as a game, not even as a game which involves the participants in a most intimate way, touching symbolically on themes capable of stirring profound responses in them. In fact, whatever its historical origin, the word is no longer used except of sacred actions. We must therefore state exactly what such acts require and what specific characteristics they assume.

'Sacred' is one of those words which everyone feels he understands and whose content, when one seeks to define it, is seen to be polymorphous and perhaps even to be evanescent. According to Otto's classical analysis,[7] the sacred is something that is first experienced as an attitude made up of fear and attraction (*horrendum* and *fascinosum*)—an attitude in which man has the impression of being taken out of himself, drawn from the condition proper to him and confronted with a world which surpasses him (*numinosum*). At once attracted and repelled, he withdraws into himself, a prey to emotion which, if he is of a lively sensitivity, or if the shock has been violent, may express itself in various physiological phenomena—suspension of breathing, then panting, and increased pulse-rate, bristling of the hair, sweating, and, in extreme cases, the onset of a trance which may go as far as loss of consciousness. Many different causes may provoke such an attitude which furnishes no reliable notion of their nature and objective value. That is the first ground of ambiguity. There is another, more serious one: the danger of being satisfied with this

[7] R. Otto: *The Sacred*, Penguin, 1959.

attitude because of the feelings which accompany it and the escape it provides from the commonplace circumstances of everyday life. This leads to the quest for the experience for its own sake, a quest that receives illusory justification from the access it gives to another world, which is itself regarded as sacred. The frontiers of this world and the rites enabling them to be crossed without danger must be determined. And because conditions of paroxysm—struggle, sexual extremes and drunken excess—arouse physiological reactions similar to those of the sacred, there are psychologists and sociologists who do not hesitate to draw the conclusion from the ritualization and integration of these things into religious ceremonies that this ambiguity can never be overcome.[8]

If this were so, the sacred would be incompatible with true religion—this is an attitude quite common among Protestants, anxious to preserve the evangelical faith from all compromise with a world of men tainted through and through by the disorderly lure of concupiscence. The Catholic Church has always refused to take this course, for she considers that the notion of the sacred, even though it can be perverted and remains in itself ambiguous, can and must, like every feeling natural to man, be corrected and orientated towards the divine realities, towards the order of sanctity.

Sacred, religious and *holy*, are closely related concepts and must be integrated one with another. The *sacred* is fundamentally subjective; it arises spontaneously from the depths of man, before any intervention of reason or will. The *religious,* on the other hand, urges man in his higher capabilities to recognize his dependence on powers superior to himself. *Holiness,* finally, means the objective transcendence of absolute moral perfection. By using each word only in its proper sense, much misunderstanding would be avoided. In particular, it will be seen that many of the dangers we have had occasion to denounce with regard to the liturgy come from a perverted or atrophied sense of the sacred, for want of being set right by a religion which itself is ordered towards the practice of holiness.

[8] R. Caillois: *L'homme et le sacré*, Gallimard, Paris, 1959.

It is not to be wondered at that before this rectification could be perfectly respected and recognised, there was needed the complete revelation of the mystery of divine holiness in Christ. And when you get Christians, as in modern times, allowing this lively sense of holiness to fade, the idea of the sacred falls back into its first ambiguity. Only by considering the stages of revelation will it be possible to restore it to its true perspectives.

The revelation of divine holiness has its origin in a manifestation of power within a liturgical setting. Hinted at in the brilliant vision of the burning bush at Horeb, it burst forth in the theophany at Sinai.[9] There, Moses prophetically grasped the symbolic significance of the storm through which the awesome presence of the transcendent God allowed itself to be discerned in the form of irresistible might. It aroused such a feeling of the sacred that death seemed inevitable. But at the same time the community saw itself constituted as a 'holy people', enabled to enter into intercourse with God the holy One. It was able to cross the bounds of its profane existence. A surpassing of self, a paroxysm—but it led towards the fulfilment of the most genuinely human powers and not to their disintegration. In this first liturgy of the covenant it is already possible to discern the essential lines along which every liturgy would have to be organized if it was not to betray its mission.

It is not surprising, therefore, to discover them again, not only in various accounts of the covenant at Sinai and the theophanies which stand out as landmarks in the obscure centuries of the times of the Judges, but also in the account of the dedication of Solomon's temple. This last is of less interest to us here for its own sake than because it provides the framework for the inaugural vision of Isaias, an episode decisive in the revelation of the true nature of holiness and the purification of the idea of the Sacred. In reliving the theophany of the Dedication, the prophet reveals its true meaning: the God to whom the whole of the Temple liturgy is directed, the God who should be the principal source of life for the 'holy people' is not simply an almighty power who manifests himself in the clash of terrifying cosmic forces; he is Perfection of an unsullied purity, and he jealously demands up-

[9] Cf. Exodus 19.16 ff.

rightness; he requires from the community dedicated to him an absolute gift of self, free from any egoistical self-seeking. The liturgy cannot be limited to the meticulous observance of ceremonies and the respect of ritual prohibitions; it must burst forth from purified hearts, wholly given to God.[10]

In this way the fundamental personal requirements of a sacredness which does not falsify man's vocation were established. They were revealed completely only when Christ came to replace the symbolic presence of God in the secret place of the Holy of Holies by the effective presence of the Incarnation in his complete humanity. Then he inaugurated authentic spiritual worship in the oblation of his own body, the new and final temple wherein dwells the fullness of the All-holy God. To all appearances, he eliminated the sacred by doing away with the boundary—before him, insurmountable—separating the creature, by nature profane, from the divinity beyond. In fact he perfected the sacred by setting free the vocation of humanity for the sacred of holiness, which alone is capable of affording a firm foundation for the dignity of the person. As Fr. Doncoeur wrote:

One of the criteria of the worth of a civilization is the harmony of its sacred order with a purer and nobler human order. A fine form of paganism, professing respect for springs, forests, seasons, guests, and kings goes together with a harmonious and wise human order. But Christian civilization, which extends its respect even to the poor and to transcendent things which are despised by a sensual and proud world, humanises, spiritualises and divinises its sacred order. It renders its sacred order the more just and effective because, if it is true that the sacred is that for which a society demands absolute respect as a condition of its existence and proper functioning, then the more fully the sacred coincides with the refined and essential human values, the more definitely and solidly will such a society establish its rule over the natural order. Conversely, a paganism which takes into account the sacred nature of wealth but

[10] Dedication of the Temple: III Kings 8 and 9. The Vision of Isaias: Isaias 6, 'Be ye holy for I am holy' had in fact been constantly re-echoed since the Exodus.

despises that of work or charity, may know an apparent and passing splendour, but it will inevitably crumble under the pressure of the invincible forces it despised. Such was the aesthetic paganism of Greece or the imperialist paganism of Rome. Such are the paganisms of the modern world, which are so much the more precarious because they depend more on violence and their systems so often are founded on lies.[11]

That is why 'Christians, in so far as they are Christians, in the very order in which they live, by supernaturally sacred realities, ought . . . to set the example of personal consciences fundamentally identified with the social conscience in the life of the Mystical Body'.[12] As we shall see this is exactly what the Christian liturgical celebration should bring about if it has been lived by its participants in accordance with its essential requirements. In Christianity, in fact :

the sacred implies far less prohibition (as in the beginning) than communion. For when Christ consecrated the bread and the wine, it was no longer to make them 'loaves of proposition' to be enclosed within the sacrosanct Ark, but to break it and give it to be eaten: 'Take,' he said, 'and eat. This is my body.' The sacred is no longer something inert and remote; it has become for us something interior, the source of life. Essentially, it is the Spirit which is identified with holiness. 'The wall has been broken down,' St Paul was to say (Eph. 2. 14). And because it is no longer I, but Christ who lives in me, with what respect ought I to respect the limbs which are as sacred to me as those of Christ himself! In this way was introduced into the world a human sacredness that even the most devout in antiquity had misunderstood and of which it was sometimes completely ignorant. The sacredness of the person founded a new civilization. However mighty Caesar's power, it sees untouchable dignity ranged before it. Man, even man in chains, opposes to every kind of threat the sovereign right of the truth he bears within him. . . . Force and the State learn their limitations for

[11] P. Doncoeur: *Péguy, la révolution et le sacré*, p. 73, n. 1.
[12] P. Régamey: *La Maison-Dieu*, 17, 1949, p. 48.

the first time. However wretched the man, however deprived of any semblance of greatness, yet his weakness holds that which makes him most inviolable. So was effected the revolution which was henceforward to govern all civilization.[18]

But it was also from this revolution that sprang a liturgy without common measure with those in which, until then, human communities had tried to express their sacred communion with transcendent reality.

LITURGY AND TRANSCENDENCE

And here, immediately, we find ourselves at the tragic heart of the human adventure. For such is our paradox: we cannot fulfil our destiny and satisfy our inmost aspirations without appealing to someone other and greater than we. God himself, and God alone, can fill this gaping void, a veritable vessel of the Danaïdes that not even the whole world could satisfy. *Abyssus abyssum invocat*: 'Deep—our deep—calls to the deep—the deep of the divine fullness', as Psalm 41 says. Such, at least, is the Christian conviction, based on unanimous tradition and the evidence of Scripture itself. From the dawn of mankind, the choice has ever been set before us: are Adam and his descendants capable of finding their fulfilment in themselves, or must they obey God? Refusal of this subjection caused the primordial catastrophe of original sin and from that time onwards this fundamental choice has ceaselessly been offered to each one of us.

So we must not be surprised to find the same issue on the plane of the community and its liturgy: can men and groups of men find in themselves and express through means which are wholly theirs the last word of their being and their destiny? Can they project themselves, hypostatise themselves in an ideal 'I' which they can go on worshipping, into which they can learn to transform themselves by contemplation and imitation? Or must they call on a God who, surpassing them in all his transcendence, suffers

[18] Cf. P. Doncoeur, *ibid* p. 108: J. Lefeuvre *Les enfants dans la ville*, Casterman, Paris-Tournai, 1956.

them to surpass themselves and find the complete fulfilment which they could not attain in any other way?

In our own time this question has become more acute through the conscious and sometimes brutal confrontation of the merely human liturgies of social groupings which affect a common destiny with religious liturgies whose very *raison d'être* lies in living communion with God and consciousness of a common fate that cannot be brought within merely historical bounds (for this community is of truly eternal scope). Totalitarian regimes of every kind (Fascism, Nazism, Marxism) have accustomed us to these spectacular godless 'liturgies'. Who does not remember the monstrous gatherings at Nuremberg? Or that extraordinary May Day of 1957 at Pekin of the same order, if not in the same style, as Hitler's parades. Fortunately it was possible, in the same country, to set over against it that other liturgy of the Christians of Shanghai: in the midst of persecution, all these believers instinctively realised the need to meet together in order to pray together and affirm their faith—in both senses of the word, that is, both to strengthen it and to profess it. And in the same vein we could quote of course what is at present happening in the Churches of Hungary and Poland.

In this brutal form, opposition is something new. It would not have been possible if the two millenia of Christianity had not slowly made clearer the repercussions of the distinction between two planes of reality: on the one side, the human plane with its profane dimensions, on the other, the holiness of a personal God, clearly distinct from all the ambiguities of the 'sacred', but who, without in any way shedding his transcendence, calls on mankind to share in his own life. In this light we can better understand the ambiguous polyvalence of the 'natural' liturgies, the confusion in which they are always more or less involved, from which Christian worship has not always succeeded in keeping itself unscathed.

Three examples will emphasise the various aspects of this ambiguity. First, the *worship of agrarian religions* which, from Neolithic times, gradually established themselves over the greater part of the planet, following the growth of agricultural civilizations. Every day we see more clearly the more or less secret survivals that are still to be found in the midst of more complex cultures. Even to this day, they form the traditional mould of the religion followed by a vast body of human beings. Its aim is assuredly religious, based on a conception of the world made explicit at an early date in the myths. In such a perspective, the industrious activity of men has as its purpose not only the satisfaction of temporal needs; it claims to imitate and sustain the acts of higher powers, especially when this activity is concerned with foodstuffs, themselves living and the sources of life and charged with life-giving cosmic energy. Moreover, agriculture, linked as it is with the mystery of life, is equally bound up with that of death. And, because agriculture is fundamentally concerned with the lot of man and the very ordering of the universe, because it touches on the ultimate secrets of existence, ritualised in some of its basic actions, it tends to become a religion. Because its rites of life and death unleash the most powerful and least controllable instincts, it can degenerate into strange and monstrous aberrations which in their turn can—as may be seen with the religions of outer Asia or Hindu Tantrism—become ritualised into sheer magic.

In other words, men begin by putting God everywhere, even in their most profane activities, at the risk of losing their awareness of his transcendence. Hence, human actions assume, it is true, a much greater significance, which we could call 'religious'. They become *rites*—but addressed to whom? Their first object—God— is no longer present to the mind to any great extent. Being no longer seen as transcendent, he tends to become confused with the omnipotence with which the rite is charged, and this efficacy seems henceforward to be sufficient to itself. Now a rite efficacious in itself, without reference to any power greater than its own, is the very definition of magic. So we have come to the end of the process of degradation—at the outset God was closely bound up with everything we did. By this transfer, everything we do becomes imbued with magic and seems to open up wider horizons. But in reality the worship of a transcendent God and religion itself are obscured, for they must be both dialogue and union between man and this personal God. So, in the end, they give way to those superstitious practices which are themselves the corruption of earlier magical beliefs. In this form they are to be found even in our own countryside—Christianised, but with a Christianity grafted onto the remains of the agrarian religions. As soon as the faith grows weak this revival of old superstitions can be observed. The same thing is to be found in Islamic North Africa, or in Central Africa, which is open to both influences. In better but nonetheless ambiguous circumstances, we notice the intellectualised transplanting of Egyptian or Greek, and even of Hindu, mysteries.[14]

Civic cults, of which Periclean Athens shows us the most perfect example and the Roman empire a monstrous caricature, are quite a different matter. In classical Greece, the cultus of the city was already political rather than religious. It must be examined at its source, as for example in the royal cults of the Fertile Crescent. We can see it born, like the city itself, from the agricultural community and its worship of cosmic forces which tend—for reasons we have no space to go into here—to become centred in the King, who is mystically identified with some divine power. This religion of the city, complex and confused in the East, revealed its specific characteristics in Greece. But at the same time it tended to become a purely formal religion. From the time of the Panathenaea, it was to itself that Athena's city offered worship or, more precisely, festivals to that ideal city in which it recognised its deepest vocation. It was only a step to the political worship of Rome and of the Emperor,[15] a worship that was the mortar which held the Empire together, to which an appeal to the astral religions failed to give religious significance. Henceforward this worship became an end in itself and the great totalitarian liturgies of our own century are able to feed on myths rich from another source in the echoes they awaken in depths of the human mind, while at the same time yielding themselves to this same self-deification.

[14] It is enough to compare the purity of the account in Genesis (which, from the first verse, proclaims the transcendence of the Creator) with the mythical narratives of all these religions, where authentically religious themes, parallel to those which find expression in the Old Testament, are mixed with unacceptable crudities.

[15] See P. Fabre: *Aspects politiques et psychologiques de la religion romaine*, Payot, Paris, 1956.

Finally, in extreme contrast to this ritualism, we may examine the liturgical expression of the Moslem community (*Umma*) in its ritual prayers. In fact, this can hardly be called a liturgy: myth is completely absent, for Islam is a religion of pure adoration of the transcendent God, with no other reference to history than the recollection of the manifestation of his word in Mohammed, the last of the 'prophets'. In addition, the ritual expression of the life and organisation of the community is extremely reduced. Except in Morocco, prayer in the name of the Caliph is only a memory. And yet meticulous ritualism, inspired by Christian monastic traditions, ensures a liturgical character for this prayer. The ease with which powerful political passions are unleashed on the occasion of the Friday prayer or on the principal feasts points to the radically ambiguous nature of the Islamic community—a community of believers which demands political organization and has no organization proper to itself.

Thus, in agrarian religions, the myth proves self-destructive, and the rite takes on a value for its own sake at the risk of becoming debased into magic; in the civic cults, liturgical expression loses its religious significance in order to put itself at the service of politics; in Islam, as in Judaism, the act of prayer itself is in danger of becoming its own end, for want of arousing a response in the real life of the community—unless, through a debasement deeper than that of the city religions, the community forgets its fundamentally religious nature, its absolute dependence on the transcendent God, and is reduced to a nationalism without, like the totalitarian city, even the possibility of deifying itself.

LITURGICAL ACTION:
CELEBRATION AND FEAST

Before beginning the study of Christian liturgy, its nature and organisation, we must pause for a moment to consider the characteristic form assumed by every liturgical action and expressed by the word *celebration*. Here can be distinguished 'the convergence of three things, three conditions, one or other of which may, however, be lacking in exceptional circumstances. The starting point or occasion of a celebration is ordinarily an important or sensational event (*festivitas, solemnitas*). This event, whether belonging to the present or commemorated from the past leads, secondly, to the calling together of a congregation, of a meeting of greater or less importance and solemnity (*conventus, coetus, frequentia*). From this arises the festal act (*actio, effectio*), the third constituent element in a typical celebration. Generally speaking, this is a communal act, involving the joint activity of several persons or even of the whole people, in which, in some way, social, family or public life is involved. This act is sometimes the motive for the assembly, but in every case it constitutes the celebration properly so called. For '*to celebrate is above all to do something communally, solemnly and religiously*', Dom Hild, from whom we borrow this definition, explains in what sense every celebration may be called religious:

'It is not that there is constant reference to the worship of the divinity, or that every action is imbued with religious significance. But the man who takes part in a celebration sheds his own separateness and is placed on the community level, whether it be that of the nation or the family matters little. Now in the eyes of the ancients every community was sacred, holy, and every activity connected with it required a quasi-religious respect towards it, an unreserved devotion, a complete gift, similar to that owed to the divinity. Any failing in this respect is considered an attack on the honour, even on the life and existence, of the community in question. Nothing is insignificant and everything must contribute to the common good, which is the purpose of the celebration.'[16]

We shall not quarrel with a certain lack of precision to be found in these lines, for they are intended merely to disclose the characteristics—in the Greco-Roman world, which on this point did not differ from other civilisations—of this kind of communal act which we, for our part, regard as liturgical. Not until Christianity did the peculiarly religious aspect become the only one.

[16] Dom Hild: *La Maison-Dieu*, 20, 1949, pp. 114-5.

The same applies to the *feast*, which was primitively inseparable from the celebration. The word suggests a break in the pattern of daily life. Also, quite naturally, it is connected with the idea of the sacred, to the extent that we have seen in this idea an attitude bearing witness to the irruption into the common condition of humanity and its profane life of a Beyond, whose ambiguity can only be resolved by a revelation from the Holy One. Only this revelation will allow us to realise the true dimensions of the feast. The ordinary course of time is suspended, not in order to give place to chaos and leave the field free for all kinds of excess, but so that a Presence may manifest itself to men (Epiphany), 'a manifestation of divine power and grace, desiring to communicate itself and to guarantee spiritual life to men anxious to offer their collaboration by celebrating the solemnity'.[17] In this festal celebration the liturgy reveals its true significance.

[17] Dom Casel: *La Maison-Dieu*, 1, 1945, p. 26.

PART ONE

THE THEOLOGY OF
THE LITURGY

Such is the nature and object of the sacred liturgy . . .
it aims at uniting our souls with Christ and sanctifying
them through him in order that the most holy Trinity
may be glorified.

Pius XII

Chapter 2

The Christian Liturgical Assembly: The Church

THE advent among men of the redeeming Word of God implies the development of a new liturgy—a liturgy no longer intended solely to recall and maintain the natural relations of the cosmos and its Creator, but to express man's *faith* in the divine economy and perpetuate the living effects of the Incarnation. The sacred play of beings and things before God and with him is no longer founded upon some myth expressive of the primitive past or an intimate awareness of the created harmony of the world, but on a sacred history, wholly orientated towards Christ and his Cross.

The Christian liturgy makes good use of the wealth of human expression common to all sacred celebrations, but in a new order and to a transcendent end. Its mission is to express and reiterate nothing else than the mystery of the love of the Triune God for the scattered multitude of sinners. It draws its explanation of this mystery from God's own revelation, the holy Word, the Bible, developing the play of its symbols around the great, meaningful themes of the community of the redeemed, who also appear as the People of God, the Bride of God, the Temple of God and, in a word, the Body of Christ, the incarnate Word of God. Such in very truth is the new community that God has purchased for himself with the blood of Christ, a community which unceasingly brings together the multitudes called to salvation by commemorating the act of Redemption in a liturgy wholly centred on the mystery of that blood, the Eucharist.

It is from this point of view that we must learn to see our Christian meetings, however far they may seem to us from that mystical ideal outlined in Scripture. To strive towards a better understanding and sounder performance of the liturgy is no substitute for the act of faith by which we recognise in our congregations the People of God.

The two themes of this chapter—the *Parables of the Church* and *The Liturgical Assembly*—are therefore strictly complementary. We must initiate ourselves into the mystery to which it summons us—the mystery of the Bride of Christ taken from among sinners.

THE PARABLES OF THE CHURCH

Liturgy—the act of the people: we began with the idea that it is the act in which an organised community expresses itself, in the strongest possible sense of that word, setting free in its inmost depths those supreme values on which its being is founded. How great then will be the liturgy of the true people of God, of the Christian Church. To comprehend this we must first know what the Church is in reality. Now, to the believer, the Church is part of the economy of salvation, of God's plan for the world; it belongs to the order of 'mystery', of the divine secret, of its nature inaccessible to our understanding.

But we believe too that God has willed to communicate this secret and to bring it within our reach, has translated it into images, into 'parables', each of which is in itself fundamentally inadequate, but which, taken all together, being divinely inspired encompass the mysterious reality and shed convergent beams of light upon it. We must follow the themes which find their ultimate and complete fulfilment in the Church of Christ throughout the whole of biblical revelation, both in the history of the people of Israel as interpreted by the authors of the sacred book and in the prophets and the reflections of the wise men of Israel. We must learn to recognise these themes in utterances at first hesitant or fragmentary, adapted to differing situations, but which gradually arrange themselves into a coherent whole. All we have already said about symbolic thought, its characteristic processes and the course it follows—which cannot be reduced to those of logical thought—finds its application here.

We shall dwell only on the most significant themes, those which concern the Church as a worshipping community. This means that they will be dominated by the theme of the Temple in terms of which the theme of the holy People of the Covenant was made explicit, it in its turn being enriched by the theme of betrothal and the marriage union. Lastly, Christ reveals to us that under the new dispensation there is no longer any other temple than his body.

'And you shall be to me a priestly kingdom and a holy nation' (Exod. 19.6). This was the charter of the Covenant, the birth certificate of the nation of Israel: a nation with all that the word conveys of density and even of sociological weight, of historical determinism and political organisation. God's plan, the Covenant, was to be fulfilled in the thick of human existence, through all the contingencies of history, economic, social and cultural disturbance, the ever-precarious balance of international relations, the thrust of biological appetites, the ambitions of the great and the resentment of the oppressed. Never was this people to lose the memory of its beginnings in the wilderness; it was a wandering people, never to be allowed to settle into that repose which the author of the Epistle to the Hebrews tells us cannot be found here below. Hardly had it achieved a political organisation in the time of Solomon, the heir to the lands conquered and pacified by his father—with only just the time to found a temple—than that unity was broken and with it the precarious stability that might have been expected.

The history of the period of the kings shows us a gradual descent deeper into excessively worldly preoccupations. The penalty was implacable. There returned from exile a merely religious community, deprived henceforward of its political independence but keeping its national organisation. The preaching of Jesus called this national exclusiveness in question and provoked the decisive crisis from which the Church emerged.

From the beginning the Church was aware of herself as the new Israel, the true community of the Covenant, justly taking to herself the traditional titles. Freed from all national particularism, the Church remains a people whose constitution is to be found in the Gospel of St. Matthew: an organised community, open to all, showing in her gatherings the infinite variety of human conditions, yet involving all her members in the same history, that sacred history leading to companionship between God and his people, which was inaugurated by the alliance on Sinai and to which Jesus in his Paschal mystery had given the definitive dimensions.[1]

Basic as it is, the theme of the People is soon seen to be inadequate as an expression of the unique character of the community of the Covenant—the idea of the Covenant itself has too juridical a character to convey the intimacy of the bonds between God and Israel, the anticipations of a freely-given love which had called the people into being so as to be able to enter with it into a dialogue of perfect reciprocity. We know how the Prophet Osee was inspired to draw on the theme of marital love. In the beginning, and until the time of Ezechiel, it was the contrast between the divine generosity and the infidelities of Israel which held the foreground. A theme as rich as that of conjugal love was bound, one day, to be developed to the full; so too, from the beginning, divine goodness was assured of one day being repaid in kind. It was for the poetical genius to whom we owe the Canticle of Canticles to sing of the vicissitudes of waiting, of the meetings and misunderstandings before the final possessing. And it was not without reason that, to sketch in the portraits of the two partners, he turned to images which, in the case of the bridegroom, evoke the Temple, and for the bride, the land of Israel, in this way twining the parables together and emphasising the liturgical character of his hymn.[2] Christian tradition was to bring this out clearly when it realised that the bride was none other than the Church: Christ purchased her at the price of his blood; moreover she was born of that blood on the cross, with the sacraments as her dowry; it is

[1] See L. Cerfaux: *La Théologie de L'Église suivant saint Paul*, Chaps. 1, 2, Le Cerf, Paris, 1948.

[2] Cf. A. Feuillet: *Le Cantique des Cantiques*, Le Cerf, Paris, 1953.

through them that in her liturgy she celebrates for ever the mystery of her espousals.

The Temple theme grew up, as was natural, in sacerdotal circles. It assumed in the definitive edition of the Scriptures a position of primary importance. The great historical synthesis of the Chronicler is centred wholly upon it. It is closely connected with the essential vocation of the people of God, a vocation at first obscure, dimmed for long by temporal preoccupations concerning political organisation but finally revealed in all its purity and with all its exacting requirements on the return from exile, when renunciation was demanded so that the great theocratic dream could be realised without delay.

It was a painful purification, and not without its perils, as the future was to show. There is in man an invincible leaning towards the absolute, and this is even truer of human societies. Obsessed by the Temple and its worship, Israel was to erect them into an absolute, and to set worship free in spirit and in truth, the destruction of the Temple was necessary.

For, in its material form, the Temple was a sign—or, more accurately a symbol, in the sense in which we have used that word. At first, as we know, the tabernacle was the 'place of witness', the visible expression of the Covenant, the meeting place of God and his people, 'the priestly kingdom and holy nation'. The little that we know of the period before Solomon suggests that the sanctuary of the Ark kept this character rather than that of a place for worship. Not so with Solomon's temple: the influence of the grandiose liturgies of the neighbouring peoples, especially the Egyptians, brought to the fore the act of worship with its twofold daily sacrifice, the chanting of hymns to the accompaniment of musical instruments. This was the development of a decisive element in the liturgy of the Covenant, the single liturgical assembly, the single sacrifice; but not until Christ proclaimed that henceforward there would be no other Temple than his body, and offered himself in sacrifice to ratify by that unique oblation the new and eternal Covenant, did the symbol of the Temple appear in its full significance.

Thus the theme of the Temple merges into that of the Body.

We know how St Paul harmonised its various perspectives and what place it was to take in the development of Christian thought.[3] We have to consider it here only in so far as it is of importance for the liturgy. The bracketing together of body and temple whether in reference to the individual or the whole Church, was a familiar idea to St Paul. In either case, what interested him was that the body was animated by the Spirit, moulding it into the likeness of Christ. A spiritual body, it is by virtue of this fact a holy temple.

With these ideas in mind read the letter to the Ephesians, the most liturgical of the Epistles. It is also the one most concerned with the Church; in it Paul solemnly promulgates the 'mystery' revealed in Jesus Christ, the mystery which henceforward shines forth in the presence of the Powers in the manifestation of the Church.[4] After reading it in this way we can see better how contemplation, in the form of thanksgiving, of God's plan to 're-establish all things in Christ, that are in heaven or on earth', (1.10), concludes with supplication that Christians, rooted in charity, may be 'able to comprehend, with all the saints, what is the breadth and length and height and depth of love' (3.18), for they have been 'built upon the foundation of the apostles and prophets, Jesus Christ himself being the chief corner stone, in whom all the building being framed together, groweth up into an habitation of God in the Spirit' (2.20-22). Now exactly the same theme is repeated further on under the image of the body: it is Christ who has 'given it to some to be apostles, and some prophets, and other some evangelists, and other some pastors and doctors; for the perfecting of the saints, for the work of the ministry, for the edifying of the body of Christ; until we all meet in the unity of faith and of the knowledge of the Son of God, unto a perfect man, unto the measure of the age of the fullness of Christ' (4.11-13).

It was necessary to quote these fundamental passages: they form the foundation of everything we have to say about the

---

[3] L. Cerfaux: *op. cit.* bk. 2, Ch. 5-6; E. Meersch: *Le Corps mystique du Christ*, Desclée de Brouwer, Paris, 1936.

[4] See Ephes. 3. 10. (Translator).

liturgy, the action of the Church, the active presence of the 'mystery'. But it is important to notice at once that the theme of the Body, although it concerns the most profound reality of the Church, is nonetheless directed towards the eschatological manifestation of that reality. Only then will be disclosed what has been in preparation from the very beginning: Christ the Lord, radiating the fullness of the Spirit who rules absolutely over his risen humanity. As long as history lasts he acts in the very thick of humanity and the Church is the visible expression of his activity. But what she really is is not yet, and cannot become, apparent in the present state of history. Were it permissible to continue St Paul's image, it could be said that the growth of the Church is hidden and it will need the cataclysm which will bring time to an end to reveal the Church to herself and to the world. Until then, it is through signs that she expresses and lives the mystery. Here below, the Church is 'sacramental' in constitution and all her actions bear the stamp of this state. We shall see that liturgical actions, more than any others, are especially worthy of being called the 'actions of the Church' because they are directly related to her plenary, eschatological realisation and signify her presence in time, under the form that this historical state requires.

To sum up in a few words what light consideration of the chief parables of the Church sheds on our subject, we can say that the Church, the people of God, the holy nation, the priestly community, must express in her liturgy her twofold nature. She is a community organised in accordance with the basic pattern she received from Christ, the 'community of the Covenant' which must bear witness before the world to the fulfilment of God's plan to be reconciled with mankind in order to summon it to union with his holiness. As the Bride of Christ, she fulfils the rôle of mother towards mankind and inaugurates in her liturgy the dialogue of love for which man was created. She is the spiritual temple, the manifestation, visible throughout history, of the mysterious Body of Christ which extends to the limits of the universe.

33

THE LITURGICAL ASSEMBLY, EXPRESSION OF THE 'MYSTERY' OF THE CHURCH[5]

The calling together of the People of God, the dialogue between Bride and Bridegroom, the growth and education of the race of the sons of God among men, the mystical building up of the definitive Temple, which is the Body of Christ—in short, all the various aspects by which the mystery of the Church has gradually been revealed to us—are brought into play in the liturgy.

But, before going more deeply into this essential function of the Christian liturgy which distinguishes it from all other rites, we should consider for a moment the liturgical assembly itself, that body of people in which all possible types are usually to be found— men, women and children, adults and the aged, rich and poor—all met together at the Church's call to offer to God that official worship laid down and organised by the Church.

To begin with, many see no further. They are there, the whole body of them—practising Catholics, faithful to habits formed in infancy; the occasional attenders, urged by a vague feeling of religiosity; the anxious, seekers after God; those whose minds and bodies are rent by suffering; the faithful, answering to Christ's call and coming to unite themselves to his sacrifice, to draw from his nearness light and strength. There are all sorts and conditions in the Christian liturgical gathering; nothing is further removed from the coterie or sect and it is out of this mixed body that the liturgy has to make the living and worshipping Church. It is to man that the liturgy is addressed—to every man, to the whole man; neither to the intelligence of the intellectual nor to the feelings of the sensitive, although it demands from each all that he has of intelligence and feeling; it takes each man as he is, asking him only to make himself amenable to whatever Christ, through his Spirit in the Church, desires to realise in him. That is why in the sacrament of Christian initiation, after marking the catechumen with the sign of the cross and offering him the salt of

[5] Cf. A. G. Martimort: *L'assemblée liturgique, mystère du Christ* in *La Maison-Dieu* 40 (1954), pp. 5-29.

hospitality in accordance with ancient Roman practice, his ears and mouth are ceremonially opened, that he may be ready to hear and answer God's word.

Indeed, the first function of Christian liturgy is to make God's Word resound in the Church—the prophetic word, whose authentic testimony is preserved in the Sacred Books, the ever living word, which we love to hear echoed in the Fathers and of whose works the liturgical books constitute the official compilation; it is the function of him who presides over the congregation, or his delegate, by means of the sermon to adapt this living word to the actual needs of those present. Although all liturgical services do not nowadays expressly begin with a reading from Holy Scripture, they all always presuppose some word of invitation and welcome. At the Office, it is the invitatory, at sung Mass the antiphon of the introit, at low Mass the opening versicle. But it must be admitted that in the West past centuries have, perhaps, too easily trusted in the spontaneous awakening of the understanding of faith among those present. Or rather, has not the aspect of the liturgy as worship been given too pre-eminent a place at the expense of its prophetical and catechetical aspects? For it is a peculiar characteristic of the Christian liturgy that, because it is not the worship of a purely human community, but of the Church, of the people of God, convened by the Word of God in his Christ, this liturgy cannot but be first of all a hearing of the Word. It alone can teach us to adore God 'in Spirit and in truth', not by a fundamentally deficient human worship but by that sacred worship for the sake of which God constituted his people. New situations in the world, by reawakening the missionary vocation in the Church, recall in equal measure the prime importance of the word. And it is the function of this liturgy at the outset to lay hold of this gathering of all sorts and conditions, to awaken them to their vocation, to bring to their notice the great acts that God performed for the salvation of men and the actual and active presence of this mystery of salvation. Only then, as we shall see more clearly as we proceed, can there be Christian liturgy in all its fullness and reality.

But this is only the first movement. Summoned, gathered together, roused up by the Word of God, this human group comes to recognise in itself an ecclesial community. It does not receive the Word passively. The Spirit of Christ which is in it gives it the ability to reply and so to engage in a dialogue: God's People opens itself to the life of community under the sign of this person-to-person exchange, the most perfect expression of which among men is the 'I will' of the marriage ceremony, the reciprocal and total giving of that very thing which in each person is incommunicable. Such is the revelation of community which is stammered out by the voice of the choir—the blending together of a multitude of voices, without the suppression of any. Liturgy calls for singing, for music is the natural medium for unanimity. In the common harmony, every individual realizes that he is sharing in the one same Breath of life which gives rise in our inmost being to the *Abba* of sonship.

A hymn of supplication first of all, the cry of mankind acknowledging its wretchedness and calling for a saviour. It rises up in many of the Sunday introits in the Roman rite, it bursts forth in the litany of the *Kyrie,* it begins each of the hours of the Divine Office, in the invocation: 'O God come to my help! O Lord, make haste to help me'; or it asserts unshakeable confidence in the versicle 'Our help is in the name of the Lord, who made heaven and earth' which occurs so frequently in the Ritual.

But it is also a hymn of praise and adoration, evoked by the divine splendour and magnificence of the work of salvation. Such is the *Gloria* in the Masses of feast days. The magnificent invitatory of the Eastern liturgies unites both aspects in the notes of the Trisagion: 'Holy God, Holy and Strong, Holy and Immortal, have mercy on us.' In such chants the community effects its conversion; under the direction of Christ, the leader of the choir, it takes part in the symphony which in a single act of adoration unites praise from earth and the powers of heaven: *Sanctus, Sanctus, Sanctus.*

But it is given to the Christian liturgy to go still further and forge the community into the unity of all. In vain, human liturgies strive towards this at the risk of collapsing under the mystical

confusion of collective ecstasy. By contrast, it is with absolute luci-
dity, *sobria ebrietas*, that the Church, by renewing the memorial
left her by the Lord, reaches the state in which all are truly brought
into unity. The motley crowd that make up the congregation is
then mysteriously identified with the one Body of Christ by eating
of the one Bread that is this Body. It is for the preaching and the
rhythm of the celebration as a whole to make the community
aware of this mystery which is accomplished within it. St
Augustine contrived to express this in admirable terms which
deserve more frequent quotation.[6]

In fact, we have here nothing less than the presence, under a
sacramental veil and in the mystery of faith, of the eschatological
realities which will be revealed at the end of time. The liturgical
assembly—because it is the expression of the fullness of the mystery
of the Church—is really the precursor of the definitive assembly
of saved humankind, gathered together for the Messianic banquet,
which ratifies the definitive covenant, in accordance with that
symbolic theme which has its roots in the oldest accounts of the
Covenant on Sinai[7] and which first the prophets and afterwards
Christ were pleased to repeat and arrange anew. So then, it is
already apparent that the celebration of the Eucharist is the heart
and keystone of all Christian liturgy. All other liturgical gatherings
and all services for worship are arranged so as to prepare for it
or prolong it by carrying echoes of it into the various
circumstances of human life.

---

[6] See the passages quoted in E. Meersch, *op. cit.*, from *The City of God*,
X.6 and 20; Sermon 272 (P.L. 38, 1247).

[7] Exodus 24. 9-11.

Chapter 3

The Liturgy:
'Action' of The Church

WHAT is most commonly lacking in our view of the Church is *faith*, which discerns the presence of God at the heart of the most exterior aspects of the Christian mystery. We lack, too, the living experience of the unity of man with himself and with others, through which the union of body and soul and of individual and community are sharply perceived, if not explained. This lack both of living faith and of human wholeness accounts for such unsatisfactory definitions of the liturgy as: 'The liturgy is the official, public expression of the Church's worship.' What interest can a Christian who longs for God for his own sake and for his brethren in God's love have in a display or spectacle, even if it is a sacred one? Rather is he seeking unity with God, with himself and with all men. The liturgy might be defined as the giving of unity to the Church through the act of worship. Nothing is less exterior, and yet all the external elements in man's being are in the liturgy taken up into their places.

It is this wealth of the liturgical reality which the idea of *Action*, as used here, is intended to convey. *Action*, that is, realisation, making actual or real, the reality and life of the Church. *Realisation:* the Church is constituted by the liturgy, for it is the Word of God which is at work in it, the Word of which Isaias said: 'My word shall not return to me void, but it shall do whatsoever I please, and shall prosper in the things for which I sent it.' *Reality:* the very being of the Church is liturgical. The outpouring

38

of the Spirit is sacramental and there could be no Christianity without an objective and very real link with this liturgical datum. Consider, for example, that if the celebration of the Mass were to stop absolutely in the world the Church would disappear. *Life:* the whole wealth of activity and expression which flows from the fullness of a being still appertains to that being. So it is with the praise of the Church, with the charity of the Church, with the unending sacrifice of all Christians 'in a living victim, holy, acceptable to God': all this is intrinsically liturgical, for it is the living and communal expression of the Bride's love for Christ, for God. It is the ultimate realisation of the hidden mystery of which St Paul speaks. So far must we go to understand the liturgy in all its reality and effectiveness.

The first two sections of this chapter ('The action constituting the Church' and 'The action expressing the Church') are devoted to bringing understanding of this fact within the unity and diversity of the liturgical reality. The subsequent pages examine the concrete aspects of this unique and fundamental action — communal, cosmic (in St Paul's sense) and hierarchical.

How may we best define the liturgy's function in relation to the Church? One category suggests itself at once: that of activity. From the beginning we have seen that this is a constituent of all liturgy: communal, sacred action. But this does not go far enough to express the real nature of Christian liturgy. We have already seen the insufficiency of all analogies taken from the life of man and especially the image of the nation to express that unique kind of community which is the Church. A new creation, the Church regenerates man in his inmost being, making him a citizen of the divine world. Liturgical celebrations cannot therefore be put on the same plane as profane activities; they spring from the inmost being and involve man in his fullness. It seems preferable therefore to define the liturgy as a 'sacred action'.

Action means more than activity. Since Aristotle, philosophy has chosen it as a word to express reality as opposed to mere possibility, meaning immanent acts which are distinct from actions in that in them the subject is fully realised without modification of relationship to the outside world. It is obvious that the liturgy is not an action of this kind, but it too expresses and makes real the fullness of being. In this sense the liturgy can be defined as the action of the Church, for it is in it that the Church makes real the fullness of her being. And for everyone who takes part in it, although the liturgy is not at every moment an action, it is the 'action' of the servants of God, and for the baptised it is the action of the sons of God living in the Spirit of the life of Christ.

If it is abnormal that in the Church one group of the members of the community should have no more than the passive rôle of presence (there are no mere onlookers in the liturgy), it is normal that the members of a particular order—especially the lay men— should not intervene in certain liturgical actions, such, for example, as many sacramental acts. But all, from the very moment a liturgical function begins, are enacting the official service of God, a potentiality fundamental to every man is realised, or, as the scholastics would have said, becomes actual.

The liturgy is that action by which the Church as a social body becomes aware of herself as she is established in this world: as the dispenser of the mystery of salvation to mankind.

But this 'action' is effected only in activity, and it is this which gives the liturgy its special place in the dispensation of the mystery of salvation. The liturgy is not primarily a form of teaching, although, as Pius XI said, it is the *didascalia* of the Church and the chief organ of her ordinary *magisterium*;[1] it must be approached from the practical rather than the speculative stand-point. The documents of the liturgy, especially liturgical texts, however great their importance, are not the liturgy; they become the liturgy only when they are set in action, like a musical score. Less still are ceremonies, and the rubrics explaining them, the liturgy. They are only the medium for its performance, and become liturgy only when they are seasonably performed at the right time for the purpose for which they were instituted, that is for the communication of the mystery of salvation.

[1] Cf. Dom Capelle: *Revue Grégorienne*, 1937, p. 79.

THE ACTION CONSTITUTING THE CHURCH

Seen from this point of view, the liturgy has a twofold function in the Church. It *constitutes* the Church and it *expresses* the Church. The first is the work chiefly of the sacramental liturgy, the second that of the liturgy of praise.[2] And the eucharistic liturgy lies at the very heart of the life of the Church, it is pre-eminently *the* sacrament, the sign and bond of the unity of the Body of Christ.

Quite obviously the sacraments of Christian initiation occur first to the mind when speaking of the liturgical action constituting the Church. The Fathers pictured them as the fruitful womb from which Mother Church brings forth new children to Christ. But this image renders the reality only imperfectly, for the Church is herself established in this very act of generation.

It is in faith and in the sacrament of faith that there is effected the integration of the sons of God, hitherto scattered abroad, into the Body of Christ, the Church. The whole of the baptismal liturgy, with its diversity of rites bearing witness, through allusions to its multiform aspects, to the richness of the mystery—recruitment to the militia (the profession of faith), the struggle against the powers of evil and liberation from their ascendancy (the exorcisms and pre-baptismal anointings), the bath of regeneration and burial with Christ in the mystery of death and resurrection, admission to the nuptial feast with its eschatological implications (post-baptismal ceremonies, anointing, the baptismal robe and candle) —the whole of this liturgy, abounding in images and, in the Roman tradition, full of allusions to the most varied scriptural archetypes, forms the setting and means of admission to the Church. The essential, of course, is Christ's efficacious act operating in the properly sacramental formula and rite. But to reduce the rest to

[2] In saying this, we do not forget that the sacramental liturgy is also—and more fully than the liturgy of praise—expressive of the mystery of the Church, for in it the word, endowed with the power of Christ, effects exactly what it says.

secondary ceremonies which can be postponed even when there is no grave reason—indeed it may be wondered if there is any other save immediate danger of death—is to ignore the living nature of the liturgical acts and, to use a somewhat crude image, to resort too lightly to Caesarian operations. The birth of a Christian, and the general health of the Church, deserve closer attention than a juridical theology would generally afford the liturgy. This is even truer of confirmation, the solemn administration of which requires the direct intervention of the head of the local Church—either in person or through his delegate—for the complete integration into it of the new faithful. This sacrament is too often disfigured by a deficient liturgy which is poorly expressive of its properly 'ecclesial' character.

The Eucharist, as we said above, is worthy of especial attention. It is through the Eucharist that the life begun in baptism is, as a rule, sustained. It is the Eucharist which gathers the community of the Church together for the Lord's meal: 'For we being many are one bread, one body; all that partake of one bread' (I Cor. 10.17). There can be no question of putting in the first place, as though it were a separate value, the personal union of each individual with Christ, when all the teaching since the New Testament, the liturgy and the most strongly guaranteed doctrine of the Church, show it as the fruit of the unity of the Body which is the Church. Why then do we so often fail to show how there is found in the Eucharist not only the sign but also the immediate principle of this unity, and how in it is rooted the mystical bond between the Christian and Christ.

The eucharistic celebration brings the community together for its most fundamental action. The Body of Christ is 're-actuated' daily in this sacrament which is the effective sign of the divine and human reality which forms a single being, a multiform but coherent organism, soundly articulated, pervaded by a single sap and by an influx from him who is both its head and its fullness— or fulfilment—animated by a single Spirit which operates differently in its various members, but through the ministry of all prepares the harmonious growth of the Body to the full stature of the perfect man, until that day when there shall be but the one

Christ presenting himself to the Father in the finally perfected sacrifice (cf. Ephesians 4.11-16).

Understanding the Mass thus, as the act which at the same time constitutes and expresses the reality of the Body of the Church, should render impossible the individualism still too common among Christians and priests. To be present at Mass, to celebrate "my" Mass—these are meaningless phrases which are the result of a mistaken piety. And what deep significance really community Masses, conventual and chapter Masses, assume once more—even when, under present discipline in a community of priests they seem to duplicate the eucharistic ministry of each individual member. Even in a privately celebrated Mass, the priest bears with him, invisibly, the community of all those whom he names in his intentions, and whose reality is expressed by the sacrament; and in the community Mass it is his own membership of the body that he expresses and makes real in the most vital way imaginable. How one wishes that a slight change of discipline would make it possible to give this 'realisation' its own sign : communion in the very Bread that is consecrated at that Mass in which all are taking part.

We could follow out through the whole sacramental structure those signs which, directly or indirectly, are agents in constituting the Body of the Church : the re-incorporation of its members in Penance; the handing down of hierarchical powers and the per-petuation of apostolic tradition in the sacrament of Order, whose very name evokes the organising function in the life of the Church; and finally Matrimony, which raises to the level of the special interests of the Kingdom God's command to the species: *Increase and multiply*. Even when we come to the Sacrament of the sick, we must say that its purpose is the building up of the Church. By adapting a Christian in a spiritual manner to meet his special rôle as an invalid, it gives expression to the new function that has been entrusted to that member—a privileged function, immedi-ately expressive of one aspect of the mystery of our redemption.

But there is no reason why this mission, this 'making actual' the mystery of the Church, should be confined to the sacraments. Of course, they do do this in a very special way since the essential grace of Christ uses them as instruments which carry on the redemptive work of his humanity. The whole body of 'mysteries' which, universally or even locally, the Church has thought should be added to them, would not merit the name of 'liturgy' if they did not have a part in that great and ultimate 'mystery' which is the realisation of God's eternal plan to gather all things together in Christ. The most important among them—the consecration of places and persons—have a special part in this since they delegate their subjects—virgin, religious, church or altar—to a more direct co-operation in the priestly ministry of Christ and to the expression of some particular aspect of his mystery. In the same way, the funeral liturgy is not just a magnificent expression of the consummation, by one particular member of the Church, of his way of the Cross; it would have no meaning if it did not express the oneness of the Church here below with the congregation of saints and angels and with those who still await their final deliverance.

THE ACTION EXPRESSING THE CHURCH

However, in the case of the great sacramentals and even more with the multitude of secondary liturgical rites, it is the expressive aspect of *liturgical action* which is most prominent. What is more, the philosophical concept of 'action', to which we have already referred, insists on the indivisibility of these two aspects. It conceives of the action as both the dynamism which brings into existence what is merely possible and as the fullness which expresses the existing reality. The liturgy acts thus; and this is why it can be termed, in the strict meaning of the word, the *action* of the Church. At the same time that it constitutes her it expresses her and these two aspects can be separated only by a process of mental abstraction.

It is this second aspect of the liturgical action that most appropriately brings into play its character as 'mystery'. A mystery expresses and makes present—both functions are essential—by means of sensible signs and symbols, a divine reality which, in itself, is inaccessible to us in our present state.

It is not inconceivable that the Church should have been constituted and her life maintained without the use of signs; but God did not choose this for the economy of the Incarnation. So then, since the Church is herself a parable and a sacrament of the Kingdom, her liturgy is necessarily expressive, in mystery, of the ultimate realities of this Kingdom. And this expression is in no way accidental or an afterthought. It forms the resplendent brightness of that human and divine reality which is the Church. By the very fact of her existence, by the modality of that existence, she expresses what she is and what she brings into being. Nonetheless, it remains true that this expression will always be endowed with all those human values that the Church integrates within herself; she will always bear the mark, and the burden, of the cultures in which she has her roots. Because of this she never expresses distinctly more than one aspect of the mysterious fullness to which she bears witness and there can never be too great a variety of rites, varying with the diversity of human cultures and historical periods, effectively to emphasise the many aspects of a mystery surpassing our understanding. Too much insistence cannot be laid on the necessity of referring to all the liturgical creations, of both East and West, if we are to gain a precise idea of what the Church, in the self-awareness that she has so far achieved, intends to express in her liturgy. A characteristic emphasised in one place will appear only in outline in another. Should we discern it in one place if, more clearly delineated, it has not been encountered elsewhere? On the contrary, this comparison, rather, this synoptic view, alone enables us to recognise the fundamental constant and the secondary developments, the fruits of the local needs or tastes of a given community.[3]

There can be no question here of going into details; they are of interest only in so far as they are based on all the sources of information we have just mentioned. But it was necessary to draw attention to one aspect of the liturgy, whose theological value has not always been perceived, either because the diversity of rites was considered in their purely human aspect, such as the manifestations of folklore, or because they were arbitrarily laid under con-

[3] Cf. Part II, Ch. 8.

tribution in favour of a preconceived theological position. On the contrary it is important to see these rites for what they are, that is, expressions, albeit deficient or clumsy, of a reality of which we must bear in mind both its divine aspect—perfect and unchangeable—and the human, ever changing and dependent on the conditions of the milieu in which the Church must live. Moreover, a sign like this, insufficient, clumsy, forced though it be, very often draws attention to some aspect which the classic lines of the great liturgies in their massive equilibrium have obscured. Thus, by reason of its sobriety, the Roman liturgy is often in danger of concealing from too perfunctory an examination some nuance which it has contrived to indicate discreetly.

Despite its shortcomings and false notes, the Christian liturgy taken as a whole forms a wonderful mirror of the mystery of the Church. More faithfully than in her Fathers and Doctors, who were especially alert to the needs of their hearers and the concerns of the moment, more fully than in the acts of her magisterium, which always bear the marks of controversy and of the errors requiring correction, the Church expresses in her liturgy, her Action *par excellence*, the exercise of her ministry of Salvation, which she effects throughout the whole of time and to the profit of every human nation.

THE COMMUNAL NATURE OF CHRISTIAN LITURGY

Being the action *par excellence* of the Church, the liturgy is necessarily a social action. An individual liturgy, in the strict sense of the term, is inconceivable. Liturgy is performed by the community of the faithful; it is God's people who come to meet their Lord and stand before him. If rubrics and legal prescriptions are indispensable to liturgy, that is because they are so to every action of a human community. The meticulous ordinances of the Mosaic law and the multitudinous prescriptions of Leviticus are not unworthy of the word of God, because on grounds greatly superior to those of legislative prescriptions properly so called, these ceremonial laws organise God's people in a much more essential matter, its sacred actions. The 'convocation' at Sinai wrought a more or less turbulent association of nomadic tribes into an *ecclesia,* a holy people, worthy to come into contact with the awesome divine holiness, whose lightning flashes annihilated whosoever dared approach it without being in a state of holiness. It was the people itself that was sanctified by sprinkling with the blood of sacrifices, that was made a nation of priests. Because this holiness was social of its nature, it had to be regulated by exact laws. But these prescriptions had a religious significance only because the 'law of holiness', the apex of the code of Leviticus (ch. 17-26) is preceded by the law of offerings (ch. 1-7). And in the definitive form of the Sinaitic legislation (Exodus ch. 19-40), the whole of the considerable body of laws concerning the sanctuary (ch. 25-31, 35-40) like the second form of the code of the Covenant (34. 12-28) came to stress the capital rôle played in the life of Israel by the mysterious presence of Yahweh over the 'propitiatory' of the ark within the tabernacle.

When, after Pentecost, the first Christian community realised that it was the *ecclesia,* the 'convocation' of the people of God, the new Israel of which the Sinaitic community had been only the figurative anticipation, it organised itself at once, 'persevering in the doctrines of the apostles and in the communication of the breaking of bread and in prayers' (Acts 2.42). A new ritual quickly took shape and the Apocalypse clearly seems to bear witness to an already developed form of worship. The prominence given to ritual prescriptions in the oldest collections of Christian legislation which have come down to us (the *Didache,* the *Apostolic Tradition* of Hippolytus, the Syrian *Teaching of the Apostles,* and repeated in the great collections of the fourth century, the *Apostolic Constitutions* and Clement's *Octoteuch*) are not evidence of a Judaising tendency, but of a deep-seated need in the life of the people of God, culminating in the direct service of the Lord. The life-giving law of the Gospel, written on their hearts, the law of charity, animates the multitudinous prescriptions to which it gives rise for the safeguarding of the holiness, not only interior, but also social, of the divine service.

Because the Church lives in time, the Church is subject to the conditions of the age. In each era, its liturgy is inspired by the norms of social life proper to each community. It borrows from social life ceremonies and forms of expression, so that it can infuse into them the efficacy of the mystery of salvation. From this point of view, nothing is more revealing than a comparative study of liturgies, which show with what flexibility and how sure a touch the things universal to Christian worship—Eucharist, the Office, the sacramental rites, consecrations and blessings—are adapted to the spirit of every culture.

Provided always that the liturgy preserves its social character.[4] As soon as it becomes the business of the clergy alone, it grows rigid and fossilised and the Christian people is reduced to finding substitutes for it; devotions, which for a Christian community are the normal overflowing of its life, become the sole refuge of its piety. And, because of their very nature devotions, even when they are collective, as with confraternities, are not in themselves social, religion becomes an individual affair. Liturgy itself suffers the after-effects; even when it is not stripped of all its community character-istics (as is all too often the case today with the administration of the sacraments), and even when it is not completely abandoned by Christian people (like the Divine Office or the blessings of the Ritual), it is performed in the presence of a handful of individuals, by the ministry of the clergy alone. How can we recognise in this sort of thing the image and anticipation of the heavenly city? Can we still speak of the liturgy, of 'social worship', when the people of God is reduced to the rôle of passive spectators? Can they truly be 'enacting' the divine service when they can no longer reply *Amen* to the sacerdotal Eucharist? There can be no city worthy of the name if the citizens do not exercise their civic rights. The Church—the anticipation in time of the heavenly city—calls on all her members to take part in the liturgy that the saints cele-brate together on the heavenly mountain. For 'you are come to mount Sion and to the city of the living God, the heavenly Jeru-salem, and to the company of many thousands of angels, and to the church of the first-born' (Hebrews 12, 22-3).

[4] Cf. J. Travers: *Valeur sociale de la liturgie d'après saint Thomas d'Aquin*, 'Lex Orandi' 5, Editions du Cerf, Paris, 1946.

THE ONE LITURGY OF EARTH AND HEAVEN

The Church in her pilgrimage on earth can never forget that she is a citizen of heaven. The Epistle to the Hebrews and the Apocalypse are for her what the model of the sanctuary shown to him on the mountain was to Moses (Exodus 25.9).

The Church, the sacrament of the Kingdom of God, of which she possesses the pledge in the plenary communication of the Spirit on the day of Pentecost, is nonetheless under the law of figures for the duration of her earthly life. 'We see now through a glass in a dark manner; but then face to face' (I Cor. 13. 12); 'We are now the sons of God; and it hath not yet appeared what we shall be' (I John 3.2); 'Your life is hidden with Christ in God. When Christ shall appear, who is your life, then you also shall appear with him in glory' (Col. 3.3-4). It is in this perspective that the whole of the Christian liturgy must be understood.

This unique interplay of heaven and earth makes the liturgy what it is. There are not two liturgies, any more than there are two Churches. But just as the same Church is a pilgrim on earth and triumphant in heaven, so it is the same liturgy that is celebrated here below in figurative rites and is fulfilled without symbol 'beyond the veil' in the heavenly sanctuary. To an extraordinary degree the first generations of Christians had developed this sense of the unity of the Church on earth and in heaven. By his triumphant ascension, Christ broke the bounds of creation, triumphed over time and space, bore human nature into that transcendent sanctuary where Israel had been used to contemplate the angelic hosts performing their service around Yahweh. Henceforward, it was not merely a matter of imitating here below what was done on the 'mount of God', in the heavenly Sion; it became necessary to take part in that solemn liturgy. The ancient eucharistic prayers in every Christian rite are full of the spirit of the Epistle to the Hebrews and of the Apocalypse; the ceremonial is imbued with this spirit.[5] For example, anyone taking part in the Sunday liturgy of the Byzantine rite can feel almost physically this

[5] Cf. E. Peterson: *Le livre des anges*, Desclée de Brouwer, Paris, 1954.

eschatological character, when the doors of the sanctuary are opened for the processions of light, the Gospel or the sacred gifts; the singing of the choir emphasises that this is no mere imitative symbol, but a real participation in the heavenly liturgy—thus, the Gospel procession is followed by the Trisagion, the hymn that Isaias heard on the lips of the Seraphim at the great theophany which inaugurated his career as a prophet (Isaias 6); during the procession of the sacred gifts, the choir, in an endless vocalisation, whose repeated and complicated form seems to transcend the limitations of time, proclaims: 'We who are here the mysterious icon of the Cherubim sing to the life-giving Trinity the thrice holy hymn; let us cast aside every earthly concern, let us receive the King of the universe, invisibly escorted by the angelic hosts: *alleluia!*'

The Roman rite, more sober than those of the East, Spain or Gaul, is no less realistic where the supra-terrestrial nature of the Eucharist is concerned: as he goes up to the altar, the priest asks to be admitted to the Holy of Holies; the canon of the Mass prays that the Church's offering may be placed upon the heavenly altar by the hand of an angel. Moreover, the symbolism of the rites—and especially of the censings which are directly drawn from the Apocalypse—would have no meaning out of this context. They are as it were the visible condensation of a spiritual reality: the reality of the 'glory of God' which fills the temple. And the temple itself was consecrated on earth, because this is what the present state of man and his social life requires—that it should be the dwelling place of God, who fills all things, and the place of his manifestation.

AN HIERARCHICAL ACTION

The social and mysteriously heavenly dimensions of the liturgy so far studied are by no means the only ones. It is also an *hierarchical* action, and there must be restored to this word all the meaning Dionysius found in it, and which became a part of the language of Christians. In this case it means the sovereign priesthood sharing out its functions in degrees, in orders.

It is in this light that the liturgy of the Old Testament appears to us. Moses instituted the high priest and priests of the second rank to make sacrifices and to bless the people in the name of Yahweh. To these were soon added the Levites who were entrusted with the guarding of sacred furnishings and the service of the sanctuary. Later, with the building of the Temple and the definitive organisation of worship, new offices appeared. The work of divine praise was entrusted to singers who gradually acquired a repertory of psalms. Nonetheless, the whole nation was a holy people, a priestly race entitled to stand in the presence of God and wholly consecrated to his service.

The early Christian Communities, in freeing themselves—very quickly it would seem even at Jerusalem—from the Aaronic priesthood, formed a new hierarchy. Special powers were reserved to the Apostles, who alone apparently were empowered to communicate sacramentally to the neophytes the Spirit, of whom since Pentecost the Church had been the trustee. It was their function also, by this same rite of the laying on of hands, to regulate the *charismata* distributed out for the common needs of the Church. The Spirit could, however, intervene directly and make known by extraordinary phenomena the vocation of some particular person to an occasional ministry.

Gradually, a distinction was drawn between the ecclesiastical hierarchy to which was entrusted the maintenance of the sacramental life of the Church (power of order), the organisation of the Church herself (power of jurisdiction) and the official proclamation of the Gospel message (power of teaching), and the charismatic ministries subject to hierarchical control. At the end of the first century the letter of St Clement of Rome,[6] and at the beginning of the second, those of Ignatius of Antioch, show us the liturgy in process of being organised hierarchically, under the presidency of the bishop. When, later, the liturgy of praise was

---

[6] 'To the high priest there is entrusted a special liturgy, to the priests, a particular place is assigned, the Levites engage in the service which is theirs, the laity keep to the laity's rules. May each one of you, my brethren, perform the Eucharist before God according to the order to which he belongs, may he keep good conscience and not transgress the rule appointed for his liturgy' (I Clem. 40. 41).

arranged in definitive order in the monasteries and the churches of the great cities, it was naturally to the members of the hierarchy that fell the right to preside.

The basis for this hierarchical organisation of liturgical worship is found in what we have said above. As an act of the Church, the liturgy is modelled on the constitution of the Church; gradually we see some ministry, at first extra-liturgical, like that of the deacons (Acts 6), come to form part of the performance of Christian worship in such a way that eventually it is restricted to liturgical functions, but of such importance that the Latin church and certain of the Eastern churches more directly subject to her influence do not hesitate to have these offices performed by a priest.

For the liturgy is nothing else than the continuation 'in his body which is the Church,' of the priestly ministry of Christ, the high priest according to the order of Melchisedech.[7] The Epistle to the Hebrews expounds at length the theology of Christ's priesthood. While it emphasises its independence in relation to the Aaronic and Levitical priesthood, it shows how it fulfils them in their most characteristic features—the sacrificial rites dominated by the liturgy of the day of expiation when the great high priest alone would enter the Holy of Holies, bearing the blood of the victims, the pledge of cleansing from sin.

There was another rite, pre-eminently liturgical because it commemorated the Covenant made between Yahweh and the children of Israel after he had delivered them from bondage in Egypt. This was the rite of the Pasch.[8] This was at once the commemoration of the liberation and the Covenant, and also the agrarian liturgy of spring at the approach of the harvest, the liturgy of renewal. To a large extent it was outside the functions of the Levitical priesthood; but it was this which, because of its deep implications, Christ chose for the accomplishment of his sacrifice. The old priesthood culminated in the festival of expiation; the new and eternal priesthood of Christ reaches its full significance in the Pasch, and it is in the context of the Pasch that it is sacramentally accomplished in the Church.

[7] Cf. Pius XII's Encyclical, *Mediator Dei*.

[8] Cf. *La messe et sa catéchèse*, 'Lex orandi', Ed. du Cerf, Paris, 1948.

All the wealth contained in Christ's paschal oblation, both ritually on the evening of the Last Supper and in his body on Golgotha, was to be displayed in the diversity of the rites in the Christian liturgy and in the diversity of ministers to whom they are entrusted. Therefore, all liturgies tend to connect these rites, whether sacramental, consecratory, funerary or laudatory, to the liturgy of the Eucharist, just as they call on all degrees of the hierarchy to take part in them. In fact, just as the Christian liturgy knows only one Priest, Christ, so it knows only one rite, the paschal mystery, which is sacramentally performed in all its fullness in the celebration of the Eucharist.

We are now at the heart of the theology of liturgical action. Without the exercise of the priestly ministry of Christ there is no Christian liturgy, for there is no ritual communication of the mystery of salvation. Christ in his human nature has been consecrated mediator between God and men and anointed as Christ by the Holy Ghost. The exercise in the Church of this mediatory ministry is what constitutes the liturgy. That is why it is not enough to see in it an act of the virtue of religion. *The act of liturgy is a meeting place between the act of religion on the part of man and the saving activity of God,* who, in the offering of Christ on the cross, had mercy on the world. This is obvious for the sacramental liturgy, and especially the eucharistic liturgy; but it is also valid for the liturgy of praise, for the Divine Office which, in one way or another, according to the various rites, is also linked with the Eucharist.

Finally, a few points require clarification concerning the organisation of the Christian priesthood and its connection with the priesthood of Christ.[9] In so far as it is the new and true Israel, the entire Christian people, even more exactly than the old Israel, is a priestly race. A member of Christ through baptism, the Christian participates in the three ministries that Scripture sees in Christ—prophet, priest and king. But it is not as an individual that the Christian is moulded to Christ, but as a member of the Church, of the body of Christ 'spread abroad and communicated'

---

[9] Cf. F. Colson: *Les fonctions ecclésiales aux deux premiers siècles,* Desclée de Brouwer, 1955.

throughout time and space. The Spirit who, in his fullness resting on Christ, anointed him prophet, priest and king has, since Pentecost, rested in his fullness in the bosom of the Church. He also rests in his fullness in every Christian, but communicates his gifts to him as to a member, according to the office bestowed on him within the complete organism. As Head of the Church it is for Christ to bestow these offices and he has done so by communicating his powers to the Apostles whom he chose.

Following his example, they too have been made prophets, priests and kings, with the task of making helpers share in the exercise of these powers, as should seem good to them and of communicating their fullness to those whom they would choose to continue their exercise in time or space. To these successors of the Apostles the name bishop has been reserved since at least the fourth century, as was for a long period also that of ἱερευς or *sacerdos*. In apostolic times we see them first of all associated together in a college in which apostolic powers seem to have been vague. Then, at some quite early date, the powers were concentrated in the president of the college of presbyters and particular liturgical functions were generally reserved to him. He entrusted the vicarious exercise of these to his assistants, to whom also the title *sacerdos* came gradually to be attributed, especially when the growth of the Church made this delegation of powers permanent. The members of the *presbyterium* participated in the priestly action when gathered about the bishop's altar though whether this was what is now described as a 'sacramental' participation is not clear.[10]

In addition, certain liturgical functions were entrusted to the deacons, who were chosen by the Apostles themselves at a very early date to relieve them of the more secular external functions of their ministry. The three orders thus constituted in apostolic times and designated by the imposition of hands with or without rites more specifically defining the appointed office, together form the

[10] Nowadays, while respecting the validity of what was done in former times or what is still done in other rites, for valid concelebration the Church requires that every priest should say the words of consecration (Cf. Pius XII's Allocution to the Congress of Assisi, *Acta Apostolicae Sedis*, 1956 (XLVIII), p.718).

hierarchy properly so called. With them are associated, by virtue of a special call and blessing, coadjutors for certain subordinate ministries. Those to whom they are entrusted occupy a particular position during liturgical celebrations and live more or less wholly apart from profane occupations. In this way was established the body of the clergy, that is, the body of those set apart to devote themselves exclusively to the things of God. But, side by side with the clergy, the Christian people is also an order; it, too, has a share in the hierarchical distribution of ministeries, for it is summoned to offer its gift at the altar and to blend its voice— at the very least by the *Amen* of assent—with the priestly Eucharist. The performance of the liturgical *action* requires that all should take part, for without this participation it would not be an Action of the Church.

Chapter 4

The Liturgy:
Mystery of Worship

IF, having realised from the preceding chapter the real value of the liturgy and of the place of this action within the most intimate life of the community and of each of its members we should ask what this action is, the answer— and it is the final explanation —is that it is a Mystery. All that has gone before this apparently enigmatic answer should suffice to prevent our being upset by this paradox; since in the liturgy we are concerned with God and with men, the last word can only be an appeal to the transcendent and the final attitude, the resting of our whole being, body, mind and soul, in him who excels it in every way and reveals himself without ever reaching an end of his revelation.

The concept of Mystery is taken from St Paul, and our first step will be to clarify it. But at the outset it may be useful to construct a synthesis with the help of two sentences from St John: 'And the Word was made flesh and dwelt among us' (John 1.14). 'By this hath the charity of God appeared towards us, because God hath sent his only begotten Son into the world, that we may live by him. In this is charity, not as though we first loved God, but because he hath first loved us, and sent his Son to be a propiation for our sins' (I John 4.9-10). The Mystery is here given full expression provided that we take careful note that it concerns God.

What could God's coming into the world signify except a radical transformation of the meaning of things and of history? We are so accustomed to our catechetical formulas that we have almost reached the point of failing to see that if God has come into the world everything is in some way fulfilled, everything has received its meaning and, apart from this, nothing has any real purpose. If the plan drawn up by God in his eternal charity includes as an essential the coming among men of the Redeeming Word, how can earlier history have any meaning except as a preparation for that coming, or later history any meaning except in its reactualisation, ceaselessly renewed throughout time and space and in all possible situations? If Christ was born, died and rose again, have we anything else to do besides recount that fact to ourselves and enter into that mystery by which alone the union of time and eternity, of God and man, is brought about? All things find their consummation in Christ and their reconciliation is definitive. This is what St Paul never wearies of telling us, this is what the Church proclaims and effects in the Eucharist.

In other words, because it is a mystery of union, this single Mystery is experienced differently by those whom it unites. In God, it is the mystery of Love, willing eternally to save us and lead us to our consummation by the Incarnation of the Word. In Christ, the centre of union, the same mystery of union and of the salvation of men finds concrete realisation. It only remains for all men to enter into union with Christ, which they do by means of the worship instituted by him—such is the properly ecclesial or liturgical dimension (the two words are here synonymous) of this same, single mystery.

To attain to this liturgical dimension of the Mystery with all its extensions, three preliminary approaches are necessary. First, we must learn about the transformation wrought by the Incarnation in creation which thus receives the Word. By hypothesis, it could be said, the mystery cannot be the voiding of the first creation which would be completely replaced by something else; it is a question of salvation and fulfilment, not destruction. Sin disappeared, but not nature, and, in the sinful creature, the fundamental aspirations to salvation, the very ways in which these might be expressed in the course of the ages, will certainly be purified, not systematically rooted out. That explains why coincidences between

certain forms of worship anterior to Christ—the pagan mysteries
—and certain aspects of the truly Christian liturgical Mystery can
be encountered. This is certainly not a very serious problem. As
we have said, Christian worship uses natural means of expression.
Why should it not use means taken from the civilisations into which
it introduced the leaven of the Gospel? In fact it did not deprive
itself of these throughout the ages and the present forms of our
liturgy contain many borrowings of all kinds from milieus alien to
Christianity. After all, is it really possible to say that Christ is a
stranger to anything whatsoever, or deny any human culture the
possibility of being purified and taken up into the mystery of
Christ? Here recurs the everlasting problem of pagan rites which
missionary pioneers have always solved in a positive sense. Nor
was it otherwise right from the beginning.

For the same reason we must progress beyond the somewhat
simple view that our childhood instruction gives us about the
liturgy: that liturgy equals the sacraments. In fact, the sanctifying
power of the mystery of Christ extends to absolutely everything,
and although the sacraments are the privileged actions of the
liturgical mystery, the idea of sacrament does not exhaust that of
Mystery. There is here an extremely delicate problem in theological method—in any case, the comparison between the ideas of
Mystery and of sacrament will have been fruitful if it has con-
vinced us of the fundamental, objective link between the Christian
mystery and all concrete human reality. Thus liturgy is not
limited to reception of the sacraments, but exerts a certain
dominion over our entire lives as Christians.

Lastly—the third and final approach to the liturgical dimension of Mystery—the coming of the Eternal into time could not
occur without intrinsically altering the course of human history.
This is another and one of the most fundamental aspects of the
actual meeting between God and men in Christ. An understanding of the new division that the Incarnation introduced into time
is indispensable for an understanding of the significance of the
liturgical mystery. Through it, in fact, there is inserted at every
instant of time the definitive intervention effected by the Incarna-

tion : at all stages of its development can be realised the encounter of creation with Christ and with God.

Thus we see that these are the very problems posed for the Christian by the central object of his faith, that is, by the divinity of Jesus Christ, and encountered again when we try to penetrate further into the liturgical Mystery. This is one more sign—if one were needed—of the complete identification of the liturgical Mystery with the Christian Mystery.

Having come, if possible, to an understanding of these difficult theological problems, we shall in any case be able to grasp the essentially *paschal* nature of all liturgy and the prolongation of the Mystery, which takes place not only in the sacraments but also in the great diversity of sacramentals, the veneration of the saints and the whole temporal cycle.

On several occasions already, since we have been trying to define the original nature of the Christian liturgy as an act of the Church, we have been forced to use the word 'mystery'. It is of course familiar in Christian speech, for we have not quite forgotten to call the celebration of the Eucharist, the heart of all liturgy, by that slightly obsolete, but very significant name, 'the holy mysteries'. This is the last trace of an entire vocabulary widely used in the liturgical texts of various rites. It must be admitted that this vocabulary, by reason of its scriptural and profane origins, offers a whole field of theological reflection which has only so far just been begun. Nevertheless, even now the fruitfulness of such an effort of reflection can be clearly perceived once the preliminary work, necessary to avoid the pitfalls that beset pioneers in any field, has been carried out.

At this point must be mentioned, to avoid further reference to it, the great contribution made to the theology of the liturgy by the work of Dom Casel and the Abbey of Maria-Laach.[1] The discussion and criticism provoked by it and the necessary correction entailed have opened ever wider perspectives. We shall limit our-

---

[1] Dom Casel's work is scattered through a number of publications among which prominence must be given to the fifteen volumes of the *Jahrbuch für Liturgiewissenschaft*.

selves here to indicating the principal lines of thought.[2] The
atmosphere to which they introduce us may at first seem strange
to minds accustomed to a strictly logical presentation of doctrine,
but it is clearly the most suitable method, as has already been
remarked, for a proper understanding of supernatural reality.

THE TERM 'MYSTERY'

'Mystery' in the Christian sense of the word, has a twofold ances-
try and the numerous interactions between them (especially in
centres of Alexandran thought and under the influence of Philo)
should not cause us to forget their profound differences. The
question is important in its bearing upon liturgy, and the opposition
encountered by Dom Casel from theologians was doubtless due
to a large degree to the excessive degree of continuity he saw
between these two aspects of the Christian idea of mystery.

The first, and by far the most important, goes back to St Paul.
That it depends wholly on a scriptural concept, independent of any
hellenistic influence, is now well established.[3] In its original sense,
mystery has no other meaning than secret, but St Paul gave it a
technical meaning by reserving it for the 'secret' *par excellence,*
the secret of the divine plan of salvation, which found its fulfilment in Christ and which it was the Apostle's mission to make
known in its final phase, the restoration of the unity of the human
race by the accession of all 'nations' to the inheritance explicitly
promised to Israel alone (Ephesians 3.6).

Three successive but continuous stages may be distinguished in
the Apostle's thought. In the first, 'mystery' means only secret,
but in the sense of secret *par excellence,* the correlative of revelation. In the second, 'mystery' assumes a technical sense, the
admittance of all nations to the same rights as Israel in the inheritance of divine blessings. And in the third, 'mystery' is in some sort
personified and becomes a name for Christ (I Tim. 3.16). It was

[2] Cf. Th. Filthaut: *La théologie des mystères* (Desclée, Paris 1954) and L.
Bouyer: *Liturgy and Life,* London, 1958.

[3] Cf. *Prat. Théologie de Saint Paul,* vol. 2, note L; Deden: *Le mystère paulinien*
in *Ephem. Theol.* 1936, p. 40 Louvain.

this last definition which permitted the later integration into Christian thought of the Greek concept of the 'cult mystery', and it is noteworthy that it appears in the Epistle to Timothy in a lyrical passage which may well be a fragment of a liturgical hymn. Underlying this is the whole Pauline concept of the cosmic Christ as it is expounded in the Epistles of the captivity. If Christ was 'the mystery which was manifested in the flesh,' that was because he was also 'our peace, who hath made both one, and (broken) down the middle wall of partition, the enmities,' (Ephesians 2.14). As the 'mystery' is the divine plan of salvation, so Christ is 'the power of God for salvation,' (Eph. 1.23; Col. 1.24); even more is he himself salvation, for his name which, in Semitic thought, is the expression of his essential being, is 'God Saves'. Christ is the unique instrument of the plan of salvation and, at the same time, perfects and sums up in himself the whole of that plan. When he appeared on earth as 'God the Saviour', it was truly the mystery made manifest in the flesh. Nevertheless, it is only on the day of his resurrection, when he is made Lord, that Christ is clearly identified with the mystery and expresses it in all its dimensions, for only then does he dominate time and the rift in creation, and makes of believing humanity his own Body in his Church.

The hymn quoted in I Tim. 3.16 brings us the echo of the impression made by this revelation of the 'mystery' in the earliest Christian communities. But these communities were for the most part hellenistic and the tone of the Epistles to the Ephesians and the Colossians shows us how auspicious was the atmosphere, at any rate in Asia Minor, for speculation of the most daring kind. What, then, did 'mystery' mean to the Greeks?

The word had long been used in a technical sense in the language of religion.[4] The 'mysteries' were the old agrarian religions which, although supplanted by the cult of the Olympians, had never died out in popular practice, especially in the countryside. The religious unrest which accompanied the great era of the philosophers and the disturbances of the fourth century before Christ,

[4] The principal authority for this paragraph is Festugière: *l'Idéal religieux des Grecs et l'Evangile*, Gabalda, 1932. Cf. Bouyer: *Le salut dans les religions à mystères* (Revue des Sciences Religieuses, 1953, pp. 2-16).

which confused the autonomy of the cities with faith in their gods, led to these mysteries being given a new meaning and the discovery in them of unsuspected depths. The 'mystery' of the cult secret demanded of initiates concealed, or seemed to conceal, a revelation about the destiny of man. The old nature rites, permeated with sympathetic magic, were raised to the status of efficacious symbols of divine realities. Long before this, the Osiris cult in Egypt had been a religion of salvation. In its funeral rites, which were said to reproduce those performed for the youthful God, the dead man became a new Osiris and shared with the god the kingship of the Beyond. Greece went further. Not only in death, but also in this life the initiate was brought into the society of the gods and thenceforth assured of sharing their good fortune for ever.

In Greece, the 'mystery' was fundamentally a cult, a liturgy. But while official religion in the cities consisted primarily in sacrifices and in ceremonial processions or panegyrics accompanied by hymns of praise of the gods, the mystery cults gave pride of place to the dramatic element. The little that we know of them—for their secrets were closely guarded[5]—allows us to catch a glimpse of how a representation of the divine myth, of the history of salvation—which, in the official and public cult of Dionysus had very quickly lost its sacred character—remained for the 'mystes' more than a liturgy, the presence in this world of divine realities, from which Plato was to draw some of the finest illustrations of his concept of participation.

Using more external means, well-suited to stirring the mind and imagination, the solemn exposition of sacred objects, the *hiera,* seems everywhere to have played an important rôle. Symbol and reality were blended together in the revelation of the divine secret of nature.

The possible connections between Christianity and the mystery religions have been widely discussed of late, with more imagination and passion than psychological understanding. An hypothesis confusing the orders and transforming external resemblances into

---

[5] Our most explicit source of information remains *The Golden Ass of Apuleius,* book 19.

analogies and even into identical concepts has rightly been rejected on the grounds of the universal attitude of the earliest Christians towards paganism. Closer study has brought into evidence not only the transcendence and profound originality of the Christian 'mystery' as St Paul understood it, but also its complete independence of the Greek religions. But this rebuttal has sometimes overstepped the bounds justified by an objective study of the facts, and it may legitimately be asked whether generations of Christians imbued with hellenic culture would not have made use of modes of thought and worship familiar to them to express the newness of the Christian message.

We cannot concern ourselves here with what came from religious thought in the strict sense. It is quite clear that when they spoke to 'Greeks', some educated Christians had no scruples in adopting the customary vocabulary of the Hellenic 'mysteries'.[6] But we must restrict ourselves to the organisation of Christian worship. Liturgy, no more than art, speculation, or any other element in a culture, does not spring from nothing. Gestures and forms of prayer, even the orientation of prayer and of the whole religious life, are as it were naturalised in the setting of any given culture. When, at a very early date, the Christian liturgy began to organise into forms of worship (with all that this implies hierarchically) the essentials received from Christ—baptism, the laying on of hands, the sacrificial, eucharistic meal, and prayer in the proper sense of the word—and especially when it desired to explain for its own purposes the meaning of these rites, it was impossible, in districts where religious sensibility and understanding of rites were as strong as they were in Asia Minor and Egypt, for them not to be inspired by what was most religious in the surroundings. Christian liturgy transferred these elements to an entirely different plane, or more precisely, assumed these tentative gropings of pre-Christian consciousness into the kingdom of light which is the dowry of the Church.

There is no influence that the pagan mysteries could possibly exert on Christianity, for the Christian lives by a mystery of quite another order; but the 'mystery of salvation' did not disdain to

[6] St. Clement of Alexandria's *Protreptic* is a classic example of this.

clothe itself in, and transfigure in the process, forms providentially prepared for it, mixed with error though they might be. It seems undeniable to us that Christian sacramentalism finds not only its intellectual terms but also some expression of its worship analogous to those mysteries which also claimed to ensure the presence and efficacy of an act of salvation performed by a god; these were the prefiguration and outline in which before the Hellenistic period, and most especially during it, all that was best in the religious consciousness of man thirsting for salvation took refuge.

MYSTERY AND SACRAMENT

Dom Casel defines the liturgical mystery thus: 'A sacred and ritual action in which a redeeming work in the past is made present according to a fixed rite. In performing this sacred rite, the worshipping community enters into participation in the redeeming event which is evoked, and so gains its own salvation.'[7] This definition, which we make our own, suggests two questions. What is the connection between the 'mystery of the liturgy' and the 'mystery of Christ'? And, on the other hand, is not the concept of mystery reducible, for the theologian, to that of sacrament that was carefully worked out long ago? The first problem, which we shall consider later, presupposes a precise theology of time as well as a clear idea of the two states in the 'mystery of salvation'. A preliminary study of the connections between 'mystery' and 'sacrament' will serve to clear the field.

The classical theology of sacrament is based on the concept of the sign. Outlined, in a very special context, by St Augustine,[8] from whom Peter Lombard introduced it into his *Sentences,* it was fully formulated by the masters of the thirteenth century, and notably by St Thomas.[9] It was with difficulty that this approach

[7] Dom Casel: *Mystère du culte dans le christianisme,* 'Lex Orandi', Les Editions du Cerf, Paris, 1946.

[8] *De Doctrina Christiana, P.L.* 34; Cf. Van der Meer: *Sacramentum chez St Augustine,* art. in *Maison-Dieu,* 13, pp. 50-64.

[9] For what follows it will be valuable to refer to the technical expositions added by P. Roguet to his translation of the *Traité des sacrements* (in the *Summa. Theol.* published by *Revue des Jeunes*).

displaced the concept of sacrament-mystery introduced by St Isidore. The first essential was to safeguard the realism and efficacy of the Christian sacraments. But the very precision with which in the course of the twelfth century, this concept of efficacy was endowed, as more characteristic of the seven sacraments than of any other rite of the Church, required that they should be set apart from the whole body of 'mysteries'. And, on the other hand, the concept of mystery, being too rich and too vague, did not succeed in providing the means for the kind of investigation increasingly required by the development of a closely reasoned theology on the scholastic model. Attention has recently been drawn to the passage 'From Symbol to Dialectic':[10] perhaps it has not been sufficiently noticed that this was to some degree necessitated by the requirements of a mode of thought that had at its disposal no other means of scientific investigation than those provided by Aristotelian logic as it was handed down by Boethius. The analogy of the sign, with the definitions and shades of meaning given to it by St Thomas in the *Summa* at the climax of a laborious evolution, ensured for an important element in Christian liturgy an intelligibility and a balance by which, had they been preserved in the following centuries, the extreme reactions of the reformers might have been avoided.

But the concept of the sign no matter how it was adjusted, did not enable a complete theology of the sacraments to be formulated nor, more especially, to maintain them within the whole body of liturgical rites. The importance that attached to them when their rôle as instruments of salvation was emphasised brought out particularly their immediate connection with Christ in his work of Redemption and especially in his passion. But by the same token stress was laid on their effect and hence on causality. The theologian seeking to examine their mode of action encountered the canonist anxious to define the conditions necessary for sacramental efficacy. Everything relating to the external forms under which they were performed fell into the background; the theologian as such could ignore these forms because in themselves they are meaningless. A deeper study of the concept of 'sign' accentuated

[10] De Lubac *Corpus mysticum*, Ch. 10.

this gap by revealing the relationship between sign and understanding and by distinguishing between natural and conventional
signs. This hiatus was in fact latent in Augustinian intellectualism
from the heart of which sprang the Areopagite's *mystagogia,*
which in itself was closer to Proclus than to Plotinus. Two
radically different kinds of intelligibility came thus to be confused
with each other, and of these, one was precisely that of 'mystery',
the other that of 'sacrament'.[11]

The West has profited from this by being able to use strictly
defined concepts and precise analogies. But because of this it has
failed to formulate a theology of the liturgy which preserves the
realism of its ritual action not only in its major rites, those directly
ordained by Christ himself for the communication of salvation to
men, but in the whole development that it underwent in time and
in the various local Churches. Theological thought forms a single
whole and the predominant rôle given by the Latin Middle Ages
to the redeeming Passion and to its propitiatory and meritorious
character, did not perhaps sufficiently respect the equilibrium of
the divine plan of salvation as a whole, in such a way as to make
possible an understanding of its expression in worship.

In the end one finds oneself led to propose a twofold theology
of the Christian rites: *a sacramental theology,* according to a
descending scheme of the communication to men of the salvation
wrought directly by God; and a *liturgical theology,* according to
an ascending scheme, restoring to the Church's ceremonies their
value as external and social manifestations of the virtue of religion
as acts of worship in the strict sense.

One realizes that there is something approaching despair in this
dichotomy, for it is the entire liturgy, from the major sacraments
to the least of the sacramentals, which is the expression of this
encounter between sinful and redeemed man with God the Saviour
in Christ, whose divine and human life gradually enters into all
man's religious activities, turning them into the actions of a child
of God and an inhabitant of the heavenly city. It does not seem
that any considerable progress can be made in the order which
classical theology has adopted—that of making divine reality

[11] M. D. Chenu: *La théologie au XII siècle,* Paris, Vrin, 1957.

intelligible to our minds by analogies taken from the created world, which alone is directly accessible to us, by refining these instruments as far as possible so as to preserve only their most fundamental ontological values, without concern with their mode of realisation in nature.

From this point of view the conjunction in the sacramental theology of St Thomas of the two concepts of sign and instrument forms an incomparable masterpiece. To attempt to embellish it by introducing more complex ideas, such as that of the symbol, is to dissipate its strength for very little gain. To buttress it by a liturgical theology based on the requirements of worship in man's present circumstances means abandoning any effort at understanding the originality of Christian worship and to empty it of its substance. We fear that such attempts are the result of a one-sided view of the spiritual life and of the conditions in which human reason works.

Logical thought, the product of reasoning, is one of the functions of mind, a function of primary importance, irreplaceable in its scope which is the securing of universally applicable standards for the recognition of the real by a mind which cannot pierce directly the inmost nature of beings. Through this is made possible a science or explanatory knowledge based on those principles which alone are intelligible to us. But the human intelligence makes use of complementary functions which, though closely linked with the sensory faculties, have nonetheless their part to play in our approach to reality. It seems to us that two of these apply here—symbolic thought and poetic or 'factitive' thought.[12]

Their rôle is not to act as substitutes for logical thought, which even in their regard remains pre-eminent (as alone being capable of giving an account of its object), but to offer us access to complementary values of reality. If they come into play in our relationship with nature, in order to reveal to us what to logical thought remains inexplicable, that is in the first place existence,

[12] Some profound judgments about these functions of the mind—on which not enough work has yet been done—are to be found in J. Maritain, *Art and scholasticism* (Geoffrey Bles), and *Quatre essais sur la vie d'esprit* (Alsatia, Paris, 1956)).

6

their rôle is even greater when it comes to introducing us into the world of divine realities, for these belong to an order to which our reason can attain only by analogies, that is, by means of an interpretation which leaves their specific nature vague. Now, all too often it is forgotten that the liturgy is of the order of activity (ἔργον), not of knowledge (λόγος). Logical knowledge can have only a very feeble grasp of it; it is in the very process of performance that the liturgical act becomes intelligible, and this performance operates entirely in the realm of visible realities, not by reason of what they are, but because of the power of expression which they contain, which is able to awaken in the mind echoes of the most sublime realities. Thus, as the author of the treatise on the *Divine Names* and all who stand in the Platonic tradition have already observed, the most ordinary things are capable of expressing the divine.[13]

Now it is on this level of thought that 'mystery' operates, for it is the proper mode of the manifestation of the divine in the world. To set it at the heart of the theology of liturgy, in place of the technically formulated concept of sacrament, is to admit that we are passing from logical consideration to phenomenological—in other words instead of trying to *account for* divine realities by means of analogies drawn from creation, we shall *describe* the manifestations of the divine in the universe which is accessible to us. A similar approach on the level of pure philosophy is not without interest, for this alone can make us see the consistency of the real in so far as it is made up of existing things. But it has a still greater importance for the theologian who sees in beings the effect of the eternal divine Word manifesting in them traces of his ineffable transcendence. It is lawful for him in fathoming this secret to push to its limits the analogy of human speech, which sets forth mental concepts in words. Words are the outward expression of mental concepts. Their significance is not merely conventional or algebraic, for they carry their own over-

---

[13] This is easier to understand if we allow, with a growing number of sociologists and psychologists, that participation is a manner of thought which, possessing primitive people whom it keeps, according to J. Maritain, in a 'nocturnal state of mind' is a fundamental aspect of human thought and the expression of one form of the real.

tones which give them individuality and make perfect translation
from one language to another impossible.

We cannot dwell on this. It is enough for us to have sketched in
broad outline the plane of thought to which 'mystery' belongs,
and to have shown the originality of this idea and the additional
values it can bring to theological thought. We can see now, perhaps, why this is a truly Christian concept, for which natural
thought can provide only deficient analogies—the 'mystery' is, in
fact, *revelation*. Created things carry an echo of the divine only to
ears that have heard the word of God spoken directly to men. To
human understanding, left to its own devices, they are an inscription to which the key has been lost. But created realities enter into
the realm of mystery fully only because God, through the incarnation of the Word, has entered into the heart of visible creation.
Now we can see how the double tradition of 'mystery'—the
Pauline and the Greek—can find a meeting-place, and how Christ
can without qualification be called 'the Mystery', because he is
himself the revelation of God subsisting in a created nature. But
we see, too, the close bonds which unite this mystery to time and
cause it to be more akin to poetic knowledge than to speculation.

MYSTERY AND TIME IN THE CHURCH

The interest shown by contemporary thought in everything
relating to time, the historical viewpoint from which it delights
in seeing all things so that it even introduces duration into the
constitution of created things, has only just begun to make itself
felt in Christian thinking. It is strange that it has been possible for
Christians to lose their understanding of time to this extent and
to forget that the revelation to which they are witnesses is a history
—that not only did God decide to enter into time and accom-
modate his Word to man's development, but that the heart of
revelation consists in acts rather than in words—the covenant
with Abraham by circumcision, that on Sinai, the wandering of
the people of Israel, with the Babylonian exile as its central point
and finally the birth of Christ and his ministry, death and
resurrection.

It was recently said that: 'The specifically Christian nucleus, as one might define it after going back to the documents of primitive Christianity, is actually identical with the history of salvation.'[14] Moreover, this was the field of the first decisive struggle Christian thought had to withstand against Gnosticism. This gave St Irenaeus occasion to work out a theology of history, whose wealth has scarcely been tapped by later ages. Christianity's most far-seeing adversaries were never mistaken about this matter, however, and Celsius protested ironically against the Christians' claim to give the final explanation of events in this world. For, to the Greek, there can be no such explanation. Time generates incomprehensibility, as it does corruption. If it is not to be fundamentally inconceivable to his mind, time must form part of a cycle of never ceasing beginnings and so be a moving image of unmoving eternity.

Does not the failure of the two most intellectual civilizations the world has seen—the Greek and the Indian—to reveal the meaning of time, and the fact that, on the contrary, revelation presents itself to us as a history of salvation, suggest that the duration of time belongs in a very special way to the order of mystery, of the manifestation of the divine in the created? If this be true—and it becomes ever clearer that we must allow it to be so—if time is deeply involved in the revelation God wishes to make of himself, and if, equally, it is the means by which his creation may return to God, then it is not surprising that it bears several dimensions, to meet the demands of this twofold process of revelation and reintegration. We know that there are different times, which cannot be reduced to one another, according to the various orders of existence: cosmic time with the rhythm of sidereal motion and biological time, which touch on our lives without becoming confused with each other. We learn from revelation that there is one time for human history and one time for divine history, and that these are subject to entirely different laws.

These latter were revealed only in 'the fullness of time' when

[14] O. Cullmann: *Christ et le temps*, p. 18, Delachaux et Nietslé, 1947. On this important book and the thoughts it suggests, see the article of P. Chifflot in *Maison-Dieu*, 13, pp. 26-49.

'God sent his Son, made of a woman, made under the law, that he might redeem them who were under the law, that we might receive the adoption of sons' (Gal. 4.4-5). For Israel, time was lineal, divided into three great phases: before creation; the 'time of this age' between creation and the day of Yahweh; and the last times, beyond that day, a vague term whose meaning seems to vary from one inspired author to another. In any case, the sequence of time knew only these two decisive events capable of changing its nature—Creation and the Day of Yahweh. All the interim, historic time, is broken up by various manifestations of God and by many covenants with Noah, Abraham and Moses; nonetheless it constitutes one homogeneous sequence.

But Christ broke this continuity. The 'last times' assumed an unforeseen aspect that was calculated to disconcert anyone familiar with the thought of Israel. The 'Kingdom draws near', it is 'among you', and yet the events of history continue their course. When, on the day of Pentecost, Peter declared that God had raised 'Jesus, whom you have crucified' and made him 'Lord' and 'Christ' (Acts 2.36), he was also proclaiming that the time of the Messias, the last times, had been inaugurated right in the course of history. All that was new in Christianity was stated in these few words.

Christ's resurrection, by which he was constituted Lord, was the decisive event, the fulfilment of all that preceded it and the explanation of all that was to follow. St Paul, especially in his Epistles from prison, expounds the consequences at length. By his death, Christ triumphed over the powers, the rulers of this world; having risen, he is Lord, the head and master of creation; henceforward—as the Apocalypse was to show—it is he who guides the course of events.[15]

But there is an even more profound reality; it is not only the order of time and the meaning of history that have been changed. Even more fundamental than the substitution of the 'Lord' for the 'Prince of this world' is the ontological transformation which

[15] On this point see L. Bouyer: *Le Mystère du mal dans le christianisme antique* in 'Dieu Vivant VI' and *Initiation théologique*, Vol. 1, Ch. 12, Le Cerf, Paris, 1952.

makes mankind, and through mankind the whole of creation, pass from a period of growth and of evolution, to one of recapitulation and involution. It is this transformation which is truly characteristic of—or, rather, which constitutes—'ecclesial' time. *Cosmic* time goes on apparently uninterrupted; *historic* time is given a new direction but continues to exist as before; but a new time has appeared, *the time of fulfilment,* which is to make possible the realisation of a new and final phase in the divine plan; the formation of the Church, the Body of the whole Christ gathering in all mankind except those who voluntarily refuse.[16]

This new time was inaugurated after the short intermediate period of fifty days following the resurrection, by the gift of the Spirit on the day of Pentecost. The time of the Church is really the time of the Spirit raising up the new creation manifested on the 'Day of the Lord', corresponding to the day of the first creation, and setting a term to the unfolding of historical time. This period of the 'time of the Messias', is essentially a secret time, a time of 'mystery' which will be brought to an end by the revelation (apocalypse) of the visible presence (*parousia*) of the Lord who was invisibly guiding its course by his Spirit. The Spirit himself is given only in token of 'firstfruits' (Romans 8.23) and as a 'pledge' (II Cor. 1.22), for although the kingdom is already here, it is not yet made manifest.[17] But the Spirit has been given and that is the radical new element in the time of the Church.[18] The Spirit who came only temporarily upon the prophets, as if in anticipation, is given now in intimate connection with the death and glorification of Christ (John 7.39); he brings the Church into being by giving a single soul to the body of the redeemed, to those who 'have washed their robes and have made them white in the blood of the Lamb' (Apoc. 7.14), and have performed the Pasch with him, passing over from darkness to the Kingdom of light.

But the Spirit has been given not only on the grounds that he

[16] Cf. I. Dalmais: *Le Temps de L'Église* in *L'Église et les Églises*, Chevetogne, 1954, pp. 87-103.

[17] St Gregory of Nyssa and St Maximus the Confessor—among others—explain the meaning of the second petition of the *Pater* in this sequence.

[18] We feel that this is a point on which Cullmann's book (mentioned above) is inadequate.

is the Spirit of Jesus, to shape and animate the Body of Christ, which is the Church. He is truly himself the 'other Comforter' as really and personally present in the world, although hidden, as the Son was in his Incarnation. He reveals himself in his gifts and by virtue of this is the dowry of the Church and the earnest of the Kingdom.[19] For while the Church is the Body of Christ, she is also his Bride, she has her own personality and autonomy. That is why the Church can stand in Christ's presence and 'sing hymns (to him) as to a God' (Pliny the Younger, *Letter,* 10.96), and pray for his return, crying in the Spirit: *Marana tha*: 'Come, Lord'.

This paradoxical enlargement, this twofold dialectical momentum that will be overcome only at the Parousia when Christ 'shall have delivered up the kingdom to God and the Father' and God shall 'be all in all' (I Cor. 15. 24, 28) constitutes the mystery of the time of the Church. The Lord is both present and absent; so intimately present that he works directly through his sacraments which, as instruments, prolong his sacred humanity (St. Thomas, *Summa Theol.* IIIa, q.62,a.5), and yet absent, seated at the right hand of the Father, whence he shall return only to judge the quick and the dead. This is *eschatological time* because there is nothing radically new to wait for, and yet an *historical time,* during which the many-sided work of creation is gradually recapitulated and revelation is commemorated.

This condition and this structure proper to the time of the Church, call for a special kind of liturgy; the truly Christian element in the assemblies of the first believers appears in the purpose of their worship whose only aim is the building up of the body of Christ. That is why, in the primitive Church, the climax of all worship was the celebration of the meal in which Christ was present in the midst of his own. The commemoration of the Last Supper looked both to the past and to the future. It recalled the meal Jesus ate with his disciples before his death, and the meals that the risen Lord shared with them at Eastertide. And it looked towards the future, opening out a perspective towards the end of all things; this theme existed in Judaism in the form of a Messianic

[19] Cf. Dom Vonier: *L'esprit et l'Épouse* in 'Unam Sanctam', Ed. du Cerf, Paris.

banquet. Thus in primitive Christianity every act of worship made clear that in Christ there is revealed the whole pattern of salvation.[20]

THE PASCHAL MYSTERY

In the passage cited earlier Cullmann appears to us to have clearly indicated the essential newness of Christian worship, wholly centred about the 'Lord's Supper' which, very soon, came to be called the Eucharist. But he did not show sufficiently clearly the dimensions and the central position occupied by this act of worship. The Eucharist is the centre of Christian liturgy only because it is pre-eminently the 'memorial', the Pasch, according to one possible etymology of that word. As we have seen, the Christian

[20] Cf. Cullmann: *Christ et le temps*, p. 52. Equally interesting views are expressed in J. Mouroux: *Structure spirituelle du présent chrétien*, Rech. Sc. relig., 1956, pp. 5-25.

The liturgy of Israel, which was similar in this respect to that of most other religions, was familiar with two kinds of worship—sacrifice and prayer, especially the singing of psalms, often accompanied by processions and, in the synagogues at least, interspersed with the ceremonial reading of the sacred books. All non-Christian liturgies make use of these same two kinds of worship because—whatever their deviations and aberrations from the standards of revelation—they are all within the single stream of historical time.

Christianity required something different. Now it happened that on the fringes of the official religions of the Hellenised Mediterranean world in which its first growth occurred, there existed forms of worship which had gradually risen from magic to religion and strove to satisfy the aspirations of souls for salvation (On the Greek mysteries and their expression in worship, see L. Bouyer: *Le salut dans les religions à mystères*, Rev. Sc. Rel., 1953, pp. 1-16).

There is no cause to be astonished at the similarities the various Christian liturgies show to these forms of worship. We have seen how a similarity of vocabulary in two entirely different traditions led to the assumption by Christian thinking of one section of the images and terms used by the Hellenic mystery cults. This phenomenon for which there is clear evidence is not without interest, but it is of secondary importance. What is of prime importance if the Christian rite is to be understood, is the real analogy between the two forms of worship, and the enlightment that the religious phenomenology presupposed by the mystery cults can bring us. We feel that in this respect Dom Casel was right to suggest a return to the pregnant expressions of the patristic age and to throw light on them by analogies drawn from the kind of culture in which they originated. There is no doubt that this is the best way of entering as fully as possible into realities which are themselves irreducible to any natural standard.

mystery culminates and is summed up in the paschal mystery which completed the history of the salvation and the mission of Israel while at the same time inaugurating the time of Messias, the time of the Church.

In the first centuries of Christianity, Easter was *the* feast, not only the paramount feast, the feast of feasts as the Martyrology calls it today, but also the only feast, beside which no other feast could exist. It was a feast lasting fifty days, which together made but a single festival, mirroring the fifty days which followed Christ's resurrection and during which time was, as it were, suspended; for the old times were brought to an end by the resurrection and the new times would not begin before the coming of the Spirit. We cannot emphasise too strongly the significance of a feast which broke through the course of cosmic time in this way, through the order of its two mutable elements, the rhythmic flow of light and of the phases of the moon. Dom Casel has felicitously expressed the essence of the religious feast.

'Its characteristic is that the divine life descends in some sort effectively among those who take part in the religious celebration. This celebration is no mere commemoration, it includes also a presence. God has appeared among those who serve him in worship. They have called to him—hear, come, show yourself, be present—and he has come, he has shown himself, he is present. *Advenit, ἐπεφανὴ, adest.* His presence is by no means passive; he has come to act, to succour, to overcome through suffering, just as at his first Epiphany he suffered, he struggled, he overcame. His disciples, in the act of worship, work with him because he is in their midst.'[21] Easter is *the* feast because it is the manifestation of Jesus as the Lord. For the Christian, there can be no manifestation of God which is not linked with that manifestation and does not find there its ultimate significance.

Now the characteristic expression of a religious festival is worship. If Easter is *the* Christian feast, the whole of Christian worship will be paschal and its sole purpose will be to unfold the manifold potentialities of the paschal mystery and to ensure its efficacious presence for as long as the Church is involved

[21] Dom Casel: *Le mystère de la fête*, art. in *Maison-Dieu*, 1, p. 25, 1945.

in the time sequence of history and of the world. Thus it is the middle point and point of contact between time in the world and eternal time.

Primarily, Easter is a commemoration. In Israel, the Pasch was the commemoration of the liberation from Egypt, when God revealed himself to his people in the slaying of the first-born of Egypt and the crossing of the Red Sea. This event set in motion the destiny of the people of God which was soon to be sanctioned by the covenant on Sinai. It was the epitome of all the benefits the mercy of God had bestowed on Israel. No future event was to be of comparable importance. That is why even in Judaism the Pasch is the pre-eminent feast. But it is not the only feast. The commemoration of the deliverance was fitted into a cycle of agricultural festivals, none of which were forgotten as a result. Other feasts, too, took their places in the calendar, feasts which had no direct connection with the Pasch.

The most important was the Day of Atonement, which every year reaffirmed and guaranteed the communal holiness of Israel; 'they were a priestly kingdom and holy nation' (Exodus 19.6), enabled according to the laws of holiness to enter without peril into relationship with the awful divine holiness. This other extreme of Jewish worship occasionally tended to draw to itself the title of principal feast. It too was bound up with the memory of the events of the Exodus, of those long years in the desert which, more than any others, were for the chosen people the time of holiness, because then they were completely set apart from the Gentiles and their pernicious example.

In the Christian Pasch, the feast of commemoration and the festival of atonement become a single feast. 'Christ our pasch is sacrificed' (I Cor. 5.7) and by his immolation he has 'redeemed us from all iniquity' (Titus 2.14.). God's greatest gift is no longer free deliverance, but expiation at the cost of life. And 'the Lamb stands, everlastingly, as it were slain' (cf. Apoc. 5.6), ceaselessly interceding for us beyond the veil through which he once passed bearing, not like the Jewish high priest, the blood of victims, but his own blood poured out for us (Heb. 9.11-12).

The uniting of these two aspects of the Christian mystery helps us to understand how the Church, true to Christ's ordinance on the night of the Last Supper, has been able to centre the whole of her worship on a paschal commemoration, while the author of the Epistle to the Hebrews could contemplate Christ's priestly act in images drawn from the ritual of the day of atonement. These two approaches, irreconcilable in a figurative worship, come together as soon as commemoration and propitiation achieve their perfect expression in the Person of him whom the Baptist called 'lamb of God who taketh away the sin of the world' (John 1.29).

Nevertheless, like the Jewish Pasch, the Christian Pasch is first of all the passing over of the Lord in accordance with the etymology given to the word by the Bible. During the first three Christian centuries when it was the only feast Easter was not, as it is today, the commemoration of the resurrection of Christ, but the time when, in breaking the fast by eucharistic communion, the Church inaugurated Pentecost, the feast of the fifty days, in which the newness of the Christian era was proclaimed.[22] This feast—and through it, the whole of Christian worship which is contained in it—received from the tradition of Israel certain allusive features which at first glance obscure both the eucharistic commemoration and the fact of the Resurrection. Two ideas are dominant: *salvation,* and *presence,* and about these two crystallised the whole body of liturgical rites. These are two inseparable and complementary ideas whose conjunction constituted the originality of the Christian liturgy. It is a liturgy of salvation, intended to assure men that they share in this 'salvation of God' manifested in Christ which restores, on an infinitely higher and wider level, the creation of Adam to the divine image and likeness. But it is also a liturgy of presence for, in ascending to the right hand of the Father, Christ our Lord began his rule over all creation and assured his Church of his presence until the end of time. The pledge of this presence is twofold—the sacrament which with symbolic rites effects the building up of the Body of Christ, which is the Church: and the Spirit, given as the first-fruits of the consummation to come, when he shall also quicken our mortal bodies

[22] Cf. Dom Casel: art. *Art und Sinn der ältesten christlichen Osterfeier* in the *Jahrbuch für Lit. XIV,* pp. 1-79.

(Romans 8.11), to transform them into spiritual bodies like that which has been Christ's since his resurrection.

The passover of the Lord,[23] whereby is communicated through time and space the single act of salvation—all sacramental liturgy is the unfolding of this aspect of the paschal mystery in which, in Christ and with Christ, man passes over to the divine life and inheritance of the Father. But the liturgy is also the presence of God, inaugurating the kingdom even in this world. That is why, as we saw above, there is only one liturgy of the whole Church both in heaven and on earth.[24]

And this one liturgy has only the one priest, Christ, shown to us in the Epistle to the Hebrews and the Apocalypse presiding over the heavenly liturgy, and also presiding over the liturgies of earth through the ministry of those whom he associates with himself in his priesthood.

Feast, commemoration, passover and presence: the Christian Pasch can be all these things just because it is a 'mystery'. The paschal mystery is the expression in worship of the mystery of salvation in all its dimensions. The double concept, Pauline and hellenistic, of mystery have their meeting place in it, and in it too all the various aspects of the liturgical mystery find their unity. The paschal mystery is the fulfilment of God's great plan for the reconciliation of mankind to himself in Christ and for the summoning of men to share in heavenly benefits by causing to dwell in them the Holy Ghost who initiates them into divine life.

The expression in worship of this mystery will itself also be a mystery, not this time in the Pauline but in the hellenistic sense, if it makes truly present the work of Redemption wrought by Christ on Calvary.

But although that work culminated on the cross, its extent stretches to the whole of Christ's life. 'The nativity of Christ', said Paschasius Radbertus, 'and the whole economy of salvation, form one great sacrament, for in the visible Man the divine majesty invisibly and secretly accomplished the things useful for our con-

[23] It is a question, obviously, of Christ's passing over to his Father through the redeeming death by which he merited, together with victory over the last enemy, glorification and universal Lordship.

[24] See in Ch. 3: *The one liturgy of earth and Heaven.*

secration and sanctification. This is why the Incarnation of God is rightly called a mystery or sacrament'.[25]

The liturgical mystery should express all the dimensions of the work of salvation wrought by Christ and the various ways in which man is called to share in them. It must therefore evoke the revelation of the Incarnate Word from his appearance on earth to his glorious return to heaven. But because according to St Paul the mystery of Christ is simply the supreme revelation and perfection of a mystery of salvation embracing the whole field of human history, from the creation to the ultimate consummation, a liturgy to be adequate to the mystery of salvation ought ritually to represent the whole of this development. This is the rôle of the Temporal cycle.

The liturgy ought also to be modelled on the various moments and actions which constitute man's participation in the mystery of of salvation. Born to divine life in Christ by baptism, he must let himself be shaped by Christ's saving acts until his entry into the kingdom of the Father on that day when—as the ancient form of the Latin liturgy of the dead puts it—the flight from Egypt begun sacramentally in baptism shall be fully accomplished for each one. This is what is realised by the sacramental liturgy.

But even as mankind is entering progressively and piecemeal into the Kingdom in this way, it already possesses its pledges and shares in its life. Side by side with the mystery of the sacraments, the paschal mystery calls forth the mystery of praise, the hymn of the redeemed who 'sing the canticle of Moses the servant of God' (Paschal canticle) and the 'canticle of the Lamb' (Apoc. 15.3); thence springs the liturgy of praise, represented in its essentials by the canonical Office. Sacrament and praise are combined and culminate in the Eucharist, the characteristic rite of Christian worship which is also the pre-eminent rite of the new Pasch.

Three rites which constitute so many liturgical mysteries are the medium for the expression in worship of the paschal mystery. They are the 'mystery' of water, the 'mystery' of oil and the

[25] *Lib. de Corp. et Sang. Domini* III, quoted by Dom Casel: *Mystère du Culte*, p. 117.

'mystery' of bread and wine. Together they form the basis of Christian sacramentalism.[26]

The *mystery of water* is the mystery of the freedom-bringing Pasch. It was unknown in Israel because for Israel the Pasch was a commemoration and not a mystery. A new structure of time was necessary before every individual man could share in the one passage through the waters. The various Christian liturgies delight in emphasising the meaning of this mystery in rites and prayers in which its varied and abundant aspects are revealed. At its heart stands Christ's declaration: 'Unless a man be born again of water and the Holy Ghost, he cannot enter into the kingdom of God' (John 3.5) to which sacramental theology has increasingly devoted its attention with the consequent danger of impoverishing its breadth of meaning in the history of salvation.

Why is there this mystery of water? We may not, as has often been done, seek in it symbolism to our own liking; such a method appeals only to the imagination and though elaborations of this kind can be of assistance to piety they are deprived of all theological value. This is not the method of the Church's *mystagogia,* which sets Christ's precept in the unfolding of the story of salvation.[27] Two important prefigurings, the deluge and the crossing of the Red Sea, brought into prominence the paradox of waters, the instrument of divine judgment (Wisdom 19) for the destruction of the wicked and the salvation of the good. But Christ proclaimed (John 12.31) that his mission and death were the judgment of this world; baptism in water is clearly a Pasch, the passing over of the avenging and saving God who, through it, causes mankind to enter progressively into the mystery of the death and resurrection of Christ.

The Roman rite has developed this mystery of water more perfectly than any other. The whole paschal liturgy is built up around it, at least after mid-Lent.[28] Other Churches have been

[26] On this see L. Bouyer: *The Paschal Mystery*, London and New York, 1951.

[27] See J. Daniélou: 'The Types of Baptism,' Chs. 4-6, *The Bible and Liturgy*, Notre Dame, Ind., 1956.

[28] Cf. *Spiritualité pascale*, Ch. 4, pp. 52 ff., 75 ff. Desclée de Brouwer, Paris, 1957.

especially anxious to emphasise the effects of the mystery—admission to the kingdom of light and the adoption of sonship—and have preferred to connect it with the Epiphany, so limiting its perspectives and meaning. But all liturgies have at least preserved a commemoration of it at Easter, and are to that extent faithful to the tradition of apostolic times; above all, all have emphasised the paschal nature of penance as a second baptism; the mystery of bitter waters, of sweat and tears, which give back sinful man access to Paradise, lost yet again by his own sin.

The *mystery of oil* is intimately connected with the mystery of water and emphasises its saving character. Nothing seems to link it with the Easter mystery, and yet all liturgies give it a place of distinction. Is it merely for practical reasons since oil and chrism have their part to play in baptism, or is it to emphasise paschal *newness* which requires freshly consecrated elements, or again is it to link every consecration closely with the mystery of redemption? These arguments, which are often put forward by liturgists themselves, certainly do not go to the root of the matter, and various liturgies help towards a deeper understanding of this mystery.

Oil is the sign of the Messias, of God's Anointed. Now, although Christ was anointed Messias at the moment of his Incarnation, although he began his Messianic work when, as John baptised him, the dove—once the bearer of the olive branch—rested on him, he only placed the seal on his Messias-ship on the day of the Pasch, when he was made Lord and given universal rule. In the course of his public career he had filled the rôle of prophet; in the Upper Room and on Calvary he had acted as the priest of the new Covenant; only at Easter did he exercise his kingship. Only then did his Messianic anointing assume its full significance: it was above all a royal anointing, the sign of the reign of the Spirit over his henceforward glorious flesh.

Here again the Roman liturgy better than any other has contrived to express the mystery by bringing all the blessings and consecrations of oil together into a single rite reserved to the bishop, the sole trustee of Christ's threefold office. In the course of centuries the Eastern liturgies, which are generally so expressive of mystery, seem to have lost the significance of this. The exaggerated length of the consecration of chrism, reserved to the patriarch, which he performs only rarely, has considerably weakened its expression of the Paschal mystery, which is not merely, nor primarily, the evocation of Christ's resurrection, but rather the actual admission of men into the new and divine life inaugurated by that resurrection.

It is true that for this the Eucharist, the *mystery of bread and wine*, suffices, for it is the pre-eminent rite of the Pasch, the commemoration chosen by Christ as the expression of his mystery of salvation and the guarantee of its efficacious presence in every generation. The mystery of water and the mystery of oil which form part of the sacramental order are ordained for the purpose of the Eucharist and normally have their place within the celebration of the eucharistic liturgy. All Christian worship culminates in it and in it finds its ultimate justification as the mystery of worship. That is why the Eucharist tends quite naturally to be joined to any other celebration.

There is some danger of confusion here and it is important first to delineate clearly the dimensions proper to the eucharistic mystery before trying to understand through it the ordering of the whole liturgy. The increasing and exclusive emphasis in the West since the Middle Ages on the commemoration of the death of Christ and the expression of his sacrifice has not only raised artificial theological problems such as that of the immolation of Christ on the altar; unfortunately, it has restricted the meaning of the mystery by bringing about an almost complete neglect of its eschatological aspects.

Yet these are essential, and without them the Eucharist could not be the commemoration of the Christian Pasch nor, what is more important, a mystery of worship. The Last Supper stands at that turning point at which the time of Israel was about to be completed and to give way—still in the same historical time sequence—to the fullness of time, whose meaning was the precise opposite. The nation chosen for the salvation of the world had gradually been reduced to a remnant and this remnant itself was epitomised in the Servant who was to be given up to death for the expiation of the sins of his people: 'And not only for the nation, but to gather together in one the children of God that were dispersed' (John 11.52). Henceforward, the only purpose of the world's time was to permit the reintegration of the whole man into Christ and the constitution of the new people of God. The final act was performed and made possible the communication of the Spirit to men, that is, the coming, at first in secret, of the Kingdom of God. At the same time as the last Mosaic Pasch was being celebrated, the Messianic banquet foretold by the prophets was being inaugurated (Isaias 25.6), and Jesus himself solemnly emphasized that fact: 'With what desire have I desired to eat this pasch with you, before I suffer; for I say to you that from this time, I will not eat it, till it be fulfilled in the kingdom of God' (Luke 22.15-16). The meal taken by the risen Lord with his disciples in the course of which he 'broke bread' marked the beginning of this new presence. At Pentecost, the Spirit was given and 'there occurred from that time onwards an event which, properly speaking, should not have befallen before the end of time. Christ returns already to the midst of the gathering, just as one day he will reappear visible to all. . . . In the Supper the situation of the present time sequence is put in concrete form, so to speak, in relation to the whole history of salvation'.[29]

It remains for the Church to take advantage of the richness of this gift, far too great to be expressed fittingly in a single rite. The paschal mystery reaches its full dimensions only in the three-fold sacramental mystery of water, oil and the Eucharist, but it bears fruit in a seemingly endless variety of rites, which we are now in a position to call 'mysteries', even though they are not sacraments.

THE DIMENSIONS OF THE MYSTERY

A. The Sacramental Order.

The fact that the liturgical mystery is in essence the expression in worship of the paschal mystery helps us to understand how in classical theology the word *sacramentum* (which was for a long

[29] Cullmann: *op. cit.* p. 110; Cf. P. de Montcheuil: *Rech. Sc. Rel.*, 1946, pp. 1 ff.

7

time simply the Latin equivalent of the Greek word *mysterion*) assumed its technical meaning and was restricted to the essential rites that Christ instituted in order to ensure the communication of the mystery of salvation at all important stages of human life. What has just been said about the three principal rites of the paschal mystery—the mysteries of water, oil and Eucharist— makes it possible for us to deal in brief with the whole sacramental order itself.

That the complete theological formulation of this order was slow and difficult is well known. Even today it is completed only in the West, owing to the joint influence of the canonists and scholastic theologians. In the Christian East, wherever Latin sacramental theology has not been taken over bodily, the position is much more fluid, and the rites of funerals, the consecration of churches and monastic initiation are still regarded as mysteries. This is due not only, nor even principally, to the influence of Dionysius the Areopagite; it springs chiefly from the primacy that sacramental theology affords to the rite–word combination as the expression of a special manifestation of divine grace. By emphasising with ever greater resolution, under the influence of the Scotist and nominalist schools, efficacy *ex opere operato,* Latin theology secured the benefits of a rigid systematisation, but ran the risk of weakening the unity of the sacramental order taken as a whole, together with the concept of sign, which had proved the most useful instrument in its formulation.

To stress the concept of 'mystery', even in preference to that of sign, is to be placed in the immediate presence of the entire sacramental order as of a special mode of existence, the natural result of the divine plan of salvation through the Incarnation of the Word. It is useful, even necessary, to understand its insertion into the whole body of manifestations of Divine Providence; in this way it can be 'placed' and its importance estimated by analogies drawn from the created order. But it is also desirable to study it in itself, phenomenologically, defining as precisely as possible its own especial mode of existence by a direct study of its various realisations as proffered to us by the Church. Maximum use must be made of the comparative method, which enables us to distinguish the invariable constants from particular forms of expression which vary according to differences in cultural milieus.

There can be no question of undertaking this study here. It is desired merely to point out its importance in a theology of the mystery which refuses to separate the essence of the sacrament from its complete ritual expression. The seven sacraments form a complex unity, in which can be distinguished the three sacraments of Christian initiation—Baptism, Confirmation and the Eucharist—two sacraments of social significance—Order and Matrimony — and two sacraments directly connected with Baptism, ordained especially to overcome failings of soul and body —Penance and the Anointing of the Sick. The liturgy of the first three is similar in the various rites to a much greater degree than the others, where the emphasis is different according to varying traditions. The marriage rites are naturally the most varied, for this is the sacrament more closely bound up with a social and ritual context.[30] But Order, Penance and Extreme Unction can also be seen from aspects varied enough to reveal the wealth of the mystery which neither a single concept nor a single rite can contain.

In a strictly phenomenological study it would not, of course, be possible to discern in the sacramental order the twofold scheme whose determination was an essential stage, and perhaps the ultimate basis, of scholastic investigation—the *sacraments* themselves and what it has become customary to call the *sacramentals*. But although the theology of the sacraments has reached a surprising degree of formulation on the indications supplied by Scripture and the Magisterium of the Church, under the general term 'sacramentals' there has been confused a whole collection of different rites whose only common characteristic is a more or less remote ritual connection. The idea of mystery can help in restoring their proper value to the group of rites which form the normal complement of the actual sacraments, with which they share the common character of being a ritual expression and realisation of the mystery of salvation in Christ.

This applies principally to the rites of the dedication of churches, monastic initiation, the consecration of virgins and, lastly, funerals.

[30] Cf. *La Maison-Dieu*, 50 (1957).

At a further remove we must add to these the blessings instituted to distinguish admission to certain offices, clerical or lay, for various incidental circumstances in life and for the various objects used by man. The contingent nature of all these and their close connection with the circumstances of social and cultural life explain the apparently endless variety of these secondary sacramentals. It should moreover be noticed that the institution of liturgical rites keeps pace very unevenly with the growth of civilisation so that, for example, the Roman ritual contains blessings for the most recently introduced technical inventions although it does not seem aware of any pattern of life other than that of the Middle Ages, and especially that of the Germanic Middle Ages long before the many social changes that have since occurred.

Is it possible to establish theologically that these rites—and especially the most important among them—belong to the order of mystery? We feel that it would be of interest to make a thorough investigation in this sense of the mystery of the Church, the Body and Bride of Christ, and to distinguish the *sacraments of Christ* from the *sacraments of the Church*.

In the first of these, which are our sacraments in the proper sense of the term, Christ himself acts, in his human nature, and the Church has only an instrumental rôle, preparing and putting at Christ's disposal the material and formal elements through which his acts are performed; the influx from the head makes itself felt throughout the body but in different ways according to the different organs in which it acts.

In the second, on the other hand, the Church exercises her own powers as an autonomous personality, animated by the Spirit who permeates more fully each day the race of men ransomed by the blood of Christ. As the Bride without spot or wrinkle, she moves forward to union with the Bridegroom; as the Temple of God and the Holy City, she adorns herself to receive her Lord.

Hence arises the differing mode of efficacy of these two elements which compose the sacramental order. In the sacraments properly so called, in which Christ's own causality is exercised, this efficacy is assured provided that the subject offers no opposition, that he is united by faith to Christ, and that the rites chosen by Christ and regulated by the Church are used. In the sacramentals, on the other hand, efficacy varies in proportion as the subject participates more or less fully in the life of the Spirit, that is, according to the measure of his charity. But bearing in mind this important difference, it is possible to think of the sacramental order in its entirety, as the privileged place for the manifestation here and now of the mystery of God, remembering the twofold meaning we have already seen in the word mystery: the divine plan of salvation in Christ and the real and effective presence of this *mystery of salvation* through the *liturgical mystery*.

It will be convenient at this point to examine each of the mysteries of worship, the seven sacraments, the major and minor rites of the Pontifical and the Ritual together with the expression of them to be found in each of the local liturgies of East and West. It will then be possible to discover in them the inexhaustible riches of the mystery of Christ and the Church as it is revealed not only to the contemplation of the mind but also in its work of sanctification, whereby the whole Christ grows every day, through whom the race of men is brought into the Kingdom of the Father, living according to the Spirit (cf. part II, chapters 6-8).

salvation through the *liturgical mystery*.

The Sanctoral Cycle reveals to us another aspect of this mystery, at once a reflection and continuation of the paschal mystery. What the sacramental order gradually effects, namely, the shaping of man to Christ and even more the incorporation of man into Christ by the giving of the Spirit, is brought home to us through the liturgy of the saints.[31]

Historically, as is well known, it is made up of elements drawn from two sources—the cultus of the martyrs and, at a later date, the cultus of those who imitated them in ascetic labours or various persecutions endured for Christ; and secondly, the cultus of those pontiffs whose memory was reverently preserved in the Church they had built up by their pastoral zeal and preaching of the Word of God. The *natale martyrum* and the *depositio episco- porum* together formed a twofold commemoration dear to the

[31] Cf. *La Maison-Dieu* 52 (1957), article by Dom Hild and A. Chavasse.

devotion of the faithful who, moreover, gradually lost all idea of the differences between them and in both cases came to venerate merely the 'saint', the friend of God and powerful intercessor whose miracles, wrought through his relics, revealed that he lives for ever in the Lord.

This evolution gradually tended to make the liturgy of the saints autonomous and considerably weakened its primitive significance. Scarcely a thought is given nowadays to the close link between *natale sanctorum* and the paschal mystery, and indeed, in the common view of Christians, the liturgy of the saints is merely an official, communal expression of piety towards them, connected with 'devotion' and having nothing in common with the 'mystery' as we have defined it. But the liturgical texts remain, together with the rites which convey to us the primary significance—the only significance which can properly be called liturgical—of the cultus of the saints. Through them we can see the profound importance of St Gregory's work. He rearranged the liturgical year, forming into one cycle both the annual feasts expressing different aspects of the mystery of Christ and the commemorations of the saints. These latter were raised from the level of local commemoration and a quasi-funeral cult, to that of feasts, in the strict sense in which we used that word when speaking of the Easter feast. Thereby final sanction was given to the Christological and eschatological nature of the veneration of the saints, as it had long since been given to the martyrs: they were seen as witnesses, moulded to Christ even in their victorious deaths.

These were the grounds on which the Eucharist was celebrated on the 'birthdays' of the martyrs: it was not only—as is so often said—because no greater honour can be offered to a saint than to offer Christ's sacrifice in memory of him and to join their intercession with that of the great High Priest,[32] but because for them their 'birthday' was the true Pasch, the passage through death

---

[32] This indirect relationship between the Eucharist and the worship of the saints may be applied in the strict sense to commemorations of bishops on the day of their 'deposition', a commemoration of funerary type, in which, however, the memory of the dead man's virtues leads us to recommend ourselves to him rather than beseech the Lord's mercy for him. Yet this is not all. If the anniversary of the *depositio* of bishops is marked by a special

to the Kingdom of the Father where they are victorious with Christ. In them, the victory of faith is complete, the enemy has once more been conquered. Or rather, Christ's unique victory has been manifested under given circumstances at a given time and place, and Christ, victorious in his martyr, associates him in the universal Lordship he merited through the Cross.

As we have seen, Christ's resurrection inaugurated a new temporal order: the time of fulfilment. This time sequence did not replace historical time but entered into it to endow it with a new meaning. Henceforward, two processes were at work in the world: *evolution,* still under the domination of the 'Prince of this world' reduced now to the rank of the Lord's slave; and *recapitulation,* the especial work of the glorified Christ. The interaction and mutual opposition of these two processes are at their height when a martyr is put to death. It is fitting therefore that his anniversary should be celebrated by the mystery of the Eucharist which, properly speaking, is the memorial of the mystery of the redeeming and glorified Christ.

By celebrating it, the Christian community, with the martyr, breaks the bounds of historical time: it anticipates the 'Day of the Lord' already experienced by the martyr, and asserts the reality of the victory won. It is in communion—in the fullest sense of that word—with the heroism of him who was one of its members, and whom Christ has chosen to bear witness to his name. His was no passing act of which the memory alone remains. His witness, offered even unto death, escapes from time; it is a new facet of the witness rendered by Christ to his Father: it is integrated into the mystery of salvation and takes its place in the solemn 'thanksgiving' with which the Church celebrates the mystery.

Thus, a whole lyrical liturgy has grown up to celebrate the martyr: it is made up of hymns more realistic than the *epinikia* which welcomed the victorious athletes of Greece on their return

liturgy, that is because the Priesthood of the only Priest is exercised through them, his vicars. Having now entered with Christ 'beyond the veil', they continue to intercede for their people who, by celebrating a Eucharist on the anniversary of their deaths, associate themselves in the mystery with the great heavenly liturgy that henceforward their bishops perform in its fullness.

to their homeland. Closely connected with the eucharistic mystery which it prolongs through all the hours of the day, the liturgical praise of the saints associates the Church on earth with the triumph which welcomes to his home the martyr who has fought valiantly for Christ. There is only one act of praise because there is only one liturgy, as there is only one Church : but the part of the Church in exile here below gives it an especial tone related to the needs of man's present condition, in which neither pure contemplation nor praise alone can long be sustained. Our wretchedness is so great that a brief glance at those who have reached their goal makes it more poignant: our praise is transformed into supplication. The saint is invoked as a protector of those who are still in the struggle. It could not be otherwise, and to imagine a liturgy of the saints which consisted only in praise and thanksgiving is to ignore the psychology of man.

But a saint is not merely a protector. He is also an example. As soon as the Sanctoral developed and was properly constituted, the Church was concerned to draw examples and lessons for the faithful from the lives and deaths of the saints. The 'passions' and 'legends' do not claim to be history. Their purpose is to make those who hear understand the heroism of him they come to celebrate and pray to. And it is hardly possible to explain heroism to un-polished minds, insensitive to refined sentiments, to uncivilised people, used to striking hard and receiving harsh blows—and such was the case in the early Middle Ages, the golden age of legends about martyrs, and of their cultus—except by heaping one on another a vast mass of torments until God himself approves such heroism by bringing the martyr into his kingdom. The legends of the saints have been much attacked and, indeed, the psychology they presuppose is not ours, but legend in one form or another is a necessary element in the liturgy of the saints. Its rôle is to create the atmosphere of *mystery*, to make tangible the divine realities at work in the lives and deaths of the saints. Old legends succeeded in doing so for the milieu to which they were first addressed, but the secret seems to have been lost for centuries, ever since the sense of mystery grew attenuated.

In their absence, the poetic parts of the liturgy must take their place, and we should rejoice that the Roman liturgy, by retaining pride of place in the liturgy of the saints for the words of scripture, has kept open the living spring of the mystery of the word. The choice and arrangement of these texts, even in the offices whose structure shows a mind completely alien to the tradition of *liturgical mystery,* preserves the primary, authentic meaning of the Sanctoral of the Latin Church: the living contemplation of the mystery of Christ in his saints.

C. *The liturgy of the season*

The feasts of the sanctoral cycle are like so many independent spaces in the web of time. They emphasise the eschatological nature of the time of the Church. The liturgy of the season is intended to show how the mystery of salvation in Christ penetrates cosmic time itself. Three cycles, with varying degrees of difference in different liturgies, are involved here—and here again the Roman liturgy seems to have given the most profound emphasis to the links and differences between them.

The annual cycle is essentially Christological. Its special purpose is to manifest the dominant aspects of the *mystery of salvation* by drawing on the symbolism of the seasons. After what we have said about the paschal mystery as the liturgical expression of the mystery of salvation, the reader will find it easy to understand the importance that at a very early date the Easter feast assumed in the scheme of the liturgical year. When to what had been a largely eschatological view of the liturgy was added and in part substituted a more historical view, less profound in itself but more accessible to an era in which the decline in ancient culture was becoming more apparent, the single great feast of fifty days, the primitive Pentecost, was rearranged as a cycle commemorating the chief appearances of the risen Christ; the last weeks and especially the last days before the feast of Easter were devoted to recalling the last days of his mortal life. It is however remarkable that no liturgy has taken this tendency towards commemoration to its limits. Lent and, in the Roman liturgy, the long series of weeks after Pentecost, have been linked with the paschal cycle without being arranged according to any historical pattern.

But the most original invention of the Roman rite has of course been that of a second cycle centred on the Epiphany, the revelation of our Lord in the flesh.[33]

The paschal mystery, indeed, completely fulfilled Messianic hopes, but it did so in an unexpected way, by introducing into the very course of historical time the decisive act that inaugurated the last times. Eschatology was to some extent carried into the midstream of history. The extra-temporal aspect of prophetic Messianism was in danger of losing its significance. The development of the Christmas cycle—better called the Epiphany or Advent cycle—restored it in all its richness as in all its indeterminancy. It is a pity that since the Middle Ages the importance given in Christian devotion to the historical commemoration of the birth of Christ has led to this profound meaning being lost from view, for this is the only aspect from which the texts and rites still in use take on their full significance, from the great antiphons of Advent to the chants repeated at Mass on the Sundays after Epiphany; it is the only one which gives its true place to the symbolism of light in the advent of the 'Sun of Justice', replacing the darkness of time by the light of the 'Day of the Lord'. If Easter is the feast of hope, at the heart of cosmic time, Christmas-Epiphany is the feast of the solstice, suspending the course of time and opening a new age.[34]

This penetration of cosmic time by eschatological time is seen even more clearly in the weekly cycle inherited by the Church from Mosaic worship. In the annual cycle, the whole history of salvation is repeated and arranged around Christ as its centre; he it is who gives it its meaning and transforms into *mystery* the symbolism of the profound rhythms of the seasons. In the weekly cycle, regulated by the phases of the moon, in which the ancients saw the symbol and cause of the mutability of things here below,

[33] Dom J. Lemarié: *La Manifestation du Seigneur*, Le Cerf, Paris, 1957.

[34] We know that in the beginning the choice of the dates 25 December and 6 January was apparently due to a difference in reckoning between East and West, still in vogue in fourth-century pagan religious calendars for determining the solstice.

it is the created order which is raised to the plane of the mystery of salvation. The great saga of the Six Days of creation takes on new meaning that the different Christian liturgies make use of in varying degrees by connecting it with the cycle of redemption.

So the weekly cycle is not divorced from the paschal mystery. It is arranged around Sunday, which forms the primitive kernel of Christian worship, to such a degree, indeed, that it is impossible to decide whether, in the time of the Apostles 'the Lord's Day' was a weekly pasch or whether the feast of Easter was the first Sunday. Whether in their subsequent development the various liturgies took Sunday primarily as a weekly celebration of the Lord's resurrection (as in the East and especially at Byzantium) or as the preferred expression of the new life of the Spirit inaugurated by baptism (as in the Roman liturgy), Sunday was always a feast day, the Day of the Lord, in the strict biblical sense of that phrase, the day removed from the cosmic time sequence, when we anticipate the great rest of that day when time shall be no more, just as the Lord's return in glory is anticipated on it in the celebration of the Eucharist.[35]

At first there was no celebration on the other days, and when it was introduced on Wednesdays and Fridays in Rome, it was still closely connected with the paschal feast, the 'meal of the Lord', in the old meaning, which broke the fast still customary on those days. But at quite an early date the week became the pivot of the liturgy of praise. The synagogue had already shown the way, and it was followed spontaneously by the Christian communities. The origins of a new aspect of the mystery of worship are here to be found. Whatever may have been the first beginnings of what was later called the Divine Office, and however great the part played in its development by monasticism, it is certain that at least after the end of the fourth century the Church gave it an official place in her arrangements for worship and that from this time, as far as we can tell by comparing the different liturgies, the framework of the Divine Office was the week. In this way the praise of creation was given expression in the Church and raised to the plane of a

---

[35] *Le jour du seigneur* in *Actes du Congrès Liturgique de Lyon*, R. Laffont, Paris, 1948: Dom J. Hild: *Dimanche et vie pascale*, Brepols, Turnhout, 1949.

'mystery'. By taking from St Benedict the principle of the consecutive reading of the complete Psalter in the course of the week, by taking this principle to its final conclusion under Pius X, and by causing the Sunday collect to be repeated at each Hour, the Roman Church has expressed in particularly felicitous fashion the fullness of this cycle of Christian prayer in which inspired words of praise, thanksgiving, petition and repentance all find their place.

The daily cycle of the Hours completes the arrangement of the *mystery of worship* and brings an echo of the *paschal mystery* into the very heart of cosmic time. In fact in the course of a single day the rhythm of light evokes all the phases of time's sequence; by centring on it the expression of her contemplation, the Church bears witness to the paradoxical nature of her situation at the frontiers of time and eternity. The cosmic mystery of the Hours brings to mind the grandiose idea of Phidias who, in order to express the supratemporal nature of the birth of Athene, depicted her on the pediment of the Parthenon between the horses of Helios and those of Selene. But what for the ancient sculptor was no more than a magnificent symbol is, in the Christian liturgy, a mystery—in other words, the celebration of the Divine Office effects a real consecration of time and links it effectively with eternity.

Considered from this point of view of mystery, the prayer of the Hours is inseparable from the celebration of the Eucharist, which alone can bring about completely this intercommunication between cosmic time and eternity. The duplication which has occurred between the ancient Sunday vigil—so clearly paschal and eschatological in nature—and the adoption by the liturgy of the nocturnal psalmody of the monks, by encouraging the union between the celebration of the Eucharist and an abridged vigil (our present fore-Mass), has tightened the bonds between these two rites, once independent. These have since found multiple expression in all the liturgies. In the Roman rite this has been done by causing the Gospel of the Mass to be read at the night Office. And especially by causing the collect for the day to be read at all the Hours, except the additional Hours of Prime and Compline.

The Divine Office is not merely a prayer, the prayer of the

Church, but an act of the virtue of religion. It is the contemplation of the Bride, and, better still, the collective contemplation of
the Body of Christ, still held in part by the bonds of terrestrial
life and its distracting preoccupations. Periodically, and at as close
intervals as possible, the Church on earth attunes herself, so to say,
to the harmony of the Church in heaven. She takes her place once
more in the choir of the blessed who sing unceasingly with the
hierarchies of angels 'Holy, holy, holy is the Lord, God Sabaoth,
heaven and earth are full of his glory'; and by doing so 'realises',
sets in action, the thing most essential to her : the securing, in the
form suitable to life here below, which we call *mystery,* of the
active presence of divine realities.

PART TWO

THE FORM OF THE LITURGY

From the perfect harmony of your affections and your charity, a concert of praise arises to Jesus Christ . . . so, too, in the harmony of your concord you take, by your very unity, the note from God and sing with one voice the praises of the Father through the mouth of Jesus Christ.

St Ignatius of Antioch

Worship is organised and develops according to the needs of Christians, always to the end that we should draw instruction from these external signs and that the soul should thus be made more heedful of God.

Pius XII

INTRODUCTION

The more concrete analyses that form the subject of the second part of this study are in fact simply a different view brought to bear on the same Mystery. Already in the final pages of the first part we endeavoured to show the connection between the Mystery and the whole sacramental order, as well as the sanctoral cycle, and the liturgical year. Now we must make a more precise analysis along the same lines.

First we shall break down into its constituent elements the whole body of liturgy in which the paschal mystery of Christ is expressed and made actual, analysing it into its constituent elements of words and things whose complex symbolism is explained by their reciprocal connections (chapter 5). Then we shall examine the structure of the infinitely variable types of liturgical celebration. For there is one type of celebration which initiates into the paschal mystery, one which renders it present, and those which flow from it or express the superabundance of the life of the redeemed Church (chapter 6). And when we have looked at these in turn in their historical variations (temporal aspect) and ceremonial diversity (spatial aspect—chapters 7 and 8) we shall have formed an idea of the whole as it really is, of the unity and diversity of the mystery of faith: the creative Word of God, Incarnate in the world in order to save it, restoring it to wholeness and lifting up to a new, transcendent plane the religious aspirations of man and his need for worship.

8

Chapter 5

The Constituent Elements
of the Liturgy

HOLY SCRIPTURE

THE Christian liturgy is the Word of God, living in the people
he has summoned and gathered together for them to enter
into his own mystery. It is not surprising, then, that the liturgy
is entirely woven from these very themes and expressions through
which the Word chose to make himself heard by men. This
prominent place given to Scripture dates back to the liturgy of
the synagogue. Doubtless after the time of the exile, when an increasingly clear distinction came to be drawn between political
organisation and genuine religious traditions, devout Jews
delighted in meeting together to recall the traditions and
meditate on the texts of the 'Law'. This practice grew stronger
with the passing of the centuries. Although the official liturgy of
the Temple retained its original purpose, religious life for preference was maintained by meetings in the synagogue for readings
and prayers.

The few—all too few—pieces of evidence which remain to us
from the first centuries of Christianity reveal the Church continuing and developing this tradition. About the middle of the second
century, St Justin shows us Christians in Rome in the course of
the Sunday meeting, listening to readings from 'the memoirs of
the Apostles and the writings of the Prophets', 'as long as time
allows' (I Apol. 67), before the celebration of the Eucharist. In
the course of the third century we see in all sorts of places
meetings, sometimes daily meetings, devoted to the reading of the

Scriptures, the singing of psalms and prayer. Monasticism had only to develop and organise this primitive institution to create what came to be called quite simply 'divine service', that is, the Office.

But the whole body of Christian liturgy, texts and rites, is imbued with scriptural reminiscences. It is impossible to arrive at an understanding of this liturgy without a minimum of training in the Bible. But, conversely, it is in the liturgical celebration that the texts of the Bible disclose their full wealth.

It is therefore impossible to over-emphasise the importance of this consecutive reading (*lectio continua*) of biblical texts, which occupies so important a place at one time or another in every liturgy. The Roman rite and those directly related to it appoint it for use during the Night Office. This is a custom inherited from monasticism, which played an often determining and in some cases regrettable rôle in the definitive arrangement of the Roman liturgy.

Its first consequence in this case was that the Church's constant recourse to the whole body of sacred texts was not offered to the laity; the second was that the opportunity afforded the monks of prolonging the lessons at the Office by readings in the refectory led to a certain dislocation of the pericopes so that there was not always an opportunity of hearing the most important texts. Until the recent simplification of the rubrics, undue importance was given to the reading of the first verses of each book. It is to be hoped that the general reform now being undertaken will lead to a complete revision of the system of lessons and many would wish that 'continuous reading' might be so arranged that, at least in part, the faithful should have an opportunity of hearing the most significant passages. It would then be for the sermon to link the passages together and expound them in such a way that the Bible really occupies once more the pre-eminent place belonging to it in the liturgy.

This should be so particularly because the order of the passages traditionally adopted by the Roman rite is most felicitously chosen as an accompaniment to the various phases of the liturgical cycle: Isaias during Advent, St. Paul at the seasons of Christmas and the

Epiphany, the Pentateuch during Lent, Jeremias in Passiontide, the Apocalypse, the Acts and the Catholic Epistles at the seasons of Easter and Pentecost, the books of Kings until the month of August, the sapiential books during August, the hagiographies in September, Machabees in October, and Ezechiel, Daniel and the twelve (minor) prophets in November. Few liturgies provide reading drawn so widely from the whole of the Bible.

The choice of the lessons at Mass is more complex. It would appear that most liturgies at first had a whole sequence of lessons: the Law, the Prophets, Epistles and—always in the last place—Gospels. But this complete system, in so far as it ever existed, was simplified almost everywhere.

In the East, the Syrian, Chaldean and Armenian rites kept one or more lessons from the Old Testament; the others were satisfied with the Pauline Epistles and the Gospels preceded, among the Syrians and Copts, by a lesson from the Acts.

In the West, and especially in the Roman rite, in which two lessons usually suffice, the choice of the first is more eclectic. On Sundays it is taken from the Pauline Epistles.[1] But for the ferias of Lent and the feasts of the Lord or the Saints, passages are selected from all parts of the Bible alike, each being chosen on its own merits. The five lessons preceding the Epistle on Ember Saturdays are taken from any part of the Old Testament with reference only to their suitability for the liturgical season.

As for the order in which the lessons from St Paul and the Gospels are distributed through the Sunday cycle, none of the theories suggested is completely satisfying. We may say that as a general rule the order of the Epistles for the Sundays after Pentecost suggests a continuous reading, but the distribution of the Gospels defies all attempts at classification; various arrangements have been telescoped together as a result of the complex history of this part of the cycle. During Advent and Lent, each passage is chosen for its own sake. Here we are far from the simplicity of Eastern rites, which have always retained the consecutive reading of the four Gospels in turn or of a composite Gospel. Only one feature is common to all Christian liturgies: the Gospel of St

[1] Except during Eastertide, when the Catholic Epistles are read.

John is read during Eastertide and this custom seems to be very ancient. It fits in very well with the purpose and character of the fourth Gospel.

Not only scripture is read in the course of the liturgical offices. In varying degrees in the course of the seasons and in different parts of the world, *ecclesiastical compositions* have been admitted to them. In this instance, as in many others, the Roman rite shows exceptional reserve.

It is difficult to tell since what period 'legends' of the martyrs and saints have had a place in the liturgy, but this practice seems to be very ancient and it may have been that in Rome as early as the sixth century a collection was first made of them. In Visigothic Spain, such readings were even introduced into the Mass itself. In the East, they were usually confined to a notice read in the course of the morning office. Over and above these secondary differences, a single purpose stands revealed: to set before Christian people not historical information but the example of the great deeds of the saints, their 'virtue' in the etymological sense of the word. Feelings and tastes have changed with the times and it may be difficult for minds trained too exclusively in rational disciplines to understand this aim; it may be that these liturgical legends need large-scale revision, although it is difficult to see how this could well be done, at least as far as the oldest works are concerned. Those inserted since the Middle Ages are of far less interest.

Sometimes, instead of an anonymous 'legend', the liturgy draws on a panegyric or sermon from the Fathers. But it is as authoritative commentators on Scripture that the Fathers are chiefly called upon to make themselves heard. The Roman liturgical homiliary dates back to the time of St Gregory, but it was largely developed during the Frankish Carolingian Empire. Despite the defective form in which it has come down to us in the Breviaries, it sets a standard for liturgical preaching, an element essential to every celebration. In modern times, passages from the supreme Magisterium of the Church have sometimes been introduced although neither their origin nor their form fits them for this use.

So cursory a glance gives but a poor account of the abundance and variety of the liturgical lectionary—we should, moreover, say lectionaries, for two collections at least have always attracted special attention: the book of the Epistles and the book of the Gospels. This latter, especially, has been surrounded with extraordinary veneration in every liturgy : placed on the altar on a par with the eucharistic species, solemnly proffered to the faithful for their veneration, it is regarded as a tangible form of the presence of Christ. In the Roman rite, the singing of the Gospel is one of the deacon's most important functions, and is sometimes even reserved to the celebrant. In any case, its reading or chanting calls for a sermon, the real purpose of which is to comment on it in a way suited to the needs of the community.

The book of the Epistles cannot claim such importance. Several rites entrust its reading to a simple lector; the Roman rite reserves it to the subdeacon. But commonly the collection of Epistles (to which the Acts of the Apostles are sometimes added) forms a special book distinct from the Old Testament lectionary. The Roman 'book of legends' long ago lost its identity, if it ever had one. It has now been merged with the book of homilies to form a lectionary for the Divine Office, sometimes called the 'companion' (comes or liber comicus). It is a different matter in the East, where the synaxary has undergone a considerable development in no way comparable with that collection of brief notices (in its origin simply a topographical calendar) which forms the Roman Martyrology, one of the books whose reform is most urgently needed, so greatly have its contents and the form in which it has come down to us suffered from the labours of editors. Yet it is this book which, with its daily commemorations, keeps alive in the memory of the Church the recollection of those who by their lives and deaths have borne witness to Christ. Its brief notices are, as it were, an actual response to the preaching of the Gospel.

PSALMODY AND HYMNS

'In psalms and hymns and spiritual canticles, singing in grace in your hearts to God' was St Paul's advice to the Colossians (3. 16).

And in fact the earliest evidence that has come down to us concerning liturgical gatherings in the first centuries of Christianity stresses the place given to the singing of hymns and canticles.

Singing is one of the elements very seldom lacking in any celebration of worship. Adoration and praise, the petitions of penitence and intercession all tend quite naturally to require rhythm and melody to make them more expressive; music is one of the fundamental needs of men wherever an exclusively cerebral education has not led to the withering of the natural emotions. And the community of souls calls for community of voices, just as reverence requires a special inflexion of the voice.

More specifically, Christian hymnography is rooted in the Jewish tradition. The religious chants from the times of the Kings received from Judaism a new emphasis accentuating their permanent religious value. And finally, among the zealous groups of the *anawim* a collection of one hundred and fifty psalms was made, which is like a lyrical transposition of the whole of biblical tradition. Additional canticles were inserted here and there into the sacred books, although others, just as widely used at synagogue services, were never accorded this honour. We should also take notice of the acclamations, the most important of which is the *Kadosh* which Isaias heard proclaimed by the Seraphim in his great vision in the Temple and which is still in our own times the centre of the daily liturgy of the Jews: 'Holy, holy, holy, the Lord of Sabaoth, the earth is full of his glory.' It was not long before Christian liturgy gave this a prominent position, but, by the addition of a simple phrase *'heaven and earth'* it emphasises the new dimensions reached henceforward by the manifestation of divine glory.

Nevertheless, it would be a mistake to imagine that psalmody in the strict sense of the word occupied in primitive Christianity the place since given to it in the Christian liturgy. It seems that until the third, and perhaps the fourth, century, men preferred to sing new compositions at Christian services—those hymns and spiritual songs of which all too few examples, such as the morning hymn *Gloria in excelsis,* and that for the evening (φῶς ἱλαρον), have come down to us. Attempts have been made to identify traces of a few other canticles in the New Testament and in the oldest Christian writings. The finest group is that formed by the *Odes of Solomon,* which may have been composed as early as the beginning of the second century. But these free lyrical compositions easily turn into a form of *gnosis* destructive of the pure message of the Gospel. The *Odes of Solomon* themselves are not entirely free from this. Thus the Church came to be increasingly guarded in her use of non-Scriptural canticles in the liturgy.

From the fourth century onwards the *Psalms of David* and poems taken from the Bible, which at first were simply read like the other texts from Scripture, came increasingly to take the place of the new Christian compositions. Monasticism increased their liturgical rôle still further by making psalmody one of the chief exercises of the ascetic life. It is to the monks that we owe the introduction to the Divine Office of the integral recitation of the Psalter which was later to constitute the principal part of the Office in certain cases, especially in the Roman rite. The introduction into the West of the Syrian practice of psalm singing in two choirs —later confused with antiphonal psalmody—brought a rhythm and variation to the intoning of the psalms which to a large degree justified the widespread use attained by this kind of psalmody. In the Roman liturgy it gradually brought about the almost complete neglect of psalmody by a soloist—the psalmist—with or without the repetition of a refrain by the congregation.

The most frequently employed of these refrains was, of course, the *Alleluia* inherited straight from Judaism. All liturgies give it a place in the psalmody preceding the Gospel at the Eucharistic celebration. In the West it was regarded as the principal paschal chant and its use was determined in close connection with this interpretation. From Judaism also was derived the solemn acclamation, *Amen,* which became the obligatory conclusion to all prayers. For this reason its importance cannot be over-emphasised. In the Christian liturgy the Amen is the solemn ratification by the whole assembly of the words and deeds of the celebrant.

Verses of psalms and other Scriptural and ecclesiastical texts likewise brought a greater variety to the psalmody. It would be futile to try to reduce their abundant diversity to a few schematic types: this diversity bears witness to the freedom with which the Church has always used the Scriptures, which she knows have been entrusted to her as a living word. At certain times and places, an over subtle virtuosity led to a play on verbal correspondences. But as long as these compositions originate in a direct knowledge of Scripture and were not gleaned from Concordances, this alternation of verse and response will very often be found to arouse spiritual reflections of great value.

But it was not only by the introduction of responsories that the liturgy gave prominence to psalmody. The tones which at first seem to have been very austere and 'more like recitation than singing' in the course of centuries developed into melodies capable of giving rise (at Rome more than anywhere else) to musical compositions in which the text was endowed with a new significance by its chant. But the development of melismas meant that only a small number of verses, and as a rule only one, was kept. In this classic form the responsory is far removed from its original structure.

It was, too, in connection with psalmody that there grew up the use of the single strophes which, in the Roman rite, have been given the somewhat unfortunate name of 'antiphon' and which, in accordance with Eastern usage, it would be better to call *troparion*. Traces of this are to be found in some very ancient Egyptian *graffiti* and there is some ground for thinking that it was from Egypt that their use spread abroad. In the various eastern rites they assumed a position of ever growing importance, despite the opposition of the monks who objected to a form of singing that was too ornate and alien to traditional psalmody. Mingled with the rhythmical compositions of ancient Syrian hymnography, the invading *troparia* came to replace the 'canon' of nine Scriptural odes, between the verses of which they should normally have been inserted. From them there sprang a host of compositions which were all too often redundant and in poor taste. But the oldest compositions of Byzantine origin are for the most part very beautiful, as much by reason of the richness of their expression as by the profundity of their doctrine. It was above all through these that the essential tradition of the Fathers was passed on from generation to generation.

In general the West contrived to observe greater restraint. Rome especially for long showed an extreme reserve in the use of non-Scriptural texts: but the masters of the papal *schola* and their rivals surrounded the singing of the psalms with short antiphons which are often jewels of poetry and music. Gaul and Spain gave freer reign to ecclesiastical compositions, some of which were finally accepted into the Roman liturgy. Some antiphons for the *Benedictus* and *Magnificat,* the great processional antiphons, and the great antiphons of our Lady at Compline, play, though with greater reserve, a part in our liturgy which is not inferior to that of the Byzantine *troparia.* These poetic strophes, whether popular refrains built up on a few easily-memorised notes or original compositions, are one of the most widely encountered elements in Christian worship.

The transition from such strophes, with their close connection with psalmody, to the hymn properly so called, which assumes so many different forms in the various liturgies, is almost imperceptible in its beginnings. The form familiar to us goes back, it is asserted, to St. Ambrose. At the beginning they were merely popular hymns not intended for insertion in the liturgy. It appears however that monasticism (more particularly the rule of St. Benedict) was largely responsible for their obtaining a firm foothold in the Office. In this instance again, Rome resisted for a long time and never gave more than a secondary place to these versiform compositions which so closely imitate the most familiar rhythms of ancient poetry. She was still less indulgent towards the texts which in Frankish lands it became customary to insert into the neums of the *Alleluia* and other richly melismatic pieces. These 'proses' and 'sequences' and all the 'farcings' beloved of the Middle Ages threatened to crush with their excessive weight the essential features of the liturgy. After the Council of Trent the reformed books retained only a very small proportion of the sequences. It was otherwise in several of the Eastern rites where, as we have seen, poetic compositions of varying origins and forms all too frequently ended by invading the Office to the detriment of the scriptural lessons and the psalmody. In few fields have the varied geniuses of Christian civilisation been given such free reign. And perhaps the West itself would have been less restrained if the liturgy had there remained popular. For it is by singing such hymns, with the well marked rhythms, simple and easy to remember, that a crowd of people can associate itself most readily with a celebration. For centuries the hymn has developed on the fringe of the liturgy. This cannot be too deeply regretted. We have only to call to mind the place taken by chorales and psalms in the spread of Protestantism to realise that these form a fundamental part of pastoral liturgy. If singing is a constituent part of the liturgy, the various elements of a Christian congregation must all be able to express by it their faith and their prayer.

LITURGICAL PRAYER

Transition from hymn to prayer is often imperceptible. There are psalms, antiphons and responses whose poetic character is confined to rhythm, and even this may not emerge very clearly. Conversely, there are collects, and especially 'eucharists' (prefaces), which with the lyricism of their words and the precision of their rhythms are really hymns. Moreover in the Roman liturgy (as also in others) we may find at a later date, it is true, the text of a prayer embellished with a melody which turns it into an antiphon.

Nonetheless, this diversity of literary forms emphasises the diversity of the profound movements of the soul. In a hymn, the words tend to play a diminished part; it is the rhythm which matters most and which, in the traditional chant of the various liturgies, bursts out in melody. With prayer properly so-called, the primary purpose of the rhythm is to sustain the spoken words so that they convey the fullness of their meaning. Nowhere is this difference of orientation more clearly perceptible than in the classic liturgy of Rome. The lyricism of the 'eucharists' has always been restrained; oratorical elaboration has always been very sober. But the masterpiece of the Roman euchology is to be found in its collects where the conciseness of the Latin formulas throws into relief the richness of the thought.

More important than its form is the meaning of Christian liturgical prayer, for it must be a faithful echo of its incomparable model, the Lord's Prayer. Here adoration and supplication, praise and intercession have an inalienable place. In it the contemplation of God never causes the wretchedness and needs of man to be forgotten, but neither do human preoccupations ever obscure the theological orientation of this prayer. And, lastly, the character of liturgical prayer is marked by its reference to the mediation of Christ, the one, eternal priest of Christian worship.

Its most solemn and characteristic type is the 'eucharistic' form handed down in direct descent from Judaism. In the Church it is supremely the sacerdotal prayer and the very rare exceptions are only apparent. Its tripartite structure is also of Jewish origin, but this has been modified as the new status of the people of God required.

Normally preceded by a dialogue, which in a very special way merits the name 'preface' by which, for many and complicated reasons, this kind of prayer is often designated in the West, it opens with a solemn prologue setting out the reasons why it is especially fitting to formulate a thanksgiving (eucharist). This prologue may be entirely theological, that is, giving expression to the various attributes under which we can contemplate the mystery of divine life, or it may be the occasion for an exposition of the divine plan of salvation (economy). For Israel this was the opportunity to make a special commemoration of the delivery from Egypt and the many manifestations of divine aid at the time of the Exodus. For Christians it is a reminder of the acts of divine mercy towards sinful mankind, culminating in Christ's redemptive work. Developed to this degree, this exposition attains full autonomy and constitutes the second part of the thanksgiving, the commemoration (*anamnesis*). It then remains only to beseech the Lord as did the biblical prayers at the time of the Exile, to remember his people, the covenant he has made with them and the promises this includes. For Israel the purpose of this prayer was to ask that the scattered nation might be gathered together again. For Christians this gathering together is pre-eminently the work of the Holy Ghost, so it is not surprising that, influenced by doctrinal preoccupations and a desire to make quite obvious the rôle of the Spirit in effecting salvation, this supplication has formed part of an invocation (*epiclesis*) explicitly asking that the Spirit be sent. The thanksgiving then concludes with a solemn doxology sending up to the whole Trinity the praise of the priestly people.

Another kind of prayer is centred on petition. The usual term for this is 'collect', of which the most perfect example, as we have already mentioned, is provided by the collects of the Roman liturgy. In these we meet again, in a much shorter form and differently arranged, the elements of the tripartite pattern that we have just identified in the 'eucharist'. But instead of being directed towards thanksgiving, this prayer lays stress, sometimes from its very first words, on petition. Even the invitation—the *Oremus* of our liturgy—clearly indicates this orientation. But it does not therefore obscure contemplation of the divine mystery, however briefly this may be mentioned. Sometimes the name of God or of the Lord is enough; more often some qualification is added. It sometimes happens, at a late date in the Roman liturgy, but more usually in other liturgies, that the author permits himself a rapid doctrinal exposition, explaining the grounds on which the prayer may confidently be offered.

The body of the prayer is most frequently formed by the petition itself. The classic liturgy of Rome formulated this with equal reserve and brevity. No other liturgy expresses so perfectly the repugnance felt by Christians towards verbosity, as though God did not know better than we what we need. Here we find just one or two phrases which reveal our indigence while showing our absolute filial trust. On occasion this trust calls on the intercession of the saints, giving the opportunity, at least when the composers of the prayers lacked the tact and reserve of the Roman masters, for far too lengthy dissertations on the deeds and merits of the saints. In any case, there is one intercession or, rather, mediation, that is never lacking, the mediation of Christ. But it sometimes happens that before mentioning this we wish to indicate the results expected from the prayer, which are, as it were, its ultimate justification. This complexity of themes gives to the collects of the great period of liturgical creation an extraordinary variety.

One last kind of prayer must be mentioned although it appears to occupy only a secondary position in our liturgy. This is the *litany*, the most typical of popular prayers, in which the whole congregation is directly associated, through the repetition of a short petitionary prayer or thanksgiving after each of a series of invitations, with prayer proposed by a leader who, in the Church, is traditionally the deacon.

No form of prayer is so natural; it is found in one form or another in all religions. If the structure of the 'eucharist' is proper to Judaism, if the structure of the Roman collects is inspired by the formularies of Rome's ancient religion, it is not possible to connect Christianity's litanies with any particular model. Certainly, they must owe a great deal to customs of the synagogue, especially when they refer to some past example of the liberating power of God in order to appeal to it afresh. It is not surprising to learn that it was in the Churches of Syria, that is, in a setting imbued with Semitic traditions, that the litany developed most extensively. These Churches passed on its use to the Byzantine liturgy where the *ektene* became all invading, and while it certainly associates the people with the liturgical celebration, it also cuts them off from its true rhythm and various actions as much as if not more than the iconostasis which stands as a barrier between the celebrant and the congregation at the eucharistic liturgy. The Roman liturgy, anxious to preserve the unity of the celebration, showed great reserve towards the litanic form of prayer, clearly preferring a silent prostration before the celebrant's collect. This somewhat severe approach probably did not take sufficient account of the needs of the popular mind and may have contributed to the growing lack of interest among the masses in the liturgical services.

Although *eucharists* and *collects* are priestly prayers, it is usually the deacon who directs the congregational *litany*. Indeed, everything in the liturgy in the form of proclamation or admonition is part of the deacon's function. The extreme sobriety and impoverishment of the Roman liturgy furnishes hardly any opportunity of realising this in the same way as the Eastern rites.

Moreover, we must distinguish between admonitions properly so called, relating to the physical attitudes of the faithful or to the stage reached in the celebration, and the announcements by which the deacon is called upon to give effective guidance to the congregation's prayers. Of the first group, the Roman rite has preserved hardly any, except invitations to kneel or rise and these, apart from the paschal *triduum*, have survived only on penitential days when the presence of a deacon is exceptional. The eastern rites had the wisdom to have every change of attitude prescribed by the deacon and to call upon him to arouse the attention of the faithful at important moments in the service. The rediscovery of the community nature of the liturgy and the requirements for active participation by the congregation as a whole have led to the restoration of this diaconal function under forms which are not yet liturgical, because they have not been officially adopted by the Church.

Reserved in regard to the people's litany, the old Roman liturgy seems to have preferred to entrust to the celebrant the invitation preceding the silent prayer of the faithful. This kind of prayer, found especially in Egypt, has been preserved in all its fullness in the solemn collects of Good Friday, but a few traces of it are still to be seen elsewhere, notably in the liturgy of the dead. In other rites, and especially in that of Visigothic Spain, these admonitions reach considerable proportions, verging on homily or doctrinal exposition. They then closely approximate to the catechetical instructions encountered in various sacramental liturgies.

RITES

Because liturgy is an action of the whole man within a worshipping community, in it *word* is inseparable from *gesture* and *attitude*. Here the situation is the same as with singing: until the advent of modern Western man it was inconceivable that a word could be uttered or heard without provoking movement, prolonging it or making it explicit. And conversely, it seemed natural to elucidate the spiritual implications of the utilitarian actions that occur during the progress of the liturgical celebration.

Gesture, transformed into a rite, has sometimes been seen as the very essence of liturgy and, indeed, of religion. According to this view the narrative, the 'myth' and theological speculation have all developed from ritual gesture. Whatever is the case with natural religions—and all sorts of qualifications of this theory would be needed with them—liturgical gestures in Christianity are of very differing origin and value.

Because Christ commanded her to do so the Church repeats certain fundamental gestures which for a special reason deserve to be recognised as 'sacramental', possessing a mysterious value in accordance with all the acceptations that we discerned in the word 'mystery'; but most liturgical gestures are the hallowing, within the context of the Christian message, of human gestures whose symbolic value has gained acceptance everywhere, or of forms of behaviour which for one reason or another have assumed a sacred connotation in the civilisations in which Christianity has become rooted. And perhaps we can see in the acceptance by Christian liturgy of such patterns of behaviour a measure of the real implantation of the Church into that particular culture. Now, since the end of the Middle Ages and despite the expansion of Christianity beyond the confines of the world affected by Greco-Roman civilisation, liturgical ceremony has remained practically unchanged; at most, it has admitted certain customs borrowed at the time of the Renaissance. It is not possible here to do more than indicate this state of fossilisation, so little in keeping with the guiding principles of Christian liturgy.

Any attempt to classify under a few headings so great a variety of gestures is necessarily arbitrary. In order to see them as a whole, without claiming to put forward a typology, the gestures occurring in the principal Christian liturgies might be divided into gestures of prayer and honour, sacramental gestures and, finally, utilitarian gestures.

The most usual attitude for Christian prayer is standing, which indicates both the impulse of the whole man towards heaven and the filial trust of those who know that henceforth they have access to God. This attitude, which might be called official, is however always associated with others more clearly indicative of the creaturely state, the state of the sinful creature, in the presence of the majesty and holiness of God. Christ himself prayed on his knees and prostrated himself in the garden of Gethsemane and this attitude, familiar in biblical tradition, ever since apostolic times has been found as a mark of the intensity of supplication. But it must not be confused with kneeling, which has become habitual to us and which came into use in the Latin Middle Ages, to become finally, though wrongly, the normal attitude for prayer for Western Catholics. In fact, kneeling with head and shoulders erect, although mentioned occasionally in the Bible, comes from the Germanic world; it is the attitude of the vassal before his over-lord. On the other hand, prostration, the practice of which we have almost completely lost, hardly survives in Western liturgies except at the beginning of the very archaic Good Friday office, during ordination litanies and in certain monastic ceremonies; it is the gesture most typical of adoration, as it is of ardent supplication. Genuflection, a gesture likewise borrowed from Germanic feudal ceremonial, is far from possessing the same wealth of expression.

It is the position of hands and arms which is indicative of the various kinds of prayer. The liturgy has always preferred the gesture of the *orantes:* forearms extended, palms open wide. This is a familiar attitude in the Semitic east and is wonderfully evocative. With it should be associated the gesture of recollection: forearms crossed over the breast, but certainly not folded together as we have regrettably grown accustomed to do. The joining of the hands is another gesture indicative of vassalage which does not belong to the old tradition of Christianity, but which evokes at one and the same time reverence, recollection and supplication. In the ancient Roman tradition this last was again indicated by a profound bowing of the head and shoulders, an attitude also found in other liturgies.

So between gestures of prayer on the one hand and, on the other, those which merely indicate respect and honour fittingly offered to those who, for one reason or another are the represent-atives of the Church's sole Lord, the interplay is constant and universal. Like all others, the Christian liturgy has drawn largely on court ceremonial. It must not be forgotten that until the secularisation which characterises the modern world, the sovereign was held to be a manifestation of the divine power among men. It is quite impossible to say whether ceremonies of honour passed from gods to kings or *vice versa:* it was not a question of two different worlds, but of a single sacred universe. Christianity, which alone was able to establish the clear distinction between the two orders, did not by the same token believe that it should refuse traditional honours to those in authority, even temporal authority. But it directed towards the divine holiness those gestures of homage which seemed most fitting to mark the sovereign respect due to it. And it did not forget that those who have received from Christ the duty of being his vicars can for that reason receive honours which it would be unsuitable to offer to men. Hence the bows, genuflections and kisses of respect familiar to the ancients, which have been preserved by the liturgy down to our times. Hence also ceremonies such as the bearing of lights in procession, taken from the ceremonial with which Roman magistrates were surrounded. Perhaps we should also include some censings here, although the origins of this ceremony are particularly complex. It is not surprising that in this sphere more than any other the variety of customs in different districts has exerted an influence on the liturgies of Christianity.

By *sacramental gestures* we mean, speaking very broadly, all those rites which are meant to express the sanctification of the world by the grace of Christ. First among these are those actions which are properly Christian, baptism and the eucharistic breaking of bread, those chosen by our Lord himself and prescribed by him for his Church. Moreover, it is worthy of note that in both cases the Church regarded herself as possessing a wide margin of interpretation in the performance of these sacred actions. In every liturgy, the actual act of the breaking of the bread has passed into the background in relation to the consecratory narrative of the Institution, which may or may not be accompanied by a gesture of benediction. As for baptism, in the West it has ceased, since the Middle Ages, to be what the true meaning of the word implies, an immersion, a complete bath, and has become no more than a washing in which a few drops of water touch the catechumen's forehead.

The Church's freedom is greater still wherever apostolic tradition is less clearly stated, as is the case with the other sacramental rites. They commonly include, in one form or another, a laying on of hands, a dedicatory gesture current in Israel and attested on various occasions as familiar to the first apostolic community. After centuries of hesitation Pius XII has recently re-asserted that this is the essential rite of Ordination for the Roman Church as it is for the others. But in every case its precise application is emphasised by a complementary gesture. It was the same, probably, with the other sacraments in which this gesture has grown attenuated to the point that it has been almost completely forgotten: this is so in penance, in the sacrament of the sick and, especially in the Byzantine rite, in confirmation. In these two last cases we see a ceremonial anointing with oil assume ever-growing importance. We shall have occasion to return to this later. Further, it is anointing that accompanies many of the most solemn consecrations, while the sign of the cross has become the ordinary gesture of blessing.

Lastly, we must mention the ritualisation of the utilitarian gestures that occur in the course of the liturgy. The richest and most meaningful group is, of course, that found in the old funeral liturgy, which adopts and hallows all the gestures involved in the preparation and burial of the dead. But with consummate skill the liturgies of Christianity have recognised and given prominence to the sacred significance of the simplest actions that are a part of any action performed in common: they have made a sacred ceremony of walking in processions, of the ritual purification of things and celebrants and of all the smallest details that a rite entails. Of course, it is often a question here of later developments, and the concern to find a sacred meaning at any price in every gesture and to emphasise it with an accompanying formula has been one of the most noteworthy factors in the overloading and fossilisation of liturgies. There need only be considered, for example, the excessive development of the preparation of the offerings in Eastern liturgies and even in some mediaeval Western rites. This tendency extends even to the ceremonial dressing of the bishop in the Roman rite of recent centuries. The danger is all too obvious. But in its great period, the liturgy succeeded in raising to the level of sacred realities each of the elements in a celebration. It is a difficult balance to strike and it is by no means surprising that it has sometimes been missed, but it does show that nothing that is man's must remain outside the order of sanctification to which the liturgy is both the testimony and the means.

THE LITURGY AND THINGS

Human actions are not alone in being adopted and transfigured by the liturgy so as to become the bearers of supernatural significance and worth. Material things too, the necessary supports of the human estate, receive in the course of liturgical celebration rôles which admit them to that sacramental world which is that of the Church.

There are certainly very few religions and there is no liturgy (in the full sense we have given to the word) which do not draw on this material environment, for example, temples, sacred objects and sacrificial offerings; and we should not be surprised to discover here and there among them striking similarities to the rites with which we are familiar. There are some natural elements so bound up with human existence and so rich in symbolic reference that we encounter them almost of necessity. Such are water, fire and the foodstuffs most characteristic of any human group. And, as we have already noticed when talking about gesture, there are others which play a comparable part within a certain cultural context although they may be unknown to, or devoid of any significance for, men belonging to some other civilisation. We shall meet both types in Christian liturgies, but the sobriety that these liturgies maintain in their appeal to the material universe should be noticed.

In particular, we cannot stress too greatly the fact that such things are taken into the liturgy not for themselves or by virtue simply of their natural symbolism, but by virtue of their bearing on the mystery of salvation. Thus there are three levels of depth in Christian sacramentalism: it has its roots in a natural or cultural symbolism such as can be met with in other religions; it refers, at least indirectly, to a particular moment in the history of salvation; it is directed towards the paschal mystery of Christ and its full accomplishment at the *parousia,* when history and symbolism shall come to an end, that God may be all in all.

Water, Ashes and Dust

No element is so abundant and so rich in symbolic meaning as water, with which the existence and maintenance of life on earth are bound up. Its limpidity and natural properties at once evoke purity, and it is the favourite element in rites of purification. But it is also the most common and most indispensable drink. The theme of the spring, of living water, is inexhaustible, as is also that of the sea, the unending source of life, but also the treacherous element, the symbol of instability and death. Water dissolves, effaces, but it also renders supple and gives life; it both refreshes and stifles. Depth psychology finds in water one of the most obvious expressions of an archetype which touches the very sources of life.[2]

Biblical revelation takes to itself these symbolic values and builds them into the narrative of the creation, where water is the primordial creature over which the breath of God hovers as though brooding. Springs and wells have an important place in the accounts of the Patriarchs and the Exodus (which begins with the crossing of the Red Sea and ends with the crossing of Jordan). But the theme that is constantly recurring, the Deluge, shows water to be both the element of final separation and the instrument of the judgment of God, who leaves the sinful world to founder in it only to draw from it a new and holy world.

The Church received from Christ the sign of baptism, the cleansing bath, as the sacrament of initiation to the faith. Christian reflexion has developed this symbolism by drawing both on biblical themes and on its natural origins. In the wake of

[2] Cf. L. Beirnaert: *Symbolisme mythique de l'eau dans la baptême* art. in *Maison-Dieu* 22, pp. 94-140.

baptism, the Church was to accept rites of ablution, the use of holy water, which replaces the pagan waters of lustration. In addition, to emphasise the penitential aspect, she uses ashes or dust in place of water. Their use is mentioned by the Bible and is, moreover, rooted in a natural symbolism; this was distorted in the Middle Ages in the West by being connected with the dissolution of the body into the dust from which it springs.

Bread, Wine and Oil

Christian liturgy needs, strictly speaking, as sacramental elements, drawn from the vegetable kingdom, only these three essential constituents of Mediterranean culture. But it makes free use as decorations, as tokens of life and joyous hope in the resurrection, of the flowers and green palms which held a place of distinction in Israel at the feast of Tabernacles, which was full of Messianic import.

Bread, the basic foodstuff of all Western peoples, seems at first sight to be too closely linked to one particular culture to support a universally valid symbolism. But it discloses so great a wealth of symbolism in biblical writings that its use is bound up with the deepest level of revelation: the choice Jesus made of it, as the sign of his body delivered up for the redemption of the world, revealed the ultimate grounds for this symbolism. Bread is not merely a special example of the work of men and of their collaboration in the perfecting of creation, it is not merely the basic foodstuff, the staff of life, but it also an austere food; its characteristic is to be shared during the meal. That is why it is the perfect medium of communion.

This applies also to the wine. Many religions have selected an intoxicant as the sign of and means to the ecstasy bringing man and the divinity into communion. Biblical tradition energetically rejects excesses of this kind. But in wine 'which rejoices the heart of man' it sees a symbol of Messianic joy, a joy which wells up from suffering, for wine is the blood of the grape which must be trodden underfoot in the press and undergo the mysterious transformation of fermentation. It is greatly to be regretted that the relinquishment of communion under the species of wine by the mediaeval West, for reasons first of convenience and then of principle, has caused most of the faithful to lose sight of the meaning of these great symbols.

Oil also appears in the Bible as one of the Messianic benedictions. Our modern civilisation has some difficulty in grasping these references to the manifold uses of the element as a source of light, of suppleness and of strength, giving lustre and making the face shine. It is of course for anointings that oil takes its place among the sacramental elements. The New Testament refers to it explicitly only in connection with the anointing of the sick (James 5.14)—a remedy familiar to antiquity. But in Israel its use, whether real or metaphorical, for the anointing of priests, prophets and kings, the name Christ or Messias, St John's use of the word 'unction' (I John 2.20) to designate the gift of the Spirit, naturally all led the Church to make wider use of it, a use, moreover, varying in accordance with the rite. In the West it was particularly through its uses in Frankish lands that oil came gradually to take the place in the Roman liturgy that it has today. In early times it was connected especially with baptism-confirmation, and then with the anointing of the sick.

Lights and Incense

Except in the liturgy of the candle on Easter night, lights and incense are accessory to the liturgical action rather than part of its structure. The use of lights, which is based on a universally valid symbolism and the very necessities of the human state, is sanctioned by the Old Testament as well as by the New, which with the Apocalypse gives full meaning to the wealth of that symbolism by relating it to Christ, the true light of the world, and to the light-bringing Spirit. But the official customs of the Roman world also played a part in the use of lights in ceremonies of honour, especially in processions accompanying the celebrant, the Gospel and the Blessed Sacrament.

As for incense, its use is based on the Bible and its significance disclosed by the Apocalypse, although here too we must take into account the practices of the Greco-Roman world. If the use of incense in pagan rites retarded its acceptance by the Church, it is to antiquity that we owe censing as a rite of honour and purification, whilst the Psalms (140.3) and the Apocalypse (8.3) teach us to see in it a symbol of the prayer of the saints.

Buildings and Images

For Christians there is no longer any true Temple other than the Body of Christ, which is the Church. So it is not without reason that the meeting places of the Christian congregation are called by this name. At first, in accordance with the practice of the apostolic community, the meeting place was the principal room of a house; later the increase in the number of the faithful and the donation to the Church of some of those great halls called basilicas, together with the construction on the same pattern of buildings for the use of Christian congregations, gave birth to an architectural style which has in general survived in a multitude of forms until our own times. Various kinds of funereal monuments adopted as *martyria* erected over the tombs of martyrs or in their honour also contributed to the inspiration of church builders.

But although the primary law of Christian religious architecture is the requirements of liturgical worship, it is nonetheless true that the building is intended to be a visible expression of the mystery of the Church. The liturgy of Dedication, which originated in Palestine and Syria, but under Frankish influence assumed an incomparable form in the mediaeval Roman rite, delineates the main features of this aspect; the part played by the altar and its significance as a symbol of Christ are here brought into full prominence. This liturgy makes it possible, too, to see in what sense Christians can speak of a 'holy place'.

The same concern to sound the mystery of the Incarnation to its very depths and to proclaim the transfiguration of the visible which will form its final consequence, is to a large degree responsible for the growth of Christian iconography, the rules of which were dogmatically laid down by the Second Council of Nicaea (786), on the theological foundation propounded by St John

Damascene. Here we find the grounds for the cultus of images which, in the Byzantine East, has attained a degree of development for the lack of which the Latin Church may have come to tolerate devotions of a less firmly balanced nature.

Chapter 6

The Principal Kinds of Liturgical Celebration

THE SACRAMENTAL LITURGY

BECAUSE it gives expression in worship to a religion whose true purpose is to communicate to men the plan of divine grace for their sanctification, the Christian liturgy gives prominence to the actions by which this communication is expressed. As we have seen, the present order of the economy of salvation requires this communication to be made by means of signs, which convey the grace they signify. This grace relates these signs to the fullness of salvation which will find its ultimate expression in Christ's *parousia*, which will bring history to an end.

The fundamental acts of this sacramental liturgy were instituted by Christ himself; but the Church in the course of time and in various ways, according to the customs of the peoples among whom she was implanted, has elaborated these elements in order to give greater prominence to the wealth of the mystery they effect. In some cases it took several centuries before the principles enunciated in the apostolic age achieved a distinctly defined ritual expression. And it took longer still for theological speculation, directing its attention on the practice of the Church, clearly to identify two levels of 'sacrament': the first, in which the liturgical acts themselves are vehicles of grace because they directly continue the sanctifying activity of Christ's human nature, and the second in which the liturgical act receives its sanctifying power and its efficacy in the order of salvation only through the mediatory intervention of the Church, the Bride of Christ, acting in the power of his Spirit. We have suggested that the first be called the sacraments of Christ, and the second the sacraments of the Church. Western theology and catechetics have reserved the name 'sacrament' for the first and termed the others 'sacramentals'. With this fundamental distinction firmly in mind, it will be noticed that the liturgy maintains the continuity of the sacramental system in its entirety and that, on the other hand, not all the sacraments are on the same plane. The sacraments of Christian initiation and of the Eucharist, whose essential rites were fixed by Christ himself, have the rank of major sacraments; the others, which were endowed with a liturgical form only after several centuries and which only imperfectly satisfy the definition of a sacrament[1] are in consequence, and from a liturgical point of view, minor sacraments.

Baptism

'Going, therefore, teach ye all nations; baptising them in the name of the Father and of the Son and of the Holy Ghost' (Matt. 28. 19)

Thus by Christ's will, the rite of immersion in water became the sign and instrument of entry into the community of the disciples of Jesus, the new Israel, the heir to the privileges of the People of God, henceforward the Body of Christ, born again in his redeeming death, animated by his Spirit, sharing in his sonship and carrying the seed of his glorious resurrection. This was not a new rite, wholly invented by Jesus; the cosmic symbolism of water, which we have dwelt on above, assumed new significance in the Jewish world of the first century both in the immersion of proselytes, in the rites of various baptising communities and in the baptism of penance to which John called the nation. We cannot be certain whether the necessity of invoking the Trinity, attested by St. Matthew, was explicitly realised right from the beginning. The Acts of the Apostles prefer to speak of baptism 'in the name of the Lord Jesus' although it is not possible to draw from this expression any indication of the ritual formula employed. We

---

[1] That is, matter or action whose significative value in the order of salvation is determined by a word or group of words.

know that subsequently, at least in certain Churches, a threefold interrogation on faith in the three divine Persons and their manifestation in the scheme of salvation accompanied a triple immersion. In the majority of eastern Churches an indicative formula is used even today, in baptism as in the other sacraments: 'N. is baptised in the name . . .', while the Roman Church has preferred an imperative fomula: 'I baptise thee in the name . . .' Above all, in the West, since the last centuries of the Middle Ages, baptism by infusion has been increasingly generally substituted for baptism by immersion, even partial immersion. The advantages of this practice are undeniable so far as convenience is concerned, but it is greatly to be regretted that it has directed the attention of the faithful far too exclusively towards the purifying rôle of baptism, to the detriment of its regenerative rôle and its symbolism, stressed by St Paul, of burial in death to sin in order to become a new creation (Romans 6).

The baptismal rite did not long keep its early simplicity. By the latter half of the second century we see the organisation at Rome and in other churches of a catechumate, the different stages in which soon assumed a liturgical character and became surrounded with various rites. The preliminary act of signing with the cross was universal; at Rome it was accompanied by the giving of salt, the traditional ceremony of hospitality. Liberation from the power of the devil was expressed in exorcisms, often accompanied by expressive gestures. It seems certain that before it assumed the meaning it was to keep in present baptismal liturgy, the Ephpheta rite, borrowed from popular custom and usage, was one of the rites of exorcism. Similarly the pre-baptismal anointing originated in connection with a symbolism of athletics difficult to interpret nowadays. It is interesting to see how some Churches—such as that of Ethiopia—have adapted this so as to give it a new meaning.[2] The anointing after baptism, on the other hand, has its place within the framework of the biblical symbolism of anointing and refers to the threefold spiritual anointing of the Messias (Christ means the anointed one in Greek) as

[2] The unctions are made on the joints of the limbs which are made to move in order to show their suppleness.

prophet, priest and king. The giving of the white garment, which is to be found in several rites and to which is added in the Roman rite that of the lighted candle, emphasises the eschatological nature of Christian baptism.

Confirmation

Only in Western liturgies and at a later period did the sacrament of confirmation by the use of a special rite emerge as clearly distinct from baptism. In Eastern liturgies confirmation is administered in the form of a post-baptismal anointing accompanied by a formula that signifies more or less explicitly the gift of the Spirit and the perfecting of baptismal initiation. The richest are perhaps those of the Syrian and Maronite rites : 'N. is signed with the holy Chrism, with the savour of the odour of Christ, with the sign of the true faith, with the fullness of the gift of the Holy Ghost, in the name of the Father, of the Son and of the holy and living Spirit, unto everlasting life. Amen'.

The Maronite rite has another form for unction performed by a simple priest: 'May the Almighty God, the Father of our Lord Jesus Christ, who hath regenerated thee by water and the Holy Ghost and hath brought thee remission of all thy sins, anoint thee with the chrism of salvation in that same Jesus Christ our Lord unto everlasting life. Amen.' This formula is very close to that which, in the Roman rite, accompanies the laying on of hands on the candidates for confirmation—an ancient gesture absent from, or barely discernible in, the Eastern rites.

The Roman rite is likewise the only one to make explicit mention of the seven gifts of the Holy Ghost, on the basis of Isaias's Messianic prophecy (Is. 11.2) and to recall that the gift of the Spirit was entrusted by Christ to the Apostles and their successors that it might be communicated by them to the faithful.

In other words the sacrament of confirmation in the Roman rite bears witness to a more fully formulated doctrine than those of the various Eastern rites.[3] Moreover, if we are to comprehend

[3] Cf. A. G. Martimort: *La Confirmation*, art. in *Communion solennelle et profession de foi*, pp. 159-202. Le Cerf, Paris.

the great richness of the sacrament, we must not separate the rite of confirmation from that for the consecration of the oils on Holy Thursday. The blessing of baptismal water is likewise an integral part of the liturgy of this sacrament, even when, as in the Roman rite, it is separated from it.

The Sacrament of Penance and Penitential Ceremonies

There is no human liturgy which does not contain rites of purification or expiation. But Christianity has received from biblical revelation a truly spiritual understanding of sin which brings into the foreground the virtue of penitence: 'Be converted and do penance for all your iniquities: and iniquity shall not be your ruin. Cast away from you all your transgressions, by which you have transgressed, and make to yourselves a new heart and a new spirit' (Ezechiel 18. 30-31). The Christian liturgy of penance gives an institution and ritual form to the virtue of penitence; it is something quite separate from a purification effected by the mere performance of certain ceremonies. The prophets of Israel attacked such ritualism ceaselessly, and the teaching of Christ and the Apostles rejects it, if possible even more violently.

It is in this perspective that we must understand the extremely complex history of the sacrament of penance. Above all it is important not to isolate it from the mass of penitential rites which embody it. Inherited from Judaism where they occupied a position of increasing importance, these rites can be perceived in still very fluid form at the beginnings of Christianity. They entered into preparation for baptism in the form of exorcisms; they find expression in even longer and more numerous penitential fasts from the fourth century onwards—a fast of preparation for Easter which everywhere was lengthened to one of forty days, in imitation of Christ's fasting and recalling a wealth of biblical symbolism; fasts of preparation for several great feasts; and in the Syrian East the fast of the 'Ninevites', instituted in the sixth century in imitation of that mentioned in the Book of Jonas. All these fasts occasioned a proliferation of petitions, lessons and chants to be used at the prayer meetings held to sanctify them and to recall their spiritual significance. It is a peculiarity of the Roman liturgy to break the forty day Lenten fast in the daily celebration of the Eucharist. In the East it was generally thought preferable to keep to communion of the 'presanctified', that is, of sacred species consecrated in the course of the Sunday liturgy. The Churches of Gaul and some eastern Churches also introduced the use of blessed ashes, or dust, and the Roman Church finally adopted this ceremony as the solemn opening of the Lenten fast. In the same way the sprinkling of persons and things with holy water should be regarded as a rite of purification, whose significance in Christianity could only be penitential.

The liturgy of the sacrament of penance to be understood must be seen in the context of this vast collection of rites. In the West, since the Middle Ages, the frequency and private nature of confessions 'of devotion' (as they are called), have gradually caused the solemn rite of ecclesiastical penance forming the framework of the Lenten season to be forgotten, and the whole of the liturgy of penance has been simplified to an extreme degree. On the whole the Eastern Churches have had more success in preserving the original setting.

This includes three essential elements: *the sinner's confession,* prepared for by the recitation of prayers capable of inciting him to contrition, and generally taken from the Psalter (the penitential psalms); *a prayer of petition* with which the Church as a whole is associated and the remnants of which are preserved in the second part of our Confiteor; *the reintegration of the penitent into the community of the Church and the proclamation of absolution* by the priest, acting directly in Christ's name by the virtue of the power of the keys. The imposition of a 'penance' is less an element of satisfaction than the sacramental sign of the reintegration of the penitent into the communion of saints—which explains why this penance has increasingly and commonly taken the form of a prayer to be repeated. It is a lesson which helps the penitent recover his filial attitude before God, while at the same time restoring to him the specific function of the members of the priestly nation.

The liturgy of the sick and the dead

The profound sense of the oneness of the human composite which permeates Christian anthropology is revealed in the close bond that has always linked the penitential liturgy and the liturgy of the sick. Without asserting a direct connection between sickness and sin, biblical revelation recognises in the disturbance of bodily health the outcome and reflection of that fundamental disorder which has destroyed the harmony of human nature. The liturgy of the sick is, of course, a liturgy of supplication and intercession for the return of health; it recalls the teaching of the Scriptures and the example of Christ and the saints regarding the right use of sickness and filial submission to the will of God, but it also assumes the characteristics of a penitential liturgy.

The importance of the ritual of the liturgy of the sick was only gradually revealed, until the Church clearly regarded it as a sacrament, that is a direct act of Christ's sanctifying humanity operating through a sign, the precise nature of which was only gradually determined. It takes the form of anointing the sick person with oil, to the accompaniment of the prayers of the Church. We know that for several centuries this anointing took various forms and that, despite the Epistle of St James (5. 14-15), the necessity for the ministry of a priest was not everywhere laid down from the beginning. But when this liturgy received its final form, it was clothed, especially in the East, with extraordinary solemnity. The more sober rite adopted in the Roman Church has the twofold advantage that it was easier to administer and, by reserving the blessing of the oil for the sick to the bishop within the setting of the solemn service for the blessing of Chrism on Holy Thursday, threw into greater prominence the 'ecclesial' nature of this sacrament even when it is administered in the absence of the community. On the other hand, it is to be regretted that an insufficient realisation of its meaning and the emphasis given to its penitential character have gradually led to its administration being withheld until the approach of death. A sounder appreciation of doctrine and of liturgical concepts is fortunately restoring in practice the authentic tradition of the Church.

10

Indeed, there exists, especially in the Roman liturgy, a liturgy of the dying. Some of its elements are very old and are adapted forms of the Jewish liturgy of penance. In the course of centuries it has been progressively enriched and mediaeval piety coloured it with incomparable human tenderness. But since the earliest times its essential ceremony has been the reception as viaticum of the Body of Christ, the last food given at the moment of the great 'passing over', in which every Christian accomplishes his Pasch, with the Lord, to the Father. This rite, of imposing simplicity, normally occurs within the framework of the whole body of prayers and readings that constitute the recommendation or surrender of the dying man to God. In former times these went on without interruption until the last breath in the 'commendation', which is, strictly speaking, the recommendation of the soul. It is a pity that this final element is now preserved only in the special liturgies of certain religious orders. But at least the beautiful response *Subvenite,* with the versicles and prayers which have been kept in the Roman Ritual preserve, in the absence of the deeply human tones of the old liturgy, the imposing prospects of this encounter between earth and heaven. Certain other compositions have also passed in slightly adapted forms into the liturgy of the dying; for, to the liturgy, there is no sudden rupture at the moment of death but merely a decisive moment in the slow and difficult process of the separation of soul from body.

That is why in old liturgical books and in the normal course of the Office the liturgy of the dead is a continuation without break of that of the dying. It is not easy to trace in the present arrangement of the Roman Ritual the former pattern of this liturgy, for it has been constantly recast to adapt it to the customs and outlook of each century.[4] Primitively, it was no more than an accompaniment by the prayers of the Church of the traditional stages in the preparation of the corpse and the death watch, and afterwards the burial. Although it is not certain that the watch was envisaged from the first, it has been this that has received the fullest development through the ages until it reached its final form in our

[4] Cf. the researches of Abbé H. R. Philippeau, especially in *Le mystère de la mort et sa célébration.*

Office of the dead, with its archaic structure and rather late compilation, which was used at first only as part of the suffrages for the dead.

At a very early date the funeral liturgy was interrupted by the celebration of the Mass. In the Roman world it would have been considered unfitting to bring a corpse into the Church and the Eucharist preceding the funeral meal, before taking the place of the latter, was at first celebrated after the interment and repeated on the traditional days of the ninth and thirtieth after the burial as well as on the anniversary. But in later times it was considered even more fitting to anticipate this celebration so that the body of the dead person might be present at the Eucharist for the last time.

The growing importance accorded to the Mass for the dead, the solemn absolution with which the Church dismisses her faithful child, commending him to the divine mercy, relegated the imposing liturgy of burial to the background. The liturgy of burial was a truly paschal office, hallowing each of the funeral actions. Its form in the Roman Ritual is extremely curtailed and in order to see it in its former grandeur we must study it in the liturgy of the religious Orders, which have been privileged to preserve it intact.[5]

The rites of marriage and of religious consecration

Entry to the important states of life, marriage or religious profession, was not hallowed by a strictly liturgical ceremony until a fairly late date. Christian marriage was of course raised to the sacramental order, but for several centuries the Church did not think it necessary to intervene directly in its hallowing. It is probable that at a very early date the more devout young couples asked a priest or bishop to bless their union and were anxious to sanctify it by the celebration of the Eucharist. But the marriage itself was a matter for the family; it was celebrated according to the traditional rites, stripped only of whatever in them might be unacceptable to the Christian conscience. From this springs the

[5] See, for example, the Dominican Rite, one of the most complete.

extreme diversity which exists even today, among the liturgies of East and West.[6]

The Roman Church was probably one of the first to solemnise marriages liturgically, by accompanying with a blessing the bestowing of the matron's veil on the bride—the central ceremony of matrimony in ancient Rome. This blessing was also given within the celebration of the Eucharist, and communion was substituted for the sharing of the symbolic cake (*confarreatio*). Later, Germanic customs, embellished by reminiscences of the Bible, were to bring into the foreground the blessing and giving of rings, a ceremony of Semitic origin which was at first one of betrothal, as it has remained in the East. But the Roman Church never lost sight of the fact that, as under the classical Law, it is the exchange of consent which properly constitutes a marriage.

In the East, much more slowly and much later, the Church adopted some of the most expressive acts in ancient marriage ceremonies and made liturgical rites of them. Whereas the blessing and giving of rings remained a betrothal ceremony, the crowning of the bridal pair became the characteristic marriage rite, in accordance with the interpretation given by St John Chrysostom, who saw in this ceremony a symbol of conjugal chastity and of victory over the passions.

In the West at least, the consecration of virgins was modelled on the liturgy of marriage; in the latter the imposition of the nuptial veil gradually lost its importance in favour of the rite of the exchange of rings (a rite more expressive of contract), in the consecration of virgins and widows it remained the principal act and in the end came to be its chief characteristic. Other marriage rites were added to it, but they were always considered to be of secondary importance.

For men, it is the declaration, oral or written, of religious profession and the taking of vows which constitutes the essential element in the extremely varied rituals of the many religious families. Each has coloured the rite with its own spirituality and enriched it with symbolic acts borrowed from contemporary

[6] There is a short history of the development of marriage rites in East and West in *Maison-Dieu*, 50, 1957.

secular society. Thus in Orders of mediaeval origin profession often takes the form of the vassal's homage. From a liturgical point of view, it is the 'clothing' that is surrounded by the richest body of prayers and ceremonies.

In the East, too, the bestowing of the monastic habit (and even of the different habits for monk or nun proper to each degree) is the central element in the monastic liturgy, both for men and women. Even more explicitly than in most Western rites, emphasis is laid on admission to a new life, to the angelic state: set apart from the secular world the monk becomes a witness to the world to come whose essential activities, so far as is possible here below, he anticipates, adding to them penance which points the way back to Paradise for fallen man. It is therefore not surprising to find ceremonies drawn from the penitential liturgy used on the occasion of monastic profession.

The Liturgy of Order

If the sacrament of marriage does not necessarily require the performance of liturgical rites, the same is not true of Order, whereby the Church constitutes the hierarchy of sacred ministers. It is of faith that this sacrament by divine institution includes at least the three degrees of bishop, priest and deacon; but it was in the post-apostolic age that they emerged as clearly distinct from each other. During the following centuries each Church, according to its needs, instituted the lesser ministries, admission to which was ratified by a blessing. The number of minor orders still varies in the different rites. Only the Roman rite has stressed the close bond between deacons and the subdeacons, who at an early date were associated with them, thus making the subdiaconate a major Order. On the other hand, in the East the subdiaconate has remained very close to the order of acolyte, when it was not simply merged with it. Moreover, the Roman liturgy surrounds the blessing of the acolyte with especial solemnity, a departure from the simplicity with which minor orders were conferred in former times.

In the course of the Middle Ages, the Roman liturgy adopted those expressive acts with which the Gallican Church, under the influence of Germanic law, marked entry to the different Orders, by delivering to the recipient some object characteristic of his new duties or by making him perform some symbolic action. This *porrectio,* or tradition of the instruments, much more expressive than the formula of blessing, gradually came to be seen as the essential and authentic sacramental rite. As it occurred in connection with both major and minor Orders, the distinction between the two groups unfortunately grew weaker, until such an obviously secondary rite as the great prostration of the ordinands during the litany seemed, in the eyes of the congregation, most explicitly to mark the distinction between them.

However the old tradition, which was maintained in its pristine purity in the East, still existed beneath the wealth of Romano-Germanic sacramentalism, although theologians were not always successful in seeing that this was so. In 1947 Pius XII explicitly restored it by declaring in his Apostolic Constitution *Sacramentum ordinis* that it is the laying on of hands that constitutes the real sacramental and only indispensable rite of ordination for bishops, priests and deacons.

This rite was already known, it would appear, in the Judaism contemporary with the beginnings of Christianity and played an important part in the apostolic communities. The oldest liturgical formularies which have come down to us emphasise its wealth of meaning by adapting it to the special duties of each Order. Moreover, through the successive developments they have undergone in the different rites, these formularies have preserved the essence of this primitive wealth of meaning, even though somewhat obscured, especially in the present Roman rite, by an excessive number of references and allusions to the Bible. In fact, it was the besetting temptation of the Middle Ages to add a great number of more or less false analogies between the sacraments of the new Covenant and the ceremonies of the old. There are few cases in which these comparisons are so unfortunate, despite all appearances, as in connection with the priesthood. The Christian priesthood is essentially apostolic; it is a lieutenancy held from Christ, the only priest of the new Covenant, for the evangelisation of the world and the administration of the sacraments. In this it differs from the Aaronic priesthood which is essentially a sacrificial office.

One other point worth noting is that the ordination liturgy does not refer to the ministry of Aaronic priests but to that of the Elders of Israel, thus emphasising the collegiate nature of the Christian priesthood, centred on the bishop, the guardian of the tradition of the apostles.

Rites of consecration and blessing of persons and things

In the course of centuries the essential sacramental rites came to be surrounded, in response to the needs and feelings of each successive period and each local Church, with a vast accumulation of formulas and actions intended to sanctify the most varied situations of human life. A full inventory has never been undertaken and would doubtless prove an impossible task. It is our aim here merely to set out in a few sentences the most significant elements in this conglomeration of blessings. And it will be convenient to mention with them the professional rites which stand next to them in the Roman Ritual. Here we reach the almost indefinable boundary between liturgy and devotion. The Roman and certain other liturgies have in fact given an official position to certain processions—but in general this has been to those accompanying a blessing, as at Candlemas or on Palm Sunday, and at the Rogation processions which, while petitionary, are also a blessing of fields and crops. Other processions, mentioned by the Ritual as occasional, form part of the liturgy only incidentally. They are in fact a reduced form of, or substitute for, pilgrimage. It is noteworthy that a rite which was often of considerable importance in non-Christian liturgies, and especially in those of Mediterranean antiquity, has a very slight part in Christianity.

A special place must be given among the blessings to those which withdraw an object from all profane use, reserving it for divine worship alone. For this reason they are often called consecrations, but this name is somewhat arbitrary and sometimes merely indicates greater solemnity. This is the case with the dedication of places of worship. Its full form is the solemn rite for the consecration of churches; but there is also in the Ritual a blessing which can be given by a priest delegated for the purpose, in which the essential ceremony is the sprinkling with holy water of the walls of the building. The consecration rite, reserved to the bishop, is extremely complex and is the result of the amalgamation of three dedication rites: the ancient Roman rite, the essential in which was the celebration of the Eucharist in the new church; an African rite centred on the deposition of relics at the foot of or within the altar, at the end of a triumphal procession; and a Gallo-Frankish rite drawn up in imitation of the rite of Christian initiation by baptism and unction with chrism. It is generally admitted today that it is this anointing, on twelve stone crosses marked out along the walls or pillars, which constitutes the essential act in the present rite. Eastern churches have generally kept a very simple form for the dedication of places of worship.

After the blessings of objects used in worship, those of foodstuffs and tools occupy the largest place in the ritual blessings. In the Roman Rite there is frequently only a simple prayer accompanied by sprinkling with holy water; but sometimes—although it is not always possible to discover the reason for it—the rite takes a much fuller form and includes psalmody. Recent formulas for the most typical tools of the modern scientific and industrial civilisation are an excellent proof of the vitality of the liturgy in adapting itself to a world increasingly different from that in which it has hitherto developed.

We could wish to see a similar inventiveness with regard to the blessings of persons. Although some have a timeless validity (such as those for the sick, mothers-to-be, young mothers and children) others have fallen into almost universal disuse without being replaced. Such, for instance, are the sacring of kings and the blessing of knights. In any case, study of this section of the ritual is richly informative.

THE EUCHARISTIC LITURGY

More than any other the central rite of the Christian liturgy is rooted in Jewish customs of the time of Christ. The better these are understood, the more evident it becomes that in giving his Church this commemoration of the mystery of redemption, Christ did not innovate but fulfilled. He inserted his Eucharist into a form of prayers and ceremonies long familiar to his first disciples, but in which he revealed a meaning hitherto unsuspected. What had been only evocation and hope, he endowed with Presence, the veiled but real presence of the Lord in the midst of his people; what had been for certain Jewish communities only a provisional substitute for the defiled sacrifices of the Temple became the only and true sacrifice of the New Testament. In order to understand the liturgy of the Christian Eucharist, we must see it in its original setting and notice the chief stages in its growth, whose exuberance has somewhat obscured its essential features.[7]

The Gospels agree in placing the Last Supper in a paschal context, but it has long been noticed that their short description can be harmonised only with difficulty with what we know of the ritual complexity of the paschal meal. There is no reference to its most characteristic element, the eating of the paschal lamb, a rite rich in its symbolism. Furthermore, St John expressly points out that Jesus died at the moment when the paschal lambs were being sacrificed in the Temple.[8] But there was a ceremony which has been preserved until our own day by Jewish families and well attested by ancient sources which extend its use to devout communities and especially to rabbinic brotherhoods. This is the *kiddush*, celebrated at the beginning of the Sabbath and principal feasts. It matches the celebration we see renewed every week from the first years of the Church onwards far more closely than that exceptional ceremony, the Pasch.

After the blessing of a first cup, the essential rite of the *kiddush* is, and always has been, the sharing among the guests of previously blessed bread; then, at the end of the meal, there follows a most

---

[7] A fuller exposition of the paragraphs which follow may be found in L. Bouyer: *Liturgical Piety*, Chap. 9, Notre Dame, 1954, and in N. Maurice-Denis and R. Boulet: *Eucharistie, ou la messe dans ses variétés, son histoire et ses origines*.

[8] This last difficulty has recently received a very tempting solution, based on the fact of coexistence of two calendars. See A. Joubert: art. *La date de la Cène* in *Calendrier biblique et liturgie chrétienne*, Gabalda, Paris, 1957.

solemn blessing of a final cup in accordance with the tripartite formula that we analysed in connection with the eucharistic prayers. This ritual is exactly that described briefly but clearly in the Gospel of St Luke, and no text contradicts it. If we add that the *kiddush* was commonly preceded by readings from the Bible, by the singing of Psalms and prayers and finally by the ritual washing of hands, the framework of our Mass will easily be recognised.

One point emerges with increasing clarity: in the form which we know it and which is found already in the earliest description that we possess (in St Justin, shortly after the middle of the second century) the Mass is not the result of a bringing together of two originally separate rites—a prayer service with meditative reading of Holy Scripture and the Eucharist properly so called. These two elements are already to be found together in Jewish tradition, which fact makes the uniformity of the structure of all Christian eucharistic liturgies less surprising.

If there have ever been Eucharistic celebrations without biblical lessons, it has been only on exceptional grounds and in special circumstances. The terms 'Mass of the catechumens' and especially 'fore-Mass', for this first part of the liturgy are misleading. It is a constituent part of the celebration and not a more or less optional prelude. With the almost unique exception of the Roman liturgy the various rites, in the course of their development, have emphasised this unity by placing the preparation of the offerings of bread and of wine mixed with water right at the beginning of the celebration. Several Romano-French rites of mediaeval date which had preserved this custom from the Gallo-Frankish liturgies caused it to be inserted even in the Roman liturgy. It is still to be found among the Dominicans.

In the various Eastern liturgies the preparation of the offerings underwent a late development to become as it were a Eucharistic pre-liturgy, providing an opportunity to demonstrate more explicitly the theology of sacrifice without overweighting the course of the celebration itself. An extreme case is that of the liturgy of Antioch, which has formulated a whole system of ritual speculation. The ceremonies of the preparation of the oblations and the first censings (also borrowed from Jewish tradition) are here seen as an evocation of the sacrifices of Melchisedech and Aaron. The Byzantine liturgy prefers to adhere to an evocation of the twofold mystery of the Incarnation and redemptive Passion. In the West, Germanic uses, doubtless of monastic origin, require a preparation of a penitential nature which on occasion gave rise to endless complications. The present Roman liturgy has kept this in principle, but in a form both sober and reserved and without ever raising it to the level of public liturgy.

As early as the fourth century, the celebration began with a procession: an entrance procession by the ministers in Rome, a procession to welcome persons of importance at Byzantium, which grew later to a procession for the ceremonial presentation of the Gospels. The prayer of the congregation was expressed in a litany, the form and position of which varied according to time and place, but of which at least some trace is to be found everywhere. In conformity with the basic structure of liturgical celebrations this is concluded by a prayer from the priest. In Western liturgies, and especially in the Roman, where it has attained its most perfect form, the 'collect' gives every celebration its individual tone. The lessons follow; they are only two, the first commonly taken from the Epistles of St Paul, the other always drawn from the Gospels, preceded by a verse from a psalm with the Alleluia. Only a few verses of the old psalmody still exist, and they are sung before or after the first readings, depending on the liturgy.

The singing of the Gospel, which is always very solemn, usually requires a homily. In the West, since the Carolingian era, this has also been the moment to interpolate, on Sundays and feast days, the recitation or singing of the profession of faith according to the Niceno-Constantinopolitan Creed. This first part of the service is completed by a great prayer of intercession for all the needs of mankind. For reasons difficult to define this great universal prayer has unfortunately disappeared from the Roman liturgy—or, more precisely, has been integrated into the eucharistic liturgy. This explains and justifies the continued existence of the apparently isolated *Oremus* at the beginning of the Offertory. It has survived in French churches in the prayers of the *prône* (cf. the mediaeval English bidding prayers)—although

INTRODUCTION TO THE LITURGY

this is a deformed and, for the last two centuries, neglected survival.

The structure of the eucharistic liturgy is clearly set out, as Gregory Dix has shown[9] : in the Gospel accounts of its institution Jesus took bread, uttered the blessing (eucharistia), broke and gave it. This fourfold scheme is to be found in all liturgies, although the third element, the breaking of bread so characteristic at the beginning, has sometimes tended to be reduced to a token rite either because of the lessening number of communions or because of the use of portions prepared in advance, such as the hosts used in the West since the tenth century.

In contrast, the Offertory is a development, sometimes excessive, of the very simple act of taking bread and wine and setting them aside for the oblation. As we have already said, most liturgies make this preparation right at the beginning of the service. But the Eastern liturgies have developed a most solemn procession for the presentation of the oblations. It assumes its most perfect form in the Byzantine rite in which the singing of the *Cherubikon* emphasises the eschatological nature of the celebration, which is a genuine anticipation of the *parousia:* the celebrant expressly recalls the principal intentions for which he is offering the sacrifice. At Rome, it was the faithful themselves who at this moment brought up their offerings to the singing of psalms; later, when this procession had disappeared, the celebrant filled the time left free during the psalmody with private prayers which came to form a sort of pre-Eucharist. This is a secondary growth to which it would be wrong to attach too much importance. The true 'offertory' is that following the words of consecration.

In the form that it has taken in the canon of the Roman Mass, the eucharistic prayer is inextricably combined with intercessory prayers which obscure its rhythm and profound intention. To see these in their pristine purity it is absolutely necessary to refer to the eastern anaphoras, especially those of St Basil and St James. There it is easy to recognise, after the hymn of thanksgiving, the commemoration (*anamnesis*) of divine blessings into which has been introduced the consecratory narrative of the institution of the

[9] G. Dix: *The Shape of the Liturgy*, Dacre Press, London, 1945.

sacrament; and then finally, the great petition (*epiclesis*) for the fulfilment of the divine plan. In contrast to the Roman liturgy, which has remained faithful to the old simplicity, the oriental liturgies have inserted statements of the doctrine of the Trinity and have emphasised especially the rôle of the Holy Ghost. The eucharistic prayer very soon enshrined the *Trisagion* or *Sanctus* taken from the tradition of the Jews and is everywhere completed by the recitation of the Lord's Prayer which serves more or less explicitly (depending on the liturgy) as a preparation for the communion.

This last should be immediately preceded by the fraction, the breaking of the Host, which is generally, as we have said, a token rite. Nevertheless, the chants accompanying it, and especially the *Agnus Dei* introduced into the Roman rite by the Syrian popes of the seventh century, underline its importance. In the course of centuries, the communion has been surrounded by prayers and chants the form of which often depend rather on private devotion than on liturgical style, which is to be seen again in the prayers of thanksgiving used as a conclusion. Almost everywhere a priestly blessing completes the celebration.

THE DIVINE OFFICE

At least since the time of the Babylonian Exile, liturgical assemblies of readings, psalmody and prayers became common in Israel alongside the sacrificial liturgy of the Temple. The last centuries before the Christian era witnessed an increase in the number and importance of these gatherings, while at the same time the order of the service began to be fixed. The reforming and Messianic movement, the importance of which becomes more obvious to us every day, tended to make this the essential part of its liturgical life; this was particularly so with the innumerable Jewish communities of the Diaspora, who were centred on the synagogue, which summoned them together not only for the Sabbath and for the feasts but also, at least for the more devout of the faithful, several times a week or even daily.

The first Christian community quite naturally took its place among those most assiduous in prayer. Its tenor was probably no different from that of the Jewish communities, except in the position it gave to Christ and its more sober and confident eschatological tone, for it was assured of Christ's return, and of the need to watch so as not to be taken by surprise at his sudden appearance. The rapid spread of Christianity in the Greco-Roman world, and particularly among the lower classes, made such frequent meetings impossible, though doubtless there was never a lack of ascetics and virgins to maintain the traditional rhythm of the hours of prayer taken over from the Jewish tradition and to recognise the importance of the night vigil so explicitly recommended by Jesus. At the beginning of the third century, the *Apostolic Tradition* and Origen agree in enjoining meetings for prayer at the various traditional hours, and in recommending nocturnal prayer. Still earlier, on the evidence of Pliny the Younger, Christians were assembling at the first light of dawn on Sundays to sing hymns to Christ as to a God.

It is not strictly speaking possible to talk of a liturgy of the Hours in these remote times; but the fact that these practices were rooted in the tradition of the synagogue makes it easier to understand how they gradually took on their canonical status in the Church. Official recognition of Christianity was later to make possible the organisation of a liturgy, but on the other hand the increase in conversions, by lessening the zeal of the communities, provoked ascetics to withdraw into solitude and afterwards to form special communities. The birth and growth of monasticism were among the most important factors in the liturgical organisation of prayer. It seems clear that there grew up almost everywhere, at least for some time, a twofold rhythm of liturgical prayer. The whole Christian community was called together for the morning and evening offices, for the vigils of great feasts and sometimes for the Sunday vigil. The monasteries kept a daily vigil and in the course of the day performed liturgical prayer at Terce, Sext and None, adding almost everywhere a short prayer on rising and lying down—Prime and Compline. The distinction is clearly to be seen in the descriptions of the liturgy at Jerusalem preserved for us by the travel diary of the pilgrim Etheria. There we see the body of the faithful, the clergy and the bishop taking part only at certain times, although the monks and the fervent among the faithful pray more often and at greater length.

The various Eastern liturgies still bear obvious traces of this ancient situation. Perhaps they have in this way helped the faithful to join more as a matter of course in the offices which have been arranged with them in mind. The form of the offices corresponds better with the religious outlook and needs of the people. The Roman liturgy has followed different paths. With the exception of a few rare vigils which in any case are integrated into the first part of the Mass, its office is entirely monastic in form—indeed, it is essentially made up of the continuous recitation of the Psalter which, since St Pius X's reform, has been shared between the different offices in a week, not even the extremely ancient and almost universal custom of keeping certain psalms for the daily celebration of the more ceremonial offices of Lauds and Vespers being maintained.

As we have already had occasion to point out, the biblical and patristic lessons which were so important at the ancient prayer services are to be found only at the night office, the most rigidly monastic of the offices. At the day Hours there is no more than a mere repetition of a phrase, often taken from the Epistle read at Mass and in any case needing to be replaced in its context. It should be noticed, too, that although most monastic liturgies, and especially that given in the Rule of St Benedict, allow a discreet place to the singing of hymns, generally of a popular kind, the liturgy of the Roman basilicas long refused them admission. Lastly, that part of the Office devoted to prayer of petition is extremely sober, in conformity with the constant practice of the Roman liturgy. Except on penitential days, not the least trace has been retained of the prayer of the litany or even of the Lord's Prayer which, according to the oldest evidence, formed for the early Christians an essential element in the prayer of the Hours.

It is easy to see how this austere psalmody, the dialogue form of which requires that all taking part in it should either have memorised the whole Psalter or be able to read, could become increasingly remote to almost all the faithful. In conformity— no doubt unconscious—with the oldest tradition, they first substituted for it the Lord's Prayer, recited as many times as there were psalms in the liturgical office. Later, mediaeval devotion to our Lady gave a place of ever increasing importance to the recitation of the *Ave Maria*. It was thus that there gradually grew up the 'Psalter of Our Lady', the Rosary of one hundred and fifty *Aves*. It is a paraliturgical celebration for confraternities, on the fringe of the liturgy of the Church. But every period has seen the birth of offices traditional in structure but with an abridged psalmody. We know how they are increasing today with the concern to introduce the true rhythm of the liturgy.

For it is a feature of the liturgy of the Hours that it marks the rhythm of time in its different periods—a daily, weekly, or yearly cycle. It forms an unbroken prayer, setting the various moments of time in the perspective of the fulfilment of the divine plan. In every age, devout Christians have tried in various ways to offer unceasing prayer still more effectively by forming groups which, one after the other, voice the prayer of the community and through it that of the whole Church. No liturgy has made such practices official, but certain monastic rites, such as the Byzantine, have at least tried to duplicate each of the official Hours with a short intermediate office. Others have sought to redistribute the Hours in accordance with a more effective symbolism, connected with the various events in the history of salvation.

Such indeed was the traditional pattern in the beginning, as it is attested in the oldest sources. The Roman liturgy has succeeded better perhaps than any other, in marking discreetly the harmony between the natural symbolism of the Hours and the story of salvation. In addition to the parallels with the account of the creation and fall reserved for the weekly cycle, it daily fixes the attention (especially in the texts of the hymns and little chapters) on the Crucifixion (Sext) and the death of Christ (None), his Resurrection (Lauds) and the sending of the Holy Spirit (Terce). These are discreet references with nothing in common with the often far-fetched elaboration to be met with in some Eastern liturgies. But these references are enough to bring the different parts of the day into the light of Christ, the true Sun.

The weekly cycle naturally evokes the first account of creation. In the Roman liturgy it finds a place in the office of Vespers, where the hymns are devoted entirely to extolling the successive steps in the work of creation and relating them to the redemptive plan. Here again, we must refer to the Eastern rites or even, in the West, to the Ambrosian liturgy, to find a clearer emphasis on the correspondences between the first, physical creation and the new, spiritual creation in Christ. The Roman liturgy seems more anxious to retain throughout the whole week the theme proper to each Sunday, as indicated by the collect repeated at each of the Hours, except at Prime and Compline, offices of monastic origin. In fact the rôle of the weekly cycle is not very obvious here, in contrast with the Eastern liturgies where it seems to dominate. In most of them, indeed, it includes a complete Sanctoral in miniature.

In contrast, the Roman liturgy has managed to make its annual cycle a splendid synthesis, weighed down by recent accretions but in the course of being restored in its essential outlines by the present reform. In fact, it is a double cycle. The first, the yearly celebration of the mystery of salvation, has come to full development only in the West, and especially in the Roman liturgy. It opens on Septuagesima Sunday with the evocation of the creation and the fall, and closes in the eschatological radiance of the Epiphany cycle, integrating it harmoniously with the commemoration of the Incarnation of Christ. The other cycle is linked even more directly with the mystery of history. In fact, the Sanctoral is no longer merely made up of the anniversaries of the martyrs, bishops and ascetics; by becoming universal it has been transformed into a commemoration of the most significant of the Church's answers to the problems raised by the events and predicaments of human history.

Chapter 7

Liturgy and History:
The Development of
Western Liturgy

THE liturgy being the most representative of the activities of
the Church, in which she expresses most perfectly and lives
most intensely the mystery of her being, it is natural that we should
find in it the characteristic paradox of this mystery: the reflection and prolongation of the mystery of the Word Incarnate.
Immutable in its essentials the liturgy, as a social action, bears
conspicuously the marks of differences of time and culture. It is
impossible for our appreciation of the liturgy to be accurate unless
we briefly consider this twofold aspect.

The study of the different liturgical families is reserved to a
later chapter; this present chapter is devoted to an examination
of the development of Western liturgy and, more particularly,
of the Roman liturgy, which we take as our example because it
has gradually supplanted all other liturgies in the West, while at
the same time absorbing some of their most expressive usages. It
is the most widespread of the liturgies today and by far the most
generally used in the Catholic Church—so much so that it is
commonly, but wrongly, held that being the papal liturgy this is
the true liturgy of Catholicism as a whole and that other rites are
merely tolerated. It is also the liturgy whose history is the better
known and the only one whose development it is possible to trace
without excessive conjecture.

The principal stages in its development are easily recognised, even though the dates chosen as pivotal are open to debate. But at least two of these dates are not really open to question: the pontificate of St Gregory the Great (590-604) and the promulgation of the decrees of the Council of Trent (1563) which brought unity to the liturgy and entrusted its safe-keeping to the sole authority of the Holy See. We suggest two intermediate dates: the middle of the tenth century which, with the publication of the Romano-Germanic Pontifical of Mainz and the introduction of Rhenish practices at Rome, was the beginning of a new stage of development; and the beginning of the thirteenth century, which saw the reforming work of Innocent III. The attempts of Pépin and Charlemagne to impose throughout their domains the strict Roman tradition made it possible throughout the West for a liturgy whose basis is enriched by deposits from other traditions gradually to be accepted. This is an ecumenical liturgy in the best sense of the word.

THE PERIOD OF ORIGINS

The scarcity of documents and their fragmentary condition means that we cannot follow the development of liturgical rites as fully as we should like. Until quite recently we had to rest content with all too rare hints gleaned from writers almost none of whom was concerned to deal expressly with this matter; inscriptions and monuments excited our curiosity more often than they satisfied it. It used to be thought that we could deduce that, until the peace of the Church, rites remained extremely simple; that the Eucharist, in the first place a simple appendage to the *agape,* had been separated from it quite early for reasons of seemliness and that it then became linked with the morning assembly for readings and prayers inherited from the synagogue. We have already shown how a better understanding of Jewish customs and the ritual meals of the devotional brotherhoods (*Haburah*) has led to the belief that the celebration of the Eucharist was performed from the beginning in accordance with a far more complex ritual, already substantially in agreement with what has remained in the various liturgies. So, too, the baptismal rite seems normally to have been inserted into a fully-developed office in apostolic times; I Peter and parallel texts in the New Testament show us its principal features.

But our knowledge of the Roman liturgy at the beginning of the third century was at once considerably increased when the work of Dom Connolly permitted the reconstruction, based on a late tradition, of the *Apostolic Tradition*, drawn up at the beginning of the third century by the Roman priest Hippolytus in order to establish (and perhaps also to give a more definite form to) the ancient practices of this Church at a time when important innovations had begun to be introduced.[1]

The manual so reconstructed is of extremely great value.[2] Despite its archaic character it already exhibits the essential features of the classical Roman liturgy. In particular, there is to be found in it an important Ritual for ordination to the various degrees of the hierarchy and an exhaustive description of the rites of the catechumenate, the form of which seems to have been fixed shortly after the middle of the second century. Lastly, a whole series of its prescriptions and observances find direct antecedents in the Jewish communities contemporary with the origins of Christianity. Comparison of these texts with those which have come down to us from the same period in the Syrian *Didascalia* and the works deriving from it confirms the universality of the basic points of liturgical and disciplinary tradition, as well as the differences in detail in which the variety of local situations finds expression. We learn from this that at this time in Rome, even more than in Syria, the forms of prayer and certain ceremonies demonstrate a concern to find ways of expression which, without departing from primitive tradition, would have immediate significance for the congregation.

This concern was given powerful and inspired expression in the great reform which, in the pontificate of Pope Damasus (about

---

[1] None of the objections of various kinds raised against the Roman origin of the *Apostolic Tradition* has as yet carried conviction.

[2] The text may be found in G. Dix: *The Treatise on the Apostolic Tradition of St Hippolytus of Rome*, London, 1937.

A.D. 370) substituted the use of Latin for the use of Greek as the liturgical language of the Roman community. For more than a century the Greek tongue had been losing ground among the motley and cosmopolitan throngs of the capital of the Empire, but for several generations the liturgy had resisted change. For long, however, Latin had been a liturgical language, and had almost certainly always been used in Africa and Northern Italy. It seems clear that this development was facilitated by the importance acquired by Milan, which was for a few years capital of the Empire, at the very time when Ambrose was its bishop. Ambrose was not only a skilful administrator and a figure of outstanding personality, but also an orator and writer capable of translating the prayer of the Church into forms that were accepted as much for the perfection of their language as the richness of their doctrine. Church Latin coined, mainly in Africa, by such men as Tertullian and St Cyprian who were steeped in the precious essence of the old translations of the Bible, now showed its ability to furnish the liturgy with a suitable medium of expression.

This turning point was to have far-reaching consequences and to orientate the whole development of the Roman liturgy in a profoundly original direction. In the East liturgical formulas quite quickly became stereotyped, and only poetical forms continued to flourish; but Rome adopted a type of prayer consisting of short and pointed formulas, in which the Latin tongue attains its greatest concision. These formulas varied according to the nature of each celebration. Instead of the fixed formularies of Eastern liturgies we find in Rome the growth of a wealth of interchangeable texts within an unchanging framework. Two things combined to promote this tendency. It was just about this time that Rome first began to adopt the various feasts commemorating particular events in the life of Christ. These commemorations had appeared several decades earlier at Jerusalem and throughout Palestine shrines were being raised on the principal biblical and evangelical sites. Such a liturgical cycle—embryonic as it still was—naturally called for texts adapted to each individual festival. Moreover, Pope Damasus himself was one of those pontiffs most devoted to keeping alive the memory of the martyrs, whose tombs were so numerous in the cemeteries around Rome. The increase in the number of anniversary celebrations in cemetery basilicas was a new motive for the composition of liturgical formulas proper to each. So there gradually grew up a vast treasure-house of texts which the devotion of pilgrims rapidly spread throughout the West.

An important collection of these texts has been preserved for us in a private collection, the Verona Manuscript, generally known as *The Leonine Sacramentary*.[3] Most of them seem to have come from the pontifical archives of the Lateran where, in some cases, they had already been collected into small books. Attempts made to date these prayers show that they precede the second half of the sixth century and that some of them appear to go back much further than that. So until this date there was no official and authorised collection but several collections from which extracts were made as the need arose, and to which new elements were added when the situation required it.

Unfortunately we do not possess sufficient evidence to reconstruct the ritual and ceremonial. But it is certain that at that time it was inspired by the meticulous etiquette of the later Empire and the customs of the imperial Sacred Palace, to which the papal residence at the Lateran was heir. We have equally little information about the administration of the sacraments, except with regard to Christian initiation which is described for the instruction of the newly-baptised in the reported addresses (the *De Sacramentis*) of Ambrose.[4] Cross-checking with the Eastern catecheses of the same period and with Augustine's sermons or references in other texts enables us to form a satisfactory idea of the form taken by these rites.

It was at this time also that the divine Office was taking shape in the great basilicas at Rome. It was entrusted to bodies of monks—a fact which gave it from the outset a structure of its own, very different from that which it had in the East or in other parts of the West. We know about it chiefly through refer-

[3] Latest Edition by L. C. Mohlberg, Rome, 1956; see also C. L. Feltoe: *Sacramentarium leonianum*, Cambridge, 1906.

[4] Critical edition by Dom B. Botte: *Sources Chrétiennes*, Éditions du Cerf, 1950; English trans. by T. Thompson, London, 1919, new and revised edition, 1950.

ences in the monastic rule of St Benedict, which refers now and then to Roman practices in liturgical matters. Despite the scarcity of this material it can be seen that at that time the Roman liturgy had succeeded in effecting a remarkable synthesis between the old Christian traditions and the most valuable elements in the ancient Roman ritual and the cult of the Emperor.

THE GOLDEN AGE OF ROMAN LITURGY

One figure, St Gregory the Great (590-604), dominates this period and seems to epitomise it for the generations which follow. In actual fact the accounts which have come down to us about his liturgical activities are of a later date and inconclusive on various points. But a close study of the liturgical texts does make it certain that the tradition is in accordance with his activity which was considerable. It was, no doubt, the consequence of a long period of preparation, about which unfortunately we know very little. The disorder with which the compiler of the Leonine Sacramentary has arranged his texts is proof that in the second half of the sixth century there was still no clearly defined liturgical cycle. But the oldest Roman sacramentary, the Gelasian, cannot be later than the last years of the same century. So then, it was at this particularly unsettled time that the considerable labour was undertaken of putting in order an already singularly complex liturgy. Moreover, it is possible that the various stages of this work were completed in a very few years and that the Gelasianum is no earlier than the beginning of the pontificate of St Gregory. The theory has even been put forward that the compilation of the Leonine Sacramentary was undertaken in order to gather the material together, with a view to a codification of which the Gelasianum is the first edition. But we possess only late rescensions of it, the purest of which is preserved in a manuscript of French origin which bears traces of long wandering and many retouchings.[5] Doubtless, as early as 594,[6] St Gregory ordered the

[5] Edited by H. A. Wilson, Oxford, 1894.
[6] The 'old Gregorianum' seems to be represented by the Sacramentary of Padua D.47, ed. Mohlberg, 1925.

compilation of a simpler and better arranged sacramentary. The variable prayers were reduced at every Mass to three : the collect, the secret and the post-communion; the number of variables within the eucharistic prayer of the Canon—the prefaces, and still more the forms of the *Communicantes* and *Hanc igitur* suitable for different feasts—were considerably reduced. Above all, the sanctoral cycle was introduced into the same framework as the temporal. This arrangement, badly adapted to the variations caused by the movable date of Easter, was not to survive. Lastly, St Gregory fixed definitely the text of the Roman canon.

The order of the readings from the Epistles and Gospels was likewise fixed at the same date, but this later underwent many more changes than did the prayers of the Sacramentary.

Later generations have especially retained the memory of St Gregory's activities in the reorganisation of the liturgical chant, known even today by the name Gregorian. Yet it is precisely here that the nature and scope of his activity is most debated.

Roman liturgical chant stands out from that of all the other Churches by reason of the sobriety of its style, the perfection of its melodies and their adaptation to the requirements of the accentuation and rhythm of the Latin. Its originality may clearly be perceived by comparison with the Ambrosian chant in use at Milan—the only Latin chant whose former notation can be determined with accuracy. The texts are often identical, or very nearly so, with those of the Roman collection. The relationship between the melodies is obvious, but those of the Ambrosian rite have kept much closer to oriental recitative which seems to have come from the Churches of Syria; the Roman melodies, on the other hand, show traces of complete recasting. This was surely the work of the masters of the *Schola* of the Lateran, whose reputation spread throughout the West.

But what was St Gregory's rôle in this reorganisation of the Roman chant? Clearly he could not have left it outside the scope of his great liturgical reform. Just as he shortened so far as possible the euchological part of the eucharistic celebration, so also he considerably lessened the length of the chants, in order to leave more time for preaching without wearing the patience of the faithful.

The processional chants, and even the very ancient psalmody accompanying the lessons, were reduced to a few verses. The interminable melismas brought over from the East were reduced to a few skilfully composed neums. It was only very much later that the chants of the Ordinary blossomed into long melismas. Moreover at this period they were confined to the litany, as shortened by St Gregory to the brief invocations of the *Kyrie eleison,* and the *Sanctus,* which, sung to a very simple chant, concluded the Preface. The *Gloria in excelsis* was sung only at pontifical Masses on Sunday and feasts; the *Agnus Dei* was only introduced at the very end of the seventh century by the Syrian Pope Sergius; and the *Credo* did not become part of the liturgy of the Mass until the Carolingian Empire. But the melodies we know today were written more than two centuries after St Gregory in the Benedictine monasteries of the Rhineland, and it seems certain that the chant used in the Roman basilicas was quite different.

No document informs us that St Gregory's reforming activities extended to the divine office which, in accordance with Roman tradition, remained the business of the monasteries. Not until the end of this period can we be sure of its precise structure, and even then we know it only through the monastic reform of Benedict of Aniane and the organisation of the clergy according to an analogous form. Similarly, we know very little of the development of ceremonial at Rome in these years. With the single exception of the *Ordo Romanus Primus,* which may date back to the end of the seventh century, all the documents we possess are the work of Frankish clerics and monks who were anxious to perform correctly the Roman rites which were gradually introduced throughout the West, although not without interaction with local uses.

The history of the expansion of the Roman liturgy is, in fact, the clearest characteristic of this period and the most notable result of the Gregorian reform. Two things contributed to this expansion. The first was the incomparable prestige of the Church of Rome, the guardian of the tombs of the two princes of the Apostles, and of an innumerable throng of martyrs, which drew pilgrims from all quarters. The beauty of the celebrations and in particular the splendour of the chant and the stamp of apostolic authority which was attributed to Roman practices moved the clergy to transfer them to their own churches. So, very soon, almost certainly by the end of the fourth century, these texts and ceremonies were adopted throughout Italy and beyond the mountains, as circumstances allowed. For better or worse, they were integrated with traditions which were sometimes very different and closer to Eastern usages because they had not been so completely remodelled by the genius of Rome. The crumbling of the West in the fifth to the eighth centuries and, outside Visigothic Spain, the lack of any primatial see capable of securing uniform discipline encouraged that particularism to which witness is borne by the all too rare fragments of those liturgies called Gallican, Italian or Celtic, which have come down to us. The most noteworthy characteristic of the period is the advance of Romanisation from one generation to another.

This process was hastened by the reappearance of a strong centralising power. From the beginning of his reign, Pépin the Short busied himself with the urgent reform of the Church and the reorganisation of the liturgy. From the time of his sacring in 754, he took energetic steps to impose the Roman liturgy throughout his domains. But instead of taking the Gregorian codification for foundation, he chose first of all the old Gelesian Sacramentary, which was already widespread in the Frankish lands, but far too complex and archaic. Some adaptation was imperative; it was made on the basis of a compilation from Gelasian and Gregorian texts and ancient Gallican uses. From it there arose a fairly homogeneous, but not unified family of anthologies known as the 'Gelasians of the eighth century'.[7]

Some decades later, the situation was still in the same state of anarchy. It was then that Charlemagne took the radical step of asking the pope for an authentic copy of the pontifical Roman liturgy and of using this as the foundation for a general unification of the liturgy. It is to be wondered why the pope did not have a complete Sacramentary sent, but only a festal Sacramentary

[7] Its principal representatives are the Sacramentaries of Lallane (a new edition of which is expected soon to appear), of Angoulême (ed. Dom Cagin, 1920) and St Gall 348 (ed. Mohlberg, 1939).

which was quite obviously insufficient, since it did not contain the texts for ordinary Sundays. But perhaps there was no longer a complete Sacramentary that was authoritative. For the last hundred and fifty years even at Rome the liturgy had been in a state of flux.

We know at least about the part performed by the popes and by the eastern communities expelled by Islam, to whom in particular we owe the introduction of the first feasts of our Lady with their processions, which have so little in common with the ancient sobriety of Rome. But there was no general reform and usages could vary from church to church.

This being the case, it was necessary to add a supplement to the Roman books. The compilation of this supplement was entrusted to Alcuin, who acquitted himself of this task with uncommon skill.[8] In a preface still famous, he himself explained the extent and the general trend of his undertaking. He drew largely upon the 'Gelasian of the eighth century' and from complete copies of the Gregorian Sacramentary which had crossed the Alps in earlier times. But he also preserved local practices which seemed necessary to him to satisfy a popular piety which was more demonstrative than that of the ancient Romans. Although at first carefully separated from its genuine Roman groundwork, gradually and for reasons of convenience the supplement spread into and modified it. On the other hand, the lectionary and, above all, the antiphonary (or collection of chants) remained in much stricter conformity with the Roman tradition. As for ceremonies, it was necessary to adapt them to local conditions and to the different circumstances surrounding services celebrated by a bishop, a simple priest or in the monasteries where the liturgy was being given a place of ever-growing importance. So, in a multitude of handbooks (*Ordines*), there was effected a general reorganisation of the liturgy, which considerably modified the ancient structure of the Roman rite, but which also formed the universal liturgy of the West out of a tradition more localised and particularised than any other.

[8] The supplemented *Gregorianum* was published by H. A. Wilson (London, 1915); Pope Hadrian's model has been reconstructed by H. Lietzmann.

THE ACCEPTANCE BY ROME OF FRANCO-GERMANIC PRACTICES (950-1200)

The tenth century has justly been called the century of iron. The Carolingian Empire was finally ruined as much by the weight of its internal divisions as by the blows of the Norman and Hungarian invasions. The Mohammedans achieved the conquest of Spain and, by taking Toledo in 932, gave the death blow to the magnificent Visigothic liturgy. This had been the only one which, by virtue of its coherence and the authority of its primatial see, had been able to resist penetration by the Roman Rite which at a later date the Benedictines of Cluny were gradually to make prevalent beyond the Pyrenees, as the *reconquista* proceeded. St Benedict's monks had long been among the most resolute propagators of the Roman liturgy. Brought into England by St Augustine's monastic mission as early as the reign of St Gregory the Great, it has become the special possession of Anglo-Saxon monasteries and had finally supplanted Celtic uses, which approximated to those of Gaul. It was primarily through Anglo-Saxons—first St Boniface, then Alcuin—that the Roman liturgy was firmly established on the continent, both in the Frankish lands and in Germania.

We have already indicated the part played by the monasteries of the Rhinelands in the establishment of Roman practices and in their adaptation to new habits of mind and circumstances. We must now return to this point in order to delineate more precisely just what was the work of those centres in which Western liturgy reached its final form. We are here concerned with a story the importance of which has only recently been realised. It was enacted in the two principal areas[9] of the chant and ceremonial. We have seen that, in the supplement compiled by Alcuin, the formularies of eucharistic celebration and the sacraments of Christian initiation assumed what was very nearly their definitive

---

[9] This discovery was the work principally of Mgr. Andrieu, who unravelled its complicated history in the introductions to his large critical edition of the *Ordines Romani* (Louvain, 1941-51).

form. It seems clear, on the other hand, that Gregorian chant in the form in which it has universally prevailed, was properly the work of the monasteries and churches in the districts of the Moselle and the Rhine, notably the church at Metz and the monasteries of Reichnau and St Gall. Unfortunately the lack of manuscripts with musical notation of a date earlier than the ninth century makes it impossible for us to determine precisely what their work was; that can only be learnt by comparison of their manuscripts with the oldest noted manuscripts preserved by the churches of Rome and its neighbourhood. These are very late, but are in marked contrast to the homogeneous tradition of the original manuscripts from beyond the Alps. The refinements introduced into the old cantilenas of the sixth- and seventh-century *schola* of the Lateran, whose repertory was fixed and its execution shortened by St Gregory, seems everywhere to have tended towards a more complex and harmonious melody, less rigid in its refusal to widen the range of the strictly diatonic primitive forms. The path opened in this way never ceased to broaden; the Norman school of the eleventh and twelfth centuries pushed the melodic and rhythmic possibilities of the Gregorian tradition to their utmost limits. After that time, the Gregorian tradition found itself outside the main stream of musical creation and, almost until our own times, plunged into a decadence in which its original characteristics were forgotten and only a heavy and insipid 'plain chant' was preserved.[10]

We are a little better informed about the development of the ritual thanks to the series of *Ordines Romani* which have come down to us. Mgr. Andrieu, who has unravelled the tangled skein in a masterly way, has been able to follow the work done throughout and even a little before the ninth century in describing Roman practices so that informed masters of ceremonies might comply with them, in order to adapt them to the varying conditions encountered in the episcopal, parish and conventual churches in which this liturgy was henceforward celebrated. Soon, however,

[10] The Roman antiphonary has been edited on the basis of one of the manuscripts of Compiègne (ninth century) and will be found after the works of St Gregory, P.L. 78, 648-850.

this primary concern assumed a wider dimension; both the purely Roman and Franco-Roman collections gave rise to mixed collections with a double purpose. Some were didactic and used as a basis for doctrinal instruction which was a first faint outline of future sacramental theology; others were practical, designed to put into the hands of celebrants all the information they needed for the proper performance of the liturgical services. To this second type there gradually came to be added for the convenience of those who used them, the prayers most closely associated with the ceremonies.

But the austere Roman tradition could not satisfy the new needs. Popular feeling could not give up expressive rites such as certain processions and the anointings which, in the Gallo-Frankish tradition, accompanied the consecration of churches, the blessing of objects used in worship, the ordination of bishops and priests and the sacring of kings. There were other fields, such as marriage, in which Germanic law imposed its views. In short, a completely changed form of ceremonial was gradually worked out, and this involved the composition of new formularies or the adoption of texts alien to the Roman tradition. This long drawn-out effort was to reach its consummation at the monastery of St Alban in Mainz towards the middle of the tenth century. There was composed, doubtless for the use of the new bishop, son of the restorer of the empire of Otto the Great, a voluminous collection that Mgr. Andrieu, to whom we are indebted for this reconstruction, has called the 'Romano-Germanic Pontifical'. Its implications were vast, and it was to give a new complexion to Western liturgy whilst preserving the most important elements of the old Roman liturgy.

However, before following up that story, we must notice the new emphasis which the liturgy had begun to assume and which was to weigh heavily in its future evolution. At Rome, as in all the other churches of Christian antiquity, the liturgical celebration had always possessed that communal nature on which we have laid so much stress. But perhaps more than any other church, Rome had preserved the hieratic character of its worship and the faithful there showed their participation chiefly in short acclamations and silent prayer. For this reason it found itself poorly protected against the onset of the effective and individual piety which appeared quite early in Germano-Frankish lands, owing perhaps to the persistent influence of Irish monasticism. Two things encouraged this tendency: the abandonment in the course of the eighth century, for reasons difficult to define precisely, of the solemn recitation aloud of the canon, and the continuing decline in sacramental communion, which left priests and faithful unoccupied during the chants for the Offertory, fraction and communion; and, on the other hand, the considerable curtailment, except at pontifical Masses, of the entry procession, which rendered the introit chant useless. How these voids were filled by an encroaching proliferation of private penitential prayers— the *apologiae*—and by intercessory prayers is well known.[11] The growing number of monks who were also priests from the time of the reform of Benedict of Aniane, together with the increase in clergy living in communities of a monastic kind, were no doubt equally important factors in emphasising this development of the liturgy towards becoming a purely priestly devotion, structurally complicated, in which the only rôle for the unlettered people, ignorant of Latin, was that of a passive assistance which the best of them came gradually to fill by saying the *Pater*.

This evolution was largely completed when there took place in the second half of the tenth century, by authority of the Germanic Emperors and with the help of the reformed Benedictine monasteries, a reorganisation of the Holy See and of the Church in Rome which, for almost three centuries had been in the hands of rival factions. It was in the liturgical field that this reorganisation was both most urgent and least difficult of accomplishment. Liturgical books had long been lacking in the Eternal City which had so abundantly provided the whole of the West. The Lotharingian clergy, imported to Italy by Otto and his successors to undertake the reform of the Curia, brought with them the books they had been accustomed to use. It has been shown that before the end of the eleventh century the Romano-Germanic Ponti-

[11] This kind of Romano-Germanic Mass is represented in the *Ordines* by the group called the '*Ordines* of Séez'.

fical of Mainz and the other books in use beyond the mountains spread rapidly into Italy. Gradually, they swamped the old uses—although not without being influenced by them in their turn. For almost two centuries in the Papal States and at Monte Casino (the influence of which was then at its height) the long labour continued which completed and crowned the work done in the Frankish lands during the two previous centuries. Directly or indirectly, Rome began once more to take in hand the revision of the Western liturgy in order to adapt it to new conditions. It does not appear that this work was done in accordance with any preconceived plan, nor even that, before the middle of the twelfth century, it was entrusted to persons of note. It might be called a biological activity, whereby a milieu remodelled, according to its own spirit, elements coming into it from outside. Although the continuity of Roman traditions had been broken and no one seems to have considered any kind of restoration—both the necessary documents and the inclination to do so were lacking—the genius of Rome had remained vigorous enough to set its mark on the texts and ceremonies returning to it from beyond the Alps. In proportion as the prestige of the Apostolic See was revived, the desire reappeared throughout Christendom to ask in Rome for the authoritative rules governing worship. And Rome, having absorbed syntheses effected outside her territory, lightened and rearranged rites that were now too heavily Germanic. For the first time we hear mention of Roman masters of ceremonies who codified the liturgical services to the last detail. The Basilica of St Peter may have clung to its old uses, but the Lateran to a great extent welcomed the new trends. The time for a general reform was at hand.

THE LITURGICAL REFORM OF THE ROMAN CURIA AND LOCAL PECULIARITIES (1200-1564)

This considerable enterprise formed part of Innocent III's reforming activity. It marks a turning point in the history of Western liturgy and a decisive date in its evolution towards the forms we know today. At the outset, its aims seem to have been quite modest : to put at the disposal of the clergy of the Roman Curia, which was at that time a complex administrative body forced by events to an itinerant way of life, books of a size easy to handle, which would allow the performance of the various liturgical services by reducing ceremonial to the minimum. This healthy and inspired reaction was in the most authentic Roman tradition of sobriety, against an excess of purely ceremonial rites and the proliferation of private prayers of devotion. But at the same time it was symbolic of a period in which the old concept of the liturgy as the communal and hierarchical celebration of the whole Church became finally obscured in favour of a juridical preoccupation with the task to be performed.

For several centuries already the growing influence of monastic liturgy had tended to transform the ancient episcopal liturgy into a capitular liturgy on which, so far as possible, the newly-formed parishes based their worship. The people, ill-equipped to take the active rôle that tradition envisaged for them, were eclipsed by the clergy, until they were reduced to a passive attendance. The popes of the twelfth century, formed in the habits of mind of the imperial episcopate, were first and foremost administrators, and juridical fitness was often accounted more important than theological knowledge.

Innocent III was at the same time jurist, theologian and liturgist. But his work as a liturgist before his election to the pontificate bears eloquent witness to the preferences of the period. It followed the line of allegorical commentary which had flourished since the time of Amalar of Metz. The inner meaning of the ceremonies and of genuine liturgical symbolism seems to have been irretrievably lost. The smallest detail of the service became the occasion of instruction or pious reflection—even when for this purpose it was necessary to appeal to tenuous connections wrenched from scriptural quotations and more ingenious than convincing.

Allegory, legalism and pietism : such is the background against which was achieved the work of reform of the books of the Roman Curia. For, in the first place, this was the only reform envisaged. There was no intention of touching the venerable customs of the Roman basilicas any more than those of other churches. This reform had nothing in common with the work of unification which the Council of Trent entrusted to the Roman Pontiff two and a half centuries later. The thirteenth-century reform tended principally to codification of accepted customs, as, in imitation of Cluny, the various monastic and canonical congregations had been in the process of formulating for almost two centuries in order to ensure uniformity among their members. During the twelfth century many cathedrals had done the same thing, and we still possess a large number of these Ordinaries, minutely describing the ever more complicated ceremonial they strove to establish. All these texts oscillate between two tendencies: that of diminishing the plethora of rites born of a taste for allegory and of the desire to make room for popular devotion and speak to it in forms immediately comprehensible to it; on the other hand, the desire for greater simplicity. The first course prevailed at Cluny and in most of the cathedral Ordinaries: the second asserted itself at Cîteaux and Prémontré. It also guided the composition of the ordinary of the Roman Curia and the revision of the liturgical books for its use. But the genius of Rome, and the tradition of the great pontifical masters of ceremonies of the twelfth century ensured for this reform an unparalleled style and balance, which fully justified its rapid expansion, although they are not sufficient to account for it.

In fact, it was an apparently chance happening which ensured this expansion. Innocent III's pontificate saw the birth of a new kind of religious life, in the mendicant Orders, the mobility of whose members and the itinerant ministries they performed necessitated the adoption of a single liturgy which, without grave inconvenience, could not be a purely local one. The experiment was made by the Friars Preachers. Originating in the south of France but within a few years of their foundation spread across all Europe, with supranational convents in the chief university centres and their general chapters meeting alternately in Paris and Bologna, they were led to draw up—although not without continuous difficulties of all kinds—an original liturgy, the basis of which, it seems, was practices already accepted at the University of Paris, but which incorporated other elements of diverse origin, drawn largely, in the case of ceremonial and chant, from the rites of Cîteaux and Prémontré.

The Friars Minor followed a different course. Being closely linked from the outset with the Roman Curia (by which they were granted a Cardinal Protector) they quite naturally accepted the abridged liturgical books, Missal and Breviary, which were suited to their itinerant status and poverty. The adaptations of these to the special needs of the Order and to its particular religious ethos was made by its Minister General, Haymo of Faversham. Other religious Orders such as the Augustinians and the Servites followed this example, but the rôle of the Franciscans was by far the most important.

The peculiarities of their reform were widely accepted and gradually penetrated into the very books of the Roman Curia. Here, in some measure, although on a very much smaller scale, we find once more the phenomenon that occurred in preceding ages: a liturgy of Roman origin returning to Rome and being accepted there, after enrichment by contact with non-Roman users.

The part played by the Franciscans was most clearly notable in the extension of the Sanctoral and the growth of its universalist character. Until this time the Sanctoral had remained clearly local. Of course, the ancient tradition of allowing only the feasts of those saints whose relics, fictitious or genuine, were in the possession of a church had long ago been abandoned. The adoption of Roman books in all the countries of the West, the renown of the most famous of the Roman martyrs whom all the Churches tended to celebrate, even where it had been impossible to obtain even the smallest relic, as early as the Carolingean era had brought about the compilation of a general calendar to which each church added its own list of saints. Continual exchanges and the increase in pilgrimages from the end of the tenth century onwards greatly enriched these early foundations. Nevertheless, the principles remained unchanged: the veneration of saints, like the liturgy as a whole, had a primarily local basis. The complete reversal indicated by the establishing of the liturgy of the Roman Curia was, in this respect more than in any other, decisive. Henceforward the liturgy was independent of the place of its celebration; it was regulated in accordance with the status of those who performed it.

But the Ordinary of the Curia did not derive from this principle all the consequences that it implied. In particular, its Sanctoral remained obviously Roman. Its chief characteristic, naturally enough, is the important place it gives to the cultus of the popes. Like the rest of Christendom, the Franciscans tended to favour the unrestrained development of the Sanctoral and gave a large share in it to those little known but very popular saints to whom devotion had grown increasingly since the Crusades. The cultus of our Lady, which to a large extent had developed since the eleventh century in the various religious houses, was now to take a place in the liturgy which Roman reserve had been slow to accord it. Devotion to the human nature of our Saviour and especially to the mysteries of his passion gradually found a place in the liturgy. In such ways it drew nearer to popular devotion without actually merging with it.

In fact, the debasement of the meaning and practice of the liturgy became ever more widespread in the course of the fourteenth and fifteenth centuries. This impoverishment was particularly noticeable in the eucharistic celebration. Private Masses— the number of which had grown continually with the increase in suffrages for the dead and the practice of indulgences—led to the gradual forgetting of the communal character of the celebration, even in religious communities of priests. The emphasis came more and more to be laid one-sidedly on the aspect of sacrifice at the expense of communion, the practice of which had been continually diminishing for centuries. Finally, new currents in eucharistic devotion towards affective piety, centred on contemplation of the suffering Christ, displaced the central emphasis of the celebration by laying stress on certain secondary rites and even by introducing new ones. The most important of these was the elevation of the sacred species immediately after the consecration. This ceremony, which appeared at the beginning of the thirteenth century as a declaration of faith in the Real Presence, later assumed a growing importance; it became the climax of the whole liturgical act. In sixteenth-century Italy it became the central point in worship of the Eucharist which was a close copy of court ceremonial. At length, along with the great number of hymns it inspired, it became partially detached from the celebration, to develop into exposition of the Blessed Sacrament, even during Mass.

But the treasury of liturgical tradition remained intact, awaiting better times. The most important of the books, the Pontifical, achieved its final form at the end of the thirteenth century in the recension made by William Durandus, Bishop of Mende, who returned to the work done in former times in Carolingian monasteries, in order to adapt to the needs of bishops the customs codified for the use of the pontifical Curia. It was this same William who, in his Rationale, gave definitive form to the allegorical interpretations of ceremonies—which fact in itself is noteworthy evidence of the two tendencies between which the liturgy wavered in the later part of the Middle Ages.

FROM THE VICTORY OF RUBRICISM
TO THE LITURGICAL REVIVAL (1563-1903)

From the beginning, liturgical reform was one of the concerns of the Council of Trent. Nonetheless, the Council came to an end without having been able to make more than a beginning on it, and in one of its last disciplinary canons (in the twenty-fifth session) it confided this task to the Roman Pontiff. With most of the books the work was already well advanced and only corrections were needed before their promulgation. The most difficult undertaking, on which there was a considerable conflict of opinion, was the revision of the Breviary.

Since the end of the eleventh century there had been numerous attempts to bring together in a single, manageable volume all the elements necessary for the recitation of the Divine Office, which had by then begun to be obligatory for clergy and monks even out of choir. The most important of these was the 'breviary according to the Use of the Roman Curia', published by Innocent III and adopted with some modifications by the Franciscans and other mendicant Orders. But, to a greater extent than any other, this book was increasingly modified and overloaded. At the order of Pope Clement VII, a radical reform was undertaken by the Spanish Franciscan, Cardinal Quiñonez. Whereas the Breviary of the Curia remained substantially faithful to the usage of the basilica of the Lateran (which it did no more than abridge), Quiñonez's breviary was an entirely new work, intended only for private recitation, and this was a departure from one of the fundamental principles of the liturgy. A less far-reaching reform had been undertaken at the time of their foundation by the Theatine Clerks Regular and this was given preference over Quiñonez's work. The man principally responsible for it, Giovanni Pietro Caraffa, later Pope Paul IV, had considered imposing it, after certain modifications, on the whole Latin Church. He died before he was able to give effect to his scheme, but his papers were used by the commission brought into being, shortly after the Council, by Pius IV. In 1568 his successor, St Pius V, was able to publish the new Roman Breviary, which laid down the principles of reform for all the liturgical books.

The reformers' first concern was to return to the true Roman tradition, in so far as it could then be known and as the legitimate development of the devotion of the Church allowed. For with every true liturgical reform it has always been the rule that it should avoid both archaeologism and untimely novelty. Changes were reduced to a minimum and great care was taken to preserve the old prayer forms, even when their latinity was not that of the humanists. Sixty years later, Urban VIII showed less reserve by having the texts of the hymns corrected in accordance with the rules of classical prosody. Even the legends of the saints were kept wherever there was no danger of bringing the Church into ridicule. But the Sanctoral was considerably reduced and a clear preference was shown for Roman martyrs. More than two hundred days were kept free for the ferial Office, thus allowing, in conformity with the most frequently expressed desires, the weekly recitation of the psalter and the reading of considerable sections of the various books of Scripture. But, above all, the reformers refused to admit the principle of separate offices for private recitation and for choral celebration.

Unfortunately, the errors against which St Pius V's reform had been directed were not long in reappearing. Important safeguards had, however, been instituted, for now the Holy See alone was competent in liturgical matters. In 1558, the Congregation of Rites was established to resolve any difficulties which might arise and to suggest necessary changes to the pope. In less than fifty years all the official books of the Roman liturgy had been published. In 1570 there appeared the Missal, substantially similar to that used since the thirteenth century and somewhat adapted by Clement V at the beginning of the fourteenth century. St Pius V's principal innovations lay in giving a fixed form to the rubrics, which were drawn up at the beginning of the sixteenth century by the pontifical master of ceremonies John Burchard and in making compulsory the reading of the prologue of St John's Gospel at the end of the Mass. In 1596 Clement VIII published the Roman Pontifical in the form given it a century earlier by Innocent VIII, on the foundation of the Pontifical of William of Mende. A new book appeared in 1600, the Ceremonial of Bishops; it was related to the oldest *Ordines Romani* and set out down to the last detail the ceremonies to be followed at pontifical services. An adaptation of it for use in small churches was made at the beginning of the eighteenth century by Cardinal Orsini who, in 1724, became Pope Benedict XIII; this little work took its place among the liturgical books during the pontificate of St Pius X and was promulgated by Benedict XV in 1920.

Lastly, the codifications of rites for the administration of sacraments, blessings and other occasional offices appeared in 1614 in the Roman Ritual, an essentially pastoral work which discarded many of the oldest and most valuable elements collected together by Cardinal Santorio in his over-voluminous compilation of 1584.

The pontificate of Benedict XIV (1740-58) saw the beginning of another reform, taken up again at the beginning of the twentieth century by St Pius X and not yet completed. Benedict XIV had to rest content with publishing a slightly improved edition of the Roman Martyrology promulgated by Gregory XIII

(1584) on critical foundations very insufficiently established by Cardinal Baronius. The fantastic inventions of Ado of Vienne and Usuard have very largely succeeded in surviving until our own times, despite the vast labour undertaken in the past three centuries by the Bollandists. This question of the Sanctoral, with its doubtful elements and tendency to encroachment, has been the predominant characteristic of the liturgy in modern times. To this must be added the ever increasing number of feasts for a doctrinal 'idea' and of feasts of our Lady. The various religious Orders have been unceasingly concerned to obtain the addition of their own particular saints and favourite devotions to the calendar of the Roman Church. The rules laid down by the Council of Trent, which have ever since served as the basis for papal action in reform, are thus continually in danger of being superseded.

The largely ceremonial concept of liturgy entertained until very recent times was poor protection against these encroachments. The dominating influence of court etiquette, the unquestioned sovereignty of increasingly trifling rubrics, the study of which constituted almost the whole of the liturgical equipment given to the clergy during their years of training, had ensured for divine worship a dignity not always known to previous ages. The new feasts aimed primarily at doctrinal instruction and affective devotion. But the concept of liturgy as a celebration, the idea that it was the pre-eminent activity in the life of a Christian community, was largely lost. For its revival there was needed the labour of learned men, renewing contact with ancient sources, publishing texts and explaining them. As a result of their influence, as much as through the interest in pastoral work revived by the Council of Trent, the seventeenth century witnessed a genuine liturgical revival, especially in France. But anxious to keep the treasures peculiar to their Churches and to preserve the Gallican privileges, the French bishops undertook to reform their liturgies themselves.

The result of this was the creation, in the course of the eighteenth century, of neo-Gallican liturgies which are not without great merits, but which make the unpardonable error of almost completely sweeping away ancient prayer forms, while carefully preserving the majority of traditional practices. The reshaping of dioceses following the concordat of 1801 and the growing influence of ultramontanism, together with the death of bishops and priests attached to Gallican traditions, was needed before a new orientation could take shape; but gradually this was to give rise to the liturgical revival with which we are familiar and in which pastoral considerations have once more assumed a place of primary importance.

STAGES OF THE LITURGICAL REVIVAL

Although the revival has come to full development in the last few years, it has been long prepared by the patient work of pioneers making ready the ground. It goes back even as far as the labours of scholars in the seventeenth and eighteenth centuries, and in particular of Dom Martène and Dom Mabillon, who made the ancient texts and ceremonies widely known and who added explanatory and illuminating dissertations to their editions of them. But, above all, it would be impossible to emphasise too strongly the work of Dom Guéranger and the Abbey of Solesmes which he founded, despite his exaggerations and shortcomings, the result of controversy and imperfect knowledge of the complex history of Western liturgy. Solesmes rediscovered the meaning of liturgical worship and was thus led to restore Gregorian chant, an essential element in traditional celebration. The German abbeys of Beuron and Maria-Laach were living this liturgical life for many years before the work of Dom I. Herwegen and Dom O. Casel permitted the disentanglement of its theology, and learned researches made its history better known.

Meanwhile St Pius X, animated by his acute pastoral judgment and his love for the Church's most authentic traditions, had given new impetus to this reform of the liturgy which had been so often asked for and so long neglected. But especially had he stressed the pastoral character of the liturgy and so laid down the condition essential to its revival. This new emphasis was the essential spirit of the 'Parochial Liturgical Movement', born in a newly-founded Belgian abbey, Mont-César in Louvain, a

daughter-house of Beuron. Dom L. Beauduin, a monk first trained
for the pastoral ministry, outlined its essentials at a Catholic
Congress in 1908 and became its moving spirit. Fifty years later
this view of the liturgy had prevailed in many different countries
and Pius XII, who had given it its charter in the Encyclical
Mediator Dei (1947), gave it solemn authorisation on the occasion
of the first international congress of pastoral liturgy at Assisi in
1956.

Among the most important factors in this revival there should
be noticed especially the coming together through Romano
Guardini of the German youth movement (*Jugendbewegung*) and
the ever living springs of the liturgy (*Quikeborn*). Fr. Doncoeur
and his Cadets passed on this exhilarating discovery to the youth
of France. In the scouting and youth groups with which he was
connected were formed a good many of those young people who
were to make the whole Church share as a community in these
celebrations, 'the joy of their youth'. In this they were helped by
the pastoral experience of an Austrian Canon Regular Fr. Pius
Parsch, who did more than anyone to give to the Bible its proper
place in the liturgy. So, even before biblical revival had reached
the stage at which we know it today, liturgical celebration gave
it a position in which it could find its full significance. Thanks to
Abbé Remilleux, the parish priest of Our Lady of St Alban in
Lyons, the liturgy, already once again communal at Klosterneu-
berg, was able to show its pastoral value in an ordinary parish.

The liturgical revival was slower in starting in English-speaking
countries than in Europe. It requires to be said, however, that
considerable research into origins and the evolution of liturgy was
carried out by English students (not all of them Catholics) in the
nineteenth and early twentieth centuries, though at the time the
practical importance of their work was not always realised. In
more recent years the Society of St Gregory, the Vernacular
Society and other groups have striven to promote popular participation in the worship of the Church. In the U.S.A. the pioneer
of the movement was the late Dom Virgil Michel O.S.B., of St.
John's Abbey, Collegeville, Minn. He translated Dom Lambert
Beauduin's little book *La Piété de l' Église* (*Liturgy, the Life of*

the Church, Collegeville, the Liturgical Press, 1926) and founded a monthly periodical *Orate Fratres* (its name has since been changed to *Worship*) in order to propagate the liturgical revival. The annual 'National Liturgical Conference' (the proceedings are published yearly), supported by many bishops, was largely due to his initiative.

By assimilating so many discoveries and putting this great wealth to practical use, the Centre de Pastorale liturgique, created in France in 1943, became a meeting-place for theologians, liturgists and parish priests. The same kind of initiative manifested itself in various countries, so putting at the disposal of the hierarchy the means of undertaking action on a very large scale, in order to give the liturgy its rightful place and complete significance. In this way the ground was better prepared than it had ever been before to take up again the great reform longed for through so many centuries, and for which, until now, it had been possible only to outline a few points.

The several instances of liturgical reforms instituted by the Holy See in recent years have been based on an increasingly accurate knowledge of the evidence of tradition and the main lines of liturgical evolution; they have been founded, too, on a theology of worship whose fundamental positions were approved by the magisterium of the Church in the Encyclical *Mediator Dei,* and responded to the concern of priests and people to see the restoration of a really communal liturgy.

Chapter 8

Liturgy and Human Societies: The Various Liturgical Families

FROM the example of the development of the Western liturgy, we have been able to learn how the liturgy is progressively and often clumsily adapted to the needs of different ages; we have been enabled to witness the organic growth of rites; we have seen how the peculiar genius of Rome, the organising centre and Holy City, has remodelled the rites and prayers it has assimilated and how it has been an inspiration to the creative genius of other churches from which, in return, it has taken the best they had to offer. But now we must complete this historical survey with a brief panoramic glance at the diversity of and reciprocal relationships between the liturgies which developed in connection with the differing cultures in which the Church has from time to time taken root.

Some of these differences, as we shall shortly demonstrate, may well go back to the very beginning. But most of them are not earlier than the fourth century when, with the official recognition of Christianity, there was an extraordinary development of ceremonial, the adaptation of the old and austere liturgy to appeal to the mind of those who were entering the Church in ever increasing numbers, and finally the growth of an ecclesiastical organisation fashioned on the imperial model.

We have already drawn up the slender balance sheet of our knowledge so far as the liturgy of the first three centuries in Western countries is concerned. In the East it is Syria which offers us most information, and we shall see that this was not merely a matter of chance. There is no doubt that our earliest source, the *Didache*[1], comes from Syria. It already gives an important place to liturgical regulations and preserves for us prayer forms of great antiquity, still very close in structure to the Jewish tradition. And it is certainly Syria that provided us, in the course of the third century, with the *Didascalia,* a collection as widely known as the *Apostolic Tradition* of Hippolytus of Rome. These various texts were taken up again, also in Syria, and developed into the big collection known as the *Apostolic Constitutions.* Here we have at our disposal a fair abundance of documentation covering a broad area. Yet it raises more questions than it resolves; too many of its allusions we no longer find really intelligible; too often, lacking the prayer forms, we cannot definitely interpret the rites.

We must also beware of two pitfalls : that of putting together information from different dates and origins, and that of exaggerating differences which are very often differences only of expression. The third century, with long periods of religious peace separated by the terrible Decian persecution, was undoubtedly a time of the greatest importance in the organisation of the liturgy and the formation of the various families of liturgies which are so clearly differentiated by the middle of the fourth. Unfortunately we cannot follow the course of this fruitful labour. Even in their later development, the Eastern liturgies are still too poorly understood. We must therefore rest content with taking them in their final form, which, as in the West, was established by about the thirteenth century.

THE WESTERN RITES

But so that our picture shall not be too incomplete, we must first say a few words about the various Western rites, of which we have hitherto spoken only in passing, in so far as they played a part in the final establishment of the Western liturgy inspired by Rome.

In fact very little is known about these rites, even today, except

[1] See A. Audet, *Etudes Bibliques*, Gabalda, Paris, 1958.

in the case of the Visigothic rite of Spain (which is often erroneously called the Mozarabic rite) and the late forms of the liturgy of Milan. The name 'Gallican liturgy' covers a group of dissimilar fragments of diverse origin and date, and the same is true—although the position here is even more deplorable—of the Celtic liturgies. On the other hand, we know a great deal about the complex liturgies which grew up after the tenth century by the interaction of Romano-Germanic foundations and local uses, both in local Churches and in different religious orders. Having already had occasion to assign these latter to their places, we shall content ourselves here with a brief mention of them.

The Liturgy of Visigothic Spain

This liturgy is worthy of close study on many grounds. It presents the exceptional case of a homogeneous liturgy, built up according to clearly stated principles. Its sources are obscure. At the time they settled in Spain the Visigoths were already Christians, albeit Arians. All of which would suggest that they had a liturgy bearing strong oriental influences. The appearance of Byzantine bridgeheads in the reign of Justinian reinforces this belief. Unfortunately we know almost nothing about possible liturgical uses in Spain when the Visigoths arrived; over a long period of time, Roman and African traditions had been mingling there with those of Gaul. It was this complex and barely coherent mixture which was authoritatively remodelled by the great bishops of the seventh century. Ritual splendour was joined to the wealth and theological depth of prayer to form an imposing monument assured of widespread diffusion by the close union between civil and ecclesiastical power in the Visigothic kingdom and by the unchallenged primacy of the Church of Toledo. Fortunately the most important sources have been found and published.[2] These include the ancient Pontifical and Ritual, the *Liber Ordinum Sacerdotalium*, dating from before the eighth century, the extraordinarily rich Sacramentary, a collection of prayers, the Lectionary and the Antiphonary, the musical notation of which is unfortunately still unintelligible.

[2] Edit. Dom Férotin: *Monumenta ecclesiae liturgica* vol. V-VI.

The Islamic conquest brought irreparable harm to this liturgy and after the reconquest the work of the Cluniac monks ensured the predominance of Roman practices. It was not until the end of the fifteenth century, under Cardinal Ximenes, that this ancient liturgy, adapted for the new age, was restored to a chapel in the cathedral at Toledo, where it is still in use.

The Ambrosian Liturgy of Milan

We have already had cause to speak of the part played by Milan in the formation of the Roman liturgy in the Latin tongue. The metropolis of Northern Italy has succeeded in preserving the essentials of its traditional practices until our own times and so has kept alive one of the oldest forms of Western liturgy. Indeed, as we have said, the rôle of the popes and of Roman liturgists seems to a large extent to have been to remodel, according to the liking of Roman sobriety, the too diffuse elements in the ancient Italian uses. Comparison of texts, and more still of melodies, gives us many examples of this. But while the Roman rite gradually won the peninsula for itself and then became general beyond the mountains, the perfection of the Milanese texts and the prestige of St Ambrose, who gives his name to them all, made possible their survival. Even Charlemagne in his desire for unification failed with them, and the restoration of the Romano-Germanic liturgy at the beginning of the eleventh century brought to Milan only modifications of relatively little importance. In the last years of the sixteenth century, the energetic intervention of St Charles Borromeo laid the foundation of a restoration which the eminent historians and liturgists who have occupied the throne of Milan in these last decades—Cardinal Ratti, the future Pius XI and Cardinal Schuster—were to continue. It is therefore possible in the twentieth century to see celebrated a liturgy true in its essentials to the most ancient uses of the West. For it is now quite certain that the Ambrosian rite is genuinely Western and has preserved better than the Roman liturgy—the originality of which cannot be too greatly stressed—the impress of those ancient days when customs of Syrian provenance made their mark on the whole of the Christian world.

The Gallican Liturgies

We have already mentioned the reservations with which one must speak today of the rites of the churches of Gaul. The continual splitting up of territory, consequent on the barbarian invasions, the absence of civil or ecclesiastical centres with prestige great enough to win dominance for their own particular uses, the scarcity of the sources that have come down to us and the strong romanisation of the most important of these even when, as in the case of the all too famous description of the Mass attributed to St Germanus of Paris, there is no question of fantastic reconstruction by later liturgists—all these things have contributed to consigning these traditions to oblivion.[3] In truth it would appear that there never was a 'Gallican Liturgy'. The Churches of Gaul, like those of Milan and Toledo, remained true to the old kind of liturgy that pre-dates the great Roman reforms of the fifth and sixth centuries. But the disruptions of the seventh century, the constant importation by pilgrims and monks of Roman ceremonies led, by the middle of the eighth century, to such confusion that probably there was no other remedy than that adopted, under the influence of St. Boniface, by Pépin the Short, and pursued with renewed vigour by Charlemagne: the outright adoption of the Roman rite. As for the so-called Celtic rite, there seems to have been nothing original about it except its peculiarly incoherent adoption of practices from all quarters.

The Romano-Frankish Liturgies

As we have seen, the adoption of the Roman rite did not lead to the abolition of all local customs. On the contrary, some churches were particularly faithful in maintaining intact the ancient forms of the Roman liturgy in the face of developments introduced from the Rhinelands. So it came about that (despite the changes made in later centuries) the metropolitan see of Lyons, the Carthusians

---

[3] The most important texts—*Missale Gallicum Vetus, Missale Francorum, Missale Gothicum, Missale Bobbio*—were published by Dom Mabillon (P.L.72). Critical editions are being prepared by Dom Mohlberg.

and the Dominicans still possess liturgies that are more authentically Roman than that which bears the name today.

Among the Romano-Frankish local liturgies must be included
the liturgy of Sarum (i.e., of Salisbury) in England which before
the Reformation was widely used not only in the country of its
origin but elsewhere. The similarities that have been noticed
between Sarum usages and the Dominican rite, for example, are
due to their common origins, but the former displayed a greater
elaboration of ceremonial; it owed nothing to the Cistercian
liturgical tradition which counted for more than a little in the
formation of the Dominican rite.[4]

Although Sarum was the principal liturgy in England and
Wales other rites deserve mention, particularly York, Hereford and
Bangor. All these local variants in England and Wales disappeared
at the Reformation and were never revived.

THE SYRO-ARAMEAN LITURGIES

The Churches of Syria (using that word in its widest sense) played
a rôle of exceptional importance in the organisation and earliest
development of Christian liturgy. The strength and fecundity of
their creative genius was a source of enrichment to all the other
Churches until a date late in the Middle Ages. It would be greatly
tempting to study them in fuller detail but, within the restricted
scope of this introduction, we must limit ourselves to pointing out
the principal streams of this creative activity and the most
characteristic forms of the rites into which it was gradually
canalised.

We feel it important to emphasise for a start the existence of
two traditions both going back to apostolic times. One, which
survived in Aramaic-speaking communities, remained more
closely connected with Jewish liturgical tradition. Not without
some truth it can boast of its heritage from the first apostolic community at Jerusalem. Later its principal centre of organisation was

[4] The Sarum liturgical books have been reprinted: *Missale ad Usum
Insignis et Praeclarae Ecclesiae Sarum* ed. F. H. Dickinson, 1861-83; *Breviarium
ad Usum Insignis Ecclesiae Sarum,* ed. F. Procter and C. Wordsworth, 3 vols,
1879-86. See also W. H. Frere: *The Use of Sarum,* 2 vols, 1898 and 1901.

in the kingdom of Edessa and it developed on the frontiers of the Roman Empire in regions almost untouched by Hellenism. It survives today in the liturgies of the Chaldean and Nestorian churches, as well as in the Syro-Malabar church of India. Some of its practices are to be met with again in the Maronite church of Lebanon which, as a general rule, follows the second tradition.

Next we shall study this second thread, with its beginning in the hellenised communities of which, in early times, Antioch was the most influential. From the fourth century onwards, Jerusalem, a great centre for pilgrimages and the monastic life, added new features to the Antiochene liturgy. The links between these two streams were never broken, even when they took definite form as two Churches which anathematised each other on essential points of Christological doctrine. The community of language which existed right from the beginning outside the large cities and intellectual influence of the great city of Antioch, an apostolic see, the capital of the Roman diocese of the East, ensured that there would be fruitful exchange between them. Nonetheless, we believe that the differences were great enough to justify distinguishing between two types of liturgy, the Edessene and the Antiochene.

The Edessene Liturgy

The Edessene liturgy grew up principally in the Kingdom of Edessa which succeeded in preserving its autonomy for a long time. Jews had always been numerous there. Legend attempts to connect with Christ himself the story of the beginnings of evangelisation in Mesopotamia, and at any rate it is certain that at the beginning of the third century Edessa was the foremost Christian state. It is obvious that this situation would favour the development of ecclesiastical institutions and among them the liturgy. Unfortunately the disturbances created by the wars between the Romans and the Persians and later the Islamic conquest, have deprived us of almost all ancient documents. But at least we know that Edessa played an exceptional rôle in the development of Christian hymnography. The oldest sources known to us seem to have originated in Northern Syria and Asia Minor; but it was at Edessa towards the end of the second century that Bardesanes composed his hundred and fifty hymns in imitation of the Psalter, in which he gives free reign to gnostic speculations. Such was their success that in the middle years of the fourth century, St Ephrem the Deacon is believed to have been led to compose to the same still popular tunes orthodox hymns whose influence was felt throughout Christendom. Not only are they the ever-living treasure of the Syriac liturgies; they were also the first representatives of a new kind of hymn which was to prevail in Greek-speaking Churches, and it seems clear that it was Syria that gave St Ambrose the idea of composing hymns with a metre simple enough to be easily remembered by congregations. From these grew the whole of Western hymnography.

It was only with the formation of the Nestorian Church at the end of the fifth century that our information about the liturgy begins to become more exact, owing especially to the numerous conciliar canons and canonical replies which have come down to us. They help to throw light on some at least of the poetic texts, such as the metrical homilies of the great Nestorian teacher Narsai, whose compositions enriched the hymnography of all the Syrian churches. Towards the middle of the seventh century, that is at the time of the Arab penetration into Persia, the patriarch Isho'yab III undertook a complete revision of the liturgy and gave it its final form. Fairly numerous and accurate commentaries show that since that time there have been no important changes, none in fact except the introduction, as everywhere else, of new texts and, in particular, of poetic compositions.

The Chaldean liturgy looks peculiarly conservative to us, and this characteristic seems to go back a very long way. Like all the institutions of this Church, it is in direct line of descent from Semitic traditions and is more closely continuous with Jewish practices than any other. Ritual symbolism has remained very moderate. The conditions under which this Church grew up and lived, in the midst of non-Christian empires—first Persian, then Arab—have clearly not allowed it to make use of the pageantry of Christendom. But it seems clear that the temperament of the

Chaldean peoples—eminently positive and more open to the observational sciences and to judicial definitions than to specula- tion and imaginative creativeness—predisposed them to this reserve. From this one point of view there is an abyss between the Chaldean liturgy and that of the patriarchate of Antioch.

The vast missionary undertakings of the Nestorians carried their liturgy to the eastern boundaries of Asia. But from the beginning of the fourteenth century decadence became ever more apparent and Tamerlane's expeditions gave the last blows to a form of Christianity which since that time has survived hardly anywhere except around Mosul and on the slopes of Kurdistan.

The eucharistic liturgy is celebrated in accordance with three formulas, only one of which is original, the others having been imported from the patriarchate of Antioch and attributed to Nestorius and Theodore of Mopsuestia. By contrast, the core of the 'liturgy of the Apostles', or of Addai or Mari, the first to evangelise the Edessene lands, is a very archaic prayer-form of typically Semitic flavour. In it, we recognise a Christianised form of the Kiddush thanksgiving. The narrative of the Institution does not figure in the manuscripts and there has been a good deal of debate as to whether or not it was ever known to this liturgy. A complete theory of the primitive forms of the eucharistic liturgy has been erected on this very frail foundation. In fact it seems clear that it was for fear of allowing the profanation of the most holy words of consecration that they abstained from writing them down, and the priests had to pass them on orally. This attitude is very close to that found in Judaism.

The sacramental liturgy is still very archaic, despite borrowings from the liturgies of Antioch and Byzantium and, among present- day Chaldeans, from the Roman rite. Among Nestorians, the practice of penance and anointing of the sick had long fallen into disuse and this has led Catholic Chaldeans to adopt the Roman rites. A great labour of restoration is however at present in progress on the basis of mediaeval manuscripts and especially of the Pontifical drawn up in the thirteenth century. Study of the most ancient commentators has been particularly necessary in the almost complete absence of liturgical manuscripts anterior to the twelfth century.

The Divine Office does not include the Lesser Hours. It consists chiefly in the recitation of the Psalter, which is divided into twenty sections (*marmitha*) each preceded by a prayer which reveals the principal themes of the psalms. A position of equal importance is given to the hymns and responses (*onitha*). It has remained fairly common for the people to take part in the office, including the Night Office. In the course of the centuries, moreover, this has been the principal element in religious training. Two peculiarities of the Office should be noted: the place given to veneration of the martyrs (in honour of whom hymns are sung daily at Vespers) and the absence of lessons from Scripture; these are reserved to the Mass, when they are four in number: the Law, the Prophets, the Apostle and the Gospel. At the Night Office, a metrical instruction on the theme of the season or the feast is chanted.

As we have said, in the early centuries Christianity was carried to India by missionaries from Syria and Persia. The history of these communities on the Malabar coast, which claim St Thomas as their founder, is complex and little understood. At the end of the sixteenth century, the Portuguese forced them to make a revision of their liturgical books, to adapt them to Latin practices. They then destroyed the old texts. Since that time, the Catholic portions of these groups—by far the majority—have made use of a hybrid liturgy; its revision is now in progress to restore it to the true tradition of the Churches of Eastern Syria.

A field of study even more interesting than the liturgy itself (which seems to have remained strictly true to the ancient practices, until its Latinisation) is the atmosphere of its celebration in these Indian communities. Here we can see how the survival of imported rites and an alien tongue can be allied with a way of life and thought very different from that of their homeland. So, under a restricted and usually far distant episcopate, the clergy was always almost entirely indigenous. Quite naturally they imbued their liturgy with an atmosphere suited to the mental outlook of the land. But it was not until very recent times that it was possible to see a local language in use, in the Syro-Malankarian Church. This we refer to below.

The Liturgy of the Patriarchate of Antioch

From its earliest beginnings the Church reached beyond the bounds of Palestinian Judaism and opened her arms not only to the hellenised Jews of the Diaspora but also to pagans. From the Acts of the Apostles we learn of the part played by Antioch, the great hellenised metropolis of Syria, in this broadening of outlook. It was there that the faithful were given the name Christians for the first time, and it was there too that Paul began his missionary apostolate. Tradition has it that Peter at some time fixed his apostolic Chair there. In fact, after Rome, no city was so open to ideas from all sides. It is not surprising that so lively a centre played a prominent part in the building up of the Christian liturgy. It is possible that certain New Testament texts preserve for us a few fragments of this primitive liturgy. Standing at the meeting place of the Semitic East, which penetrated as far as its outskirts, of that earlier Asia whose mystic fervour centuries of Hellenism had been unable to weaken, and the Greek world which, island by island, had through its colonies gained a footing all along the coast, Antioch was the place best fitted for the development of a liturgy which was at once faithful to its scriptural and Jewish origins, open to the mystery of the divine Unknowable revealed in Jesus Christ the God-Saviour, and imbued with that sense of proportion, order and harmony that Greece had brought to a pitch of perfection impossible to surpass.

Unfortunately, we have no means of following the earliest steps in this development, but all the evidence enables us to think that it was not less important than in the following centuries. It was no doubt at Antioch, more than anywhere else, that the Christian liturgy received those distinctive features which were later to be found in all Churches except those of Edessene Syria and, to a lesser degree, of Egypt and Rome.

After the fourth century a new factor began to affect the old Antiochene tradition. After the Peace of the Church, Jerusalem became for Christians the spiritual Mecca to which came pilgrims from all lands in great numbers. Until that time it had been a humble suffragan see of the Palestinian metropolis of Caesarea, which was itself under the sway of Antioch. But the new needs of the pilgrims and concern to give its full spiritual significance to each of the Gospel sites (on which sanctuaries had begun to be built) and, above all, the unique character of the Basilica of the Holy Sepulchre, or rather, of the Resurrection (*Anastasis*), opened new fields to the liturgy. And, providentially, it happened that in the middle of the fourth century the bishop of Jerusalem was a man whose intellect was well fitted to take the initiative the situation demanded. Cyril was imbued with a sense of tradition and yet open to new points of view. He had an exceptional grasp of the ethos and meaning of liturgical celebration. He was perhaps the first to demonstrate its character of 'mystery in worship'.

It was, it seems, from Cyril that was derived that ingenious invention which soon spread into all the Churches, the cycle of the liturgical year. Until that time Christians had known only one feast, that of Easter, in which they lived again the mystery of the presence of the Risen Lord and of the new life communicated by him to his Church. This nocturnal celebration included the initiation by baptism of the neophytes and the ceremonial breaking of a rigorous fast in the eucharistic meal. Since it was overladen with localised associations, the liturgy of Jerusalem spread them throughout the course of the year. The congregation was bidden to gather at a particular shrine chosen for its association with the Gospel event to be commemorated. Scriptural readings, psalm singing and prayer followed and then the congregation went in procession to the *Martyrium* of the Cross and to the *Anastasis* where the solemn liturgy took place according to its normal form. We can see how an entirely new orientation was thus given to the Christian celebration, one more immediately focused on the facts of the history of salvation.

In this perspective the liturgy of Antioch was to develop. The sermons of St John Chrysostom allow us to reconstruct it in broad outline as it was at the end of the fourth century and to imagine its splendour. The laity seem to have been particularly fond of nocturnal celebrations and torchlight processions; as at Jerusalem the monks, who were very numerous, played an important part and contributed to the brilliance of the ceremonies. The chant was developed and new hymns, brought in from the Euphrates district of Syria, were added to the psalms.

The sixth century was the beginning of a great change. The opposition movement against Constantinople and the ethnic nationalism which disturbed Syria took as pretext an outright rejection of the Nestorian doctrines adopted by the Christians of the part of eastern Syria that was under the Persian Empire, in order to revive St Cyril of Alexandria's most extreme statements, those which he himself abandoned and which the Council of Chalcedon had forbidden. In this way a dissident church came into being, called Monophysite, with the Patriarch Severus as its doctor, and later James Bar-Addai as its organiser.[5] Soon, the Jacobite patriarchate adopted the Syrian tongue, which until that time had been confined to the countryside; the liturgy drew more and more widely on the treasury of hymns composed by the masters of Edessa and Nisibis, the successors of St Ephrem. Compositions of all kinds became increasingly numerous as the centuries passed. Of course, we possess only a tiny fraction of these, but these are sufficient to provide the Antiochene rite with a variety and richness unparalleled elsewhere. It was carried all over Asia by missionary activity, in the same way as the rite of the Nestorians of Chaldea exerted an influence in Egypt and Armenia, before being gradually stifled by the growth of Islam. But it was to find an unexpected lease of life in India when, in the second half of the seventeenth century, one party among the Malabar Christians went into schism and joined themselves to the

[5] The Nestorians, disciples of Nestorius, bishop of Constantinople from 428-431 expressed their teaching in formulas which appeared to attribute to Christ not only two natures but also two persons, one human, the other divine. In reaction against this, the Monophysites went to the other extreme. Anxious to affirm the unity of Christ, they declared not only that there was in him only a divine Person, but also insisted on a formula which seemed to recognise only one nature, which was heresy. Every child nowadays learns from the Catechism that there is one Person but two natures in the Incarnate Word. But this exactitude was reached only after terrible doctrinal struggles.

Jacobite patriarchate, adopting their liturgy, which the Syro-Malankarian church, re-entered into the Catholic communion, was to preserve and translate into Malayalam.

As for the ancient Greek liturgy of Antioch, after surviving for several centuries among Christians who remained orthodox in faith, and were known by the name Melchites, it was finally replaced in the twelfth century by the liturgy of Constantinople. The ancient eucharistic liturgy of Jerusalem, known as the liturgy of St James, is still used in certain places on the feast of that apostle.

In addition to this form, which is considered to be the typical liturgy of Antioch, there exist more than seventy eucharistic anaphoras of which only a few are in fairly general use. Some may be linked with old Syriac forms, but the majority are mediocre mediaeval compositions. In the course of centuries the celebration has become surrounded with ostentatious ceremonial and a great wealth of symbolism. Particularly noticeable is the development in the preparation of the elements and the opening censing, called the sacrifice of Melchisedech and the sacrifice of Aaron. As in all liturgical celebrations, an important position is given to the singing of the hymns which are a characteristic mark of this rite. Equally noteworthy is a peculiar euchological form, the *sedio* (order), which unites harmoniously praise and supplication.

The sacramental ritual also is rich and varied. Tradition dates its principal elements back to the great Jacobite teachers of the seventh and eighth centuries. They were codified at the end of the twelfth century in the Pontifical of the Patriarch Michael the Great, which served as the foundation for the recent edition of the (Catholic) Pontifical of the Church of Antioch.

The Divine Office is everywhere characterised by the disproportionate place given to hymnographical compositions, which swamp the psalmody. Numerous special ceremonies, expressive and moving, mark the various feasts. In this way grew up a liturgy at once very popular and rich in instruction; yet its redundancies and repetitions seem difficult of acceptance by the western mind.

In the family of Antiochene rites we must give a place of its own to the liturgy of the Maronites of Lebanon. The origin of this church is still obscure and little is known about the first centuries of its history. Today, liturgically, it belongs without question to the Antiochene group, but it has been possible to show that it retains traces of an ancient eucharistic liturgy related to the Aramean liturgies of Chaldea. It is probable that the monastery of St Maron on the Orontes, which was the cradle of the Maronite Church, like the other monasteries of Syria, used an indigenous local liturgy which was more and more strongly marked by the influence of Antioch. Cut off among the mountains of Lebanon and thinking only itself orthodox, the Maronite Church appears to have remained conservative for a long time. This ancient Maronite liturgy would hold even greater interest for us, but unfortunately it is difficult to rediscover it under the layers of Latinisation with which it has been covered. Indeed, unlike other eastern Christians, the Maronites proclaim themselves at one with the Church of Rome and with the Crusaders who brought them knowledge of its practices. In the name of the apostolic tradition that was innocently believed to have been preserved faithfully at Rome, even in liturgical matters, the pontifical legates sent by Innocent III and his successors imposed certain rubrics and a few texts, although these were of little importance. It was only in modern times, after the Council of Mount Lebanon (1736), that the Maronite liturgy suffered the most serious damage. This went so far as to substitute for the ancient rituals an adaptation of an Italian book of devotions. On this point at least a return to a surer tradition has recently been made, but much still remains to be done and it is to be desired that the Maronite clergy would show greater zeal in preparing the restoration of a liturgy which may be reckoned among the most representative of the Syrian East.

THE LITURGY OF THE BYZANTINE WORLD

Constantine's creation of a new capital for the Empire at Constantinople on the site of the ancient Byzantium, at the entrance to

the Bosphorus, became a pole of attraction for all the Churches of
the Roman East, the consequences of which, in the liturgical
field as in so many others, have been incalculable.

Yet nothing seems to have predisposed this modest suffragan
see of Heraclea of the Bridge to the position of religious centre.
Later legends have tried in vain to assign an apostolic origin to this
Church; the province to which it belongs does not seem previously
to have played a part of any importance in the development of
the liturgy. Its rites were doubtless those of that earlier Asia, some
idea of which we can gain from the writings of the great Bishops
of Cappadocia in the fourth century. These pointers are, however,
too few, too obscure and too fragmentary for us to be able to distinguish the characteristic elements of these ancient Asian rites,
and to place them with certainty among the main streams of
development which gave birth to the various liturgical families.
We know that these Asian Churches claimed to originate with the
missionary activities of St John whose writings, both Gospel and
Apocalypse, reveal a liturgical spirit. But relations between Asia
and the metropolitan see of Antioch were continuous. Ignatius, the
great heir of the Johannine tradition, was Bishop of Antioch. This
leads us to believe that the liturgical creations of the Syrian capital
exerted a profound influence even as far away as the shores of the
Bosphorus. Later developments in the Byzantine liturgy, despite
their uniqueness, were of the same pattern. Moreover, it was
Antioch which gave Constantinople the most famous of its bishops,
John Chrysostom, whose name for centuries to come was borne
by the liturgy of the capital. And in fact—although it is impossible
to say exactly what it was—his rôle must have been great in the
organisation of worship at the beginning of the fifth century, which
everywhere saw the giving of a fixed form to the usages which
arose in the previous century.

The texts of the Byzantine liturgy are particularly rich in
doctrine and bring down to us an echo of the orthodox faith as it
was defined in the course of the great Trinitarian and Christological controversies of the fourth and fifth centuries. The dogma
of Chalcedon, on the distinction and integrity of the divine and
human natures in the single Person of Christ, the Son of God,

dominates the whole of this liturgy and stamps it as belonging to the great period of creativity.

The reign of Justinian, the most glorious in all Byzantine history and the gravest in its consequences for the Church, seems to have been particularly fruitful. The withdrawal into Asia of Syrian monks after the Arab invasion hastened the adoption by the great Church of Constantinople of many of their practices. But it certainly did not begin then. The Palestinian monasteries, especially, exercised a preponderant influence over all eastern monasticism, especially in liturgical affairs, and it is not without cause that the arrangement of the *Typicon,* which regulates the arrangement of the Offices in the Byzantine Church, is attributed to the Laura of St Sabas in the gorges of Cedron. The bitter struggle waged by the monks in the defence of orthodoxy during the iconoclastic controversy still further increased their prestige and the monastery of Soudios at Constantinople, the chief centre of resistance, played a decisive rôle in the final arrangement of the liturgy.

It was these monasteries in particular—and specially the Laura of St Sabas, with St John Damascene and his Syrian companions, and the monastery of Soudios, with St Theodore and St Joseph the Hymnographer—which were responsible for the poetic 'canons' on the scriptural odes, a literary genre which was to turn the structure of the Byzantine Offices upside down.

We must also mention the part played by the ceremonial of the Imperial court in the establishment of a liturgy which transferred to the worship of the heavenly King the etiquette laid down for the Basileus.

Other rites developed on the foundation of an increasingly slender symbolism which sometimes declined into artificial allegorism. The most typical example of this development was the growth of what was in fact a eucharistic pre-liturgy in connection with the preparation of the oblations. This office (the *proscomidie* or *prothesis*) is, moreover, performed privately, behind the closed doors of the *iconostasis.* It cannot therefore be said that it had a catechetical purpose. Another mark of this development of symbolism can be seen in the evolution of the *iconostasis.*

When the veneration of images became more general, in reaction against iconoclasm, it became customary to hang the most precious icons on the pillars in the screen which traditionally separated the sanctuary from the nave and which, it may be, here and there under Syrian influence tended to become a real wall, pierced only by two or three doors through which the celebrants might pass. But it is really only since the end of the Middle Ages and chiefly in Russia that the *iconostasis* has assumed its full symbolic significance: a projection, for the sake of the faithful, who are still bound to sensory realities, of the heavenly and spiritual world with which the liturgical celebration connects them.

These few examples are enough to give some inkling of the riches and complexity of the most fully developed liturgy of the East. By virtue of its unique position as capital of the Empire, it was able to borrow from all sides, and developed over a period of almost ten centuries.

The eucharistic liturgy makes use of two formularies; the older, nowadays reserved to a few solemn feasts, is attributed with some justification to St Basil; the other, called that of St John Chrysostom, seems to be derived from an old liturgy brought in from Antioch. We must point out the important place given to litanies which, somewhat indirectly, unite the congregation with the celebration. Also noteworthy is the development undergone by the offertory procession accompanied by the singing of the *Cherubikon*.

The liturgy of the sacraments includes no special peculiarities in comparison with that of the other Eastern Churches. But in the Divine Office should be noticed the part played by poetical compositions—the short strophes inserted between the verses of the psalms proper to each Hour, and especially the arrangement of these strophes into a single whole which has finally come to replace the recitation of the nine scriptural canticles (odes) at the morning office, between the verses of which they were originally to be performed. This is the *canon*, the Syro-Palestinian origin of which we mentioned above, and which was to furnish material for a late hymnography more remarkable for its abundance than for its poetic and doctrinal value.

Thus constituted, the Byzantine liturgy finally replaced all the rest in those Churches which remained faithful to orthodoxy. Translated first into Syriac, then into Arabic, it gained ascendancy among the Melchites of the Patriarchate of Antioch, who resisted for some time before accepting some of the accretions of the late Middle Ages. They have preserved until our own times some few special practices which may go back to the ancient traditions of Antioch or Jerusalem.

But the most noteworthy development of the Byzantine liturgy resulted in its adoption by the Slavs. We know that at the beginning of their apostolate St Cyril and St Methodius translated the texts of the Holy Scriptures and the liturgy into a Slavonic dialect, a form of old Bulgarian. A century later the conversion of the princes of Kiev opened all the Russians to the Byzantine rite and, in modern times, Russian missionaries have carried it across the whole of Syria and Central Asia as far as Manchuria, China and Japan. This prodigious expansion was facilitated by the custom of translating the liturgy into the tongue of each people as soon as possible, with the result that the liturgy was able to play its traditional rôle in catechesis. The place given to the chant, which is often composed of short, easily-remembered strophes and imbued with substantial and profound doctrine in a style full of imagery, rich with scriptural reminiscence, is one which allows the faithful to join actively in the celebration.

But despite this diversity of tongues, the Byzantine liturgy is still profoundly one, and has probably fewer variations than are accepted in the Roman liturgy of today. Of course the Slavs, like the Melchites, followed liturgical developments in the capital and the Greek provinces only from a distance. At the beginning of the seventeenth century when, after a period of disturbance, the Russian Church, now become an autonomous patriarchate, undertook its own reorganisation, it seemed imperative to revise the Slavonic texts to bring them into conformity with the latest Greek editions. The circumstances under which this revision was made and the brutality with which the ecclesiastical authorities in Moscow caused it to be imposed by the civil authorities deeply disturbed the mass of the population, who were strongly attached to the old practices, the only ones they considered orthodox. This was the beginning of a schism or *raskol* which was immeasurably prejudicial to the authority of the Church and the purity of doctrine throughout the Russian Empire.

At the same period, the metropolitan see of Kiev and the western Slavonic provinces in closest contact with the Latins and sometimes subject to Catholic princes, undertook a reform which opened the door to Latinising practices. The authority and learning of the Metropolitan of Kiev, Peter Moghila, introduced some of these into liturgical books accepted by all the Orthodox Churches speaking Slavonic languages. The dioceses which re-entered the Roman communion following the agreement of Brest-Litovsk (1599), and for that reason called Uniate, unfortunately pushed this Latinisation much further and, like the Catholics of Malabar, created a hybrid and artificial liturgy, which recent revisions have attempted to restore to a form more in keeping with the spirit of the Byzantine rite.

THE ARMENIAN RITE

A separate place must be given to the profoundly original liturgy of the Church of Armenia. The geographical situation of this nation, its complex history, the circumstances of its evangelisation, are all reflected in the structure of its liturgy, whose origins and sources are still incompletely known. The most ancient elements seem to have come from Edessene Syria, but the influence of Antioch and, above all, of the Asian churches, were not long in making themselves felt. In the end, just when the Armenian Church was assuming its own individuality and a brilliant group of translators, poets and teachers was enriching it with a magnificent religious literature, the prestige of Byzantium began to exert its influence.

Like Syria, Armenia chose Monophysitism, no doubt in order to set an insuperable barrier between itself and the dreaded Empire, but it has now been clearly proved that doctrinal divisions did not prevent exchanges, liturgical or otherwise. Finally, the migrations of the unfortunate Armenians throughout the centuries, and their close alliance with Frankish crusaders, encouraged the introduction of Latin practices, which are especially numerous among that fraction of them who have re-entered Catholic communion. It should also be noticed that as a result of the part played in this region by the Friars Preachers, who instituted a special congregation for the Armenians, the Brothers of Union, certain practices taken from the Dominican rite are to be met with in Armenia.

This liturgy, which is widespread throughout the world as a result of the number of colonies of emigrant Armenians in Europe and America is characterised especially by the splendour of its ceremonial, the brilliance of its liturgical vestments and its music, the wealth of hymns which have so large a place even in the celebration of the Eucharist. Despite its composite and somewhat hybrid nature, an Armenian solemn liturgy is one of the most magnificent celebrations in which it is possible to take part.

THE EGYPTIAN LITURGY: COPTIC AND ETHIOPIAN RITES

As far back as it is possible to go, the liturgy of Egypt has been cut off from that of other Eastern churches by a number of characteristics which are related to those of the Roman liturgy. Now it happens that the oldest liturgical formulary which has come down to us, the *Apostolic Tradition,* which is attributed, it seems certain with justice, to Hippolytus of Rome, is preserved for us principally in an adapted form called 'The Egyptian Church Order'. Moreover, the *anaphora* of the eucharistic celebration has survived until our own times in the Ethiopian liturgy, the Egyptian origins of which we shall shortly mention. These, and a few other facts, are somewhat puzzling: they have still never been really satisfactorily explained.

Even the very origins of the Egyptian Church are quite obscure. An old and well-attested tradition made Alexandria the apostolic see of St Mark, the disciple and interpreter of St Peter. But it is not only Mark's name that sounds Roman; the purpose of his

Gospel, the sobriety and concrete nature of his language, agree
with the statements of Papias in leading us to see in this text the
Gospel of Jesus Christ, the Power of God and his Son, an expression of the faith of the first Christian community at Rome.

Whatever its origins, the Church appears to have been well
organised, at least in Alexandria which was more Greek than
Egyptian, by the beginning of the third century. From the
beginning of the following century the deep roots Christianity
had put down among the lower classes, the fellahin, are evidenced
by the extraordinary growth of monasticism. It is probable that,
as in Syria, there have been two kinds of liturgy since the beginning: the one Greek in style and the other Coptic. But we have
no indication that there was any difference between these two
types except in language and, no doubt, in the extent to which
ceremonial was developed. We have the good fortune to possess
a copy of the Euchology composed in the fourth century by
Serapion, the Bishop of Thmuis, a friend of St Athanasius. The
prayers it contains give some idea of the richness of Egyptian
liturgies at this period. Not all of them, of course, have the same
doctrinal density; it is however probable that the highly centralised
character of the organisation of the Egyptian Church, the renown
of the apostolic see of St Mark and the prestige of teachers such
as St Athanasius and St Cyril ensured a wide diffusion of
Alexandrian customs and prayers. Fragments of liturgies preserved
on papyrus and texts from later collections in the ruins of monastic
libraries, corroborated by inscription and ostraca, give us a sufficient idea of Egyptian liturgy before the Arab invasion.

As in Syria, and even more completely than in that country, the
second half of the fifth century was a decisive turning point in the
life of the Church. Strongly attached to absolutely literal interpretations of the ambiguous expressions of St Cyril, and above all,
violently opposed to the Patriarchate of Constantinople and the
Byzantine administration, the clergy and monks of Egypt were
almost unanimous in rejecting the definitions of the Council of
Chalcedon and founded a dissenting church, Monophysite in line.
The results of this schism were not long in influencing liturgical
development. There followed universal adoption of the Coptic

tongue in place of Greek, which in the chief town had been the only language in use; close relations with sister Churches in Syria, which through the mediation of the monastery of St Mary of the Syrians in the desert of Scété, an important centre of Syrian culture in the heart of Egypt, transmitted to the Coptic Church a number of their practices and prayers; and finally, the increasingly marked influence of monasticism, a particular expression of the Egyptian Christian sensibility. All liturgies have been affected, although in varying degrees, by monastic practices. We have noticed their influence in the establishment of the Byzantine rite and it could be demonstrated likewise in Syria. Nowhere, however, does it seem to have been so great as in Egypt.

In the form it finally took in the Middle Ages and as the greatest liturgists of those times interpreted it, this liturgy is characterised by its simplicity, its popular character and the unrivalled importance it reserves to the reading of the Scriptures. The eucharistic liturgy has three forms. The most authentically Egyptian, today called the liturgy of St Cyril, derives from the Greek liturgy of St Mark; the liturgy of St Basil appears to have been derived from the same source as the Byzantine liturgy of the same name; and the liturgy of St Gregory Nazianzen, which has the peculiarity of being addressed to Christ. We note in these liturgies the importance given to intercessions—they occur even within the eucharistic *anaphora*. Also noteworthy is the number of times the people join in, either at the deacon's instigation or spontaneously; they show their adherence in *Amen, Kyrie Eleison* and other exclamations. The chants, with an accompaniment of percussion instruments, are for the most part reserved to professional singers. The melodies are very strange and may in part date back to Egyptian antiquity.

The administration of the sacraments made use of rites and prayer-forms on the whole rather like those of other eastern Churches, particularly the Church of Syria. On the other hand, the Divine Office has a form of its own, deriving from the traditions of Pachomian monasticism. Basically, each Hour consists in the recitation of twelve psalms; the place given to hymnody is relatively restricted and even the hymns, which are rather like our responsories, are made up principally of scriptural cantos. The most original element in Coptic hymnography is the *theotokia,* hymns to our Lady, whose cultus has always held an important place in Egypt.

The Alexandrian liturgical tradition has undergone in Ethiopia a strange development just outside the range of the Coptic rite of Egypt. According to tradition it was missionaries sent by St Athanasius who undertook the evangelisation of this country and until very recently the only bishop with power to ordain in Ethiopia was an Egyptian monk, the *Abuna,* who moreover had hardly any other duty, for the native Ethiopian clergy are fiercely devoted to their own especial customs. Many of these customs show the influence of Judaism or are still very close to the traditions of paganism. It is often difficult to determine exactly where the boundaries between liturgy and superstition lie.

The history of this liturgy is still almost entirely unknown. Most of the ancient documents seem to have disappeared during the great era of upheavals in the fifteenth century, and the rich monastic libraries are far from being completely explored. Seventeen formularies are now used for the celebration of the Eucharist. One of them is none other than the ancient *anaphora* from the *Apostolic Tradition;* others are adaptations of Coptic or Syrian liturgies; some are original compositions, remarkable for their wealth of poetry. The celebration is extremely long and is, moreover, inseparable from that of the Offices, in which an important place is given to hymns, some of which are even today improvised by clerical scholars, the *dabtaras.* Their literary genre, full of scriptural reminiscences, is akin to that of the negro spiritual. On the whole one is struck by the African feeling which impregnates this liturgy, which is without a doubt the only one to include ritual dances. As a remarkable example of adaptation, this rite deserves to be more widely known. Few demonstrate to such a degree the flexibility of the most traditional liturgies.

INDEX

INDEX

Action, constituting the Church, **38ff,**
    95, 125
    expressing the Church, **44ff,**
    125
    hierarchical, **51ff**
    liturgy is action, 68, **114ff,** 125
Abraham, 69, 71
Acts of the Apostles, 126
Advent, 92
Agnus Dei, the, 155
agrarian liturgy of renewal, 52
agrarian religions, 18ff, 61
Alcuin, 157
Allelulia, the, 107
altar, the, 123
Ambrosian chant, 154
    rite, *see* Milan
Amen, the, 107
Andrieu, P, 158n, 159
anointing, 127, 128, *see also* Oil
Antiochene rite, 180, **184-188**
antiphons, 92, 107, 109
Apocalypse, the, 47, 49, 71, 72, 78, 122
Apostles, the, 51, 54-5, 129
Apostolic Constitutions, The, 47, 175
Apostolic tradition, 118
Apostolic Tradition of Hippolytus, The,
    47, 144, **150,** 194, 197
Apuleius, 62n
archetypes, 6, 10
Armenian rite, 103, **193-194**
Ashes, 121, 130
Audet, A, 175n

Bachelard, G, 7
Baptism, 34, **41ff,** 53, 63, **79-80,** 81, 85,
    93, 118, 120, 122, **126ff**
Benedictines, 158, 161

Beuron, Abbey of, 171
Benedictus, the, 109
bishop, the, 51, 54, 88n, 119, 131, 135,
    137
blessings, 86, **137-8,** *see also* consecrations
body, the, 2, 32
Body of Christ, the Church, 33, 37, 52,
    53, 61, **72ff,** 77, 95, 123
    're-actuated' in the
    Eucharist, 42,
    see also Eucharist
Book of the Epistles, the, 105
Book of the Gospels, the, 105
'book of legends', 105
Bouyer, L, 60n, 71n, 74n, 80n, 139n
bread, 10, 79, **82-3, 121-2**
breviary, the, 104, **167ff**
Byzantine rite, the, 113, 124, **188-193**
    Sunday liturgy of, 49-50, 93
    psalmody in, 108
    confirmation in, 118

Caillois, R, 13
Candlemas, 137
candles, 122, 128
canticles, *see* singing, psalmody
Carolingian era, 104, 141, 158, 165
Carthusian rite, 179
Casel, Dom, 59ff, 64, 74n, 75, 77n, 171
catechumens, 127
celebration, 22, 119, **125ff**
ceremonies, 40, 46ff, 110, **117-119,** 157
ceremonial, 117
Ceremonial of Bishops, The, 169
Cerfaux, L, 30n, 32n
Chaldean rite, the, 181
charismata, 51
Charlemagne, 177, 178

201

chrism, 81-2, 131
Christ, 69, 73, **74ff,** 80, 92
  priestly ministry of, 44, 53
  broke bounds of creation, 49, 71
  high priest, 52, 76, 88
  paschal oblation of, 53, 73, 77-8
  mediator, 53, 111-112
  prophet, priest and king, 53, 128
  encounters man in the liturgy, 66
  in history, **69ff**
  Head of the Church, 54, 77
  the 'mystery' of, 64, 69, 87
  centre of union, **56ff,** 58
  in St Paul, 60ff
  Messias, 81, 83, 127
  sacraments of, 86, 125-126
  glorified, 89
  gestures of, 116, 117
  inaugurates Eucharist, **139ff**
  devotion to, 166
Christian liturgical assembly, 34, 37,
  107, 110, 113-4
Christian liturgy, the
  its mission, 27
  the action of the Church, 33, 38ff,
    44ff, 52ff, 68
  distinct from all other rites, 34
  primary function, 35
  agent for unity, 37-8
  unsatisfactory definitions of, 38, 53,
    58
  definitions of, 39ff, 53, 58
  dispenser of salvation, 40, 46, 48, 53,
    66, **77**
  constitutes the Church, **41ff**
  expresses the Church, **44ff**
  a 'mystery' 44, **56ff, 64ff,** 79
  communal nature of, **46ff,** 58, 160
  bears mark of milieu, 48, 58, 62-4, 74n
  liturgy of heaven and earth, **49ff,** 78
  an hierarchical action, **50ff**
  has only one priest, 53, 78, 89
  ecclesial dimension of, **57ff**
  essentially paschal, 59, **78**
  encounter between God and man, 66,
    78, 132
  sacramental order in, **83ff**
  fossilisation of, 115, 118
  and things, **119ff**
  sacramental, **125ff**
  of the dying, 132
  and history, **148ff**
  reform of, **162ff**
  pastoral nature of, 171ff

  see also Rite, Roman Rite, Byzantine
    Rite etc.; Baptism, Confirmation
    etc; Liturgy
Church, the
  part of the economy of salvation, 28,
    45
  as worshipping community, 29, 30
  the new Israel, 29ff, 33, 47, 52, 53, 83,
    126
  sacramental in constitution, 33
  variety essential in, 45, 110
  the spiritual temple, 33, 49
  a new creation, 39
  liturgical in essence, 38
  bears marks of human milieu, **45ff,**
    47, 86, 115, 125-6, 166
  citizen of heaven and earth, **49ff,** 90,
    95
  hierarchical organisation of, 50ff
  trustee of the Spirit, 51, **72ff**
  and time, **69ff**
  and mystery, **69ff**
  see also the Body of Christ
church, (the building), 123-4
Church Latin, 151
Cîteaux, Abbey of, 164, 165
civic cults, 20
clergy, the, 48, 55
clothing of religious, the, 134-5
Cluny, Abbey of, 164
collects, the, 110, 112, 113, 114, 141
comes, 105
commemoration, the, 111
communal meal, 6, 63, 73, 83, 139
communal nature of the liturgy, 46
community at worship, 143-4
community of God's people at Mass, 36,
  46ff
community of the redeemed, 27, 126
Community Masses, 43, 172
Compline, 109
concelebration, 54
confession, see Penance
Confirmation, 42, 51, 85, 122, **128-9**
Confiteor, the, 130
Congregation of Rites, the, 169
consecration, 48
  of things, places and persons, 44,
    137-8
  of oil and chrism, **81-2,** 129
  of churches, see dedication
  of virgins and monks, 85, **134-5**
Coptic rite, the, 195
Council of Trent, 109, 164, 167

Covenant, the, 29, 76, 111, 136
  liturgy of, 31
  ratified in the Eucharist, 37, 52
  code of, 47
  commemorated in the Pasch, 52
Creed, the, 141
Crusades, the, 166
Cullmann, O, 70, 72n, 74n, 82n, 83n
cult of our Lady, 166
cult of the fertile Crescent, 20
cycle of the Hours, 94

Dalmais, I, 72n
Damasus, Pope, 150, 151
Daniélou, J, 80n
Day of Atonement, the, 76
'Day of the Lord, the', 89
deacon, 52, 55, 105, 113, 135
dedication of Churches, 85, 123, 137-8,
  160, 184
depositio episcoporum, 87
de Sacramentis, 152
devotions, 48, 88, 146, 164, 166
Didache, the, 47
Didascalia, the, 150, 175
Diocletian, 7
Dionysius, 50, 62, 84
Dix, Gregory, 142, 150n
Dominican order, 164ff
Dominican rite, 133n, 140, 179
Doncoeur, P, 15ff, 17, 172
Durandus, William, 167
dust, 121

early Christian communities, 51, 61, 63,
  73, 101, 106, 118, 123, 135, 149ff
Easter, 75ff, 81, 91,
  vigil, 122
Eastern Churches, the, 52, 84, 87, 92,
  105, 114
  invitatory in, 36
  liturgies of, 81, 93, 103, 119, 140ff
  martyrology in, 104-5
  psalmody in, 107ff
  baptism in, 127
  confirmation in, 128
  lenten fast in, 130
  sacrament of the sick in, 131-3
  marriage in, 134
  consecration of religious in, 134-5

ordination in, 135-7
dedication of Churches in, 138
divine Office in, 145
Liturgical formulas in, 151
ecclesiastical compositions, 104, 109
Edessene rite, the, 180-4
Egypt
  influence on Solomon, 31
  deliverance from, 52, 76, 111
  Osiris cult of, 62
  flight from, 79
  influence on Christian psalmody, 108
Egyptian rite, the, 194-5
ektene, the, 113
Eliade, Mircea, 3n, 10n
Ember Saturdays, 103
ephpheta, the, 35, 127
Epiphany, 75, 81, 92
Epistles, the, 103, 105
Ethiopian rite, the, 127, 197
Eucharist, the, 42, 48, 59, 63, 73, 79, 82,
  85, 88, 93, 94, 117, 122
  keystone of Christian liturgy, 37, 74ff
  essential to existence of Church, 39
  the principle of unity, 41, 42
  focus of all rites, 53, 57, 82
  sacrament of salvation, 77
  sacrament of presence, 77
  eschatalogical aspects of, 82
eucharistic liturgy, 138-147, 166
eucharistic prayer, 111
evolution, 89
Exile, the, 69, 101
exorcisms, 127, 129

faith, 38, 41, 127
Fathers of the Church, 104, 109
feast, 23, 78, 88
Feuillet, A, 30n
Filthaut, T, 60n
fire, 12
Franciscans, the, 165, 166
funeral rites, 44, 62, 79, 84, 85, 88, 118,
  133

Gallican rite, the, 135, 156, 176, 178
game, and liturgy, 4, 8
Gaul, church of, 109, 130
Gelasian Sacramentary, the, 154
'Gelasians of the eighth century', 156

Germanic influence on Christianity, 116, 134, 136
Germanic rite, the, **158-162**
gesture, 5, **115**
Gloria, the, 36, 106, 155
Golgotha, 53
Gnosticism, 70
Good Friday, liturgy of, 114, 116
Gospels, the, 103, 105
  at Mass, 107, 141
Greek
  concept of 'mystery', 61ff
  concept of time, 70
  influence on early Christianity, 74n, 122
Greece, classical, 20, 22
Gregorian chant, 154ff, 158
Gregorian Sacramentary, the, 157
Guardini, R, 172
Guéranger, Dom, 171

hierarchy, 51ff
hiera, 62
high priest, 51, 76
Hild, J. Dom, 22, 87n, 93n
history
  sacred, 30
  the Church expressing Christ in, 33
  in relation to the Incarnation, 56ff, 58, **69ff,** 75, 79, 89
  theology of, **70ff,** 74n, 75
  and liturgy, **148ff**
holy people, the, 14, 33, 47, 51, 76
'holy, the', 13
Holy Spirit, the 53-4, **72ff,** 75, 77, 83, 93, 111, 122, 126, 128
Holy Thursday, 129, 131
Hours, the cycle of, 144-6
hymns, 105, **109ff,** 145
  of praise, 79
  in 1. Tim., 3, 61
  to martyrs, 89
  to the Blessed Sacrament, 167
  Edessene, 180-1

iconography, 123
iconostasis, 113
Incarnation, economy of, 45, 57, 58ff
incense, 122-3
Indian concept of time, the, 70

individualism, 42-3, 48, 161
Innocent III, Pope, 162ff, 167
Isaias, 106
Islam, 20, 21, 156, 177
Israel, 28, 47, 49, 76, 82
  nation of, 29, 69
  the Church emerges from, 29, 60
  and the Temple, 31
  concept of time in, 71
  see also Judaism

John the Baptist, 126
Judaism, liturgy of, 74n, 101, 122, 132, 143
  influence on Christian worship, 106, 107, **111ff,** 126, 136, **138ff, 149ff,** 179, 181
  see also, Israel
Jugendbewegung, 172

Kadosh, 106
kiddush, the, 139, 182
kneeling, 116
kyrie eleison, the, 36, 155

Last Supper, the, 53, **138ff**
  see also, Eucharist
law, the, 47, 101
laying-on of hands, the, 55, 63, 118, 128, 136
lay order, the 102
  part in liturgy of, 39, 48, 55, 160, 163
Lefebvre, J, 17
Lent, 103, 129, 130
Leonine Sacramentary, the, 152
lessons, 102, 103
Levites, 51
Levitical priesthood, 51-2
Leviticus, Code of, 47
Liber Ordinum Sacerdotalium, 176
light, 11, 92, **122**
litany, the, 113, 114, 141
liturgical lectionary, **101ff,** 154, 157
liturgical prayer, **110ff**
liturgical revival, 167, **171ff**
liturgical texts, 40, 88, 91, 132, 152, 171
  history of, **148-173**

liturgy, the,
   what it is, 1ff
   the work of the people, 3, 28
   elements important for the celebra-
      tion of, 4
   and human action, 5ff
   and sensory phenomena, 6
   and material things, 10, 119
   what it effects, 16
   and transcendence, 17
   and celebration, 22
   and feast, 23
   of the Old Testament, 51-2
   of Israel, 74n, 76, 101
   of praise, 53, 79, 93, *see also* Office
   see also Christian Liturgy
Lord's prayer, the, 111, 161
Lotharingian clergy, the, 161

Mabillon, Dom, 171
magic, 4n, 9, 19
Magisterium of the Church, the, 85,
   104
Magnificat, the, 109
Maison-Dieu, La, 23n, 64n, 85n, 87n,
   120n, 134n
Maria-Laach, Abbey of, 59, 171
Maritain, J, 67n, 68n
Maronite rite, the, 128, 180,
marriage union,
   image of the Covenant, 29
   in Old Testament, 130
Martène, Dom, 171
martyrs, 87-88, **89,** 151-2, 168
   legends of, 104-5
   tombs of, 123
Mass,
   lessons at, 103
   in the Middle Ages, 166
   see also Eucharist
material things in the liturgy, 10, 86
matrimony, rites of, **133ff**
   sacrament of, 43, 85
meal of the Lord, 93
Mediator Dei, x, 26, 52n, 98, 172, 173
Meersch, E, 37
Melchisedech, 52, 141
melisma, 108, 155
melody, 105, 108, 154
mendicant Orders, 164ff
Middle Ages, the, 86, 90, 92, 104, 109,
   115, 117, 121, 135, 136

Milan, Ambrosian liturgy of, 147, 151,
   154, 176, **177**
ministry
   threefold Christian, 53
   of priest in sacrament of the sick, 131
Missal, the, 169
Missale Bobbio, 178n
Missale Francorum, 178n
Missale Gallicum Vetus, 178n
Missale Gothicum, 178n
monasticism, 52, 93, 102, 107, 109,
   144ff, 152, 155, **158ff,** 163
monastic initiation, 84, 85, 134-5
Moses, 51, 71
Mouroux, J, 74n
'mystery', **64ff,** 70, 72, 78, 84, 115
   St Paul's concept of, **60ff,** 69, 78
   Greek concept of, **61ff,** 69, 78
   and sacramental order, **87ff**
   of Christ, 64ff
   of the Church, 43, 46, **58ff**
   of God's love, 27, 44, **56ff**
   revealed in Christ, 32, 59
   of salvation, 63
   Paschal, *see* Paschal mystery
mystery religions, the, 62-3, 74n
myth, 3, 9, 115
   and the Passion, 4n
   and magic, 4n, 9
   and rite, 9

natale martyrum, 87
natale sanctorum, 88
nature religions, 6, 62
nature, sacredness of, 7
naturalism, danger of, 7
Nestorian rite, the, 181, **182**
Noah, 71

Octateuch, the, 47
Odes of Solomon, the, 107
Offertory, the, 142
Office, the, 35, 36, 48, 52, 79, **93ff,** 102
   105, 107, 109, 132, **143ff,** 152
oil, 79, **81-2,** 118, **121-1,** 131
Old Testament lectionary, 105
orantes, gesture of, 116
Orate Fratres (Worship), 173
Order, sacrament of, 43, 85
   power of, 51
   liturgy of, **135-7**

Orders, in the Church, **50ff**
Ordination, ceremony of, 118
Ordines Romani, 157, 159-60, 169
Ordo Romanus Primus, 155
Origen, 144
Otto, R, 12n

processions, 141
prophets, 72, 129
prostration, 116, 136
Protestantism, 110
Psalms, the, 107, 123, 140
Psalmody, **105ff**, 138
Psalter, the, 94, 107, 130, 145

pagan mysteries, 58, 61
Palm Sunday, 137
'parables'
    God's way of communicating with men, **28ff**
    the Church a p. of the kingdom, 45
Parochial Liturgical Movement, the, 171
parousia, 72, 73, 120, 125
Parsch, P, 172
Pasch, the, 52, 72, 74, **76ff**, 80, 82, 83, 88, 132
Paschal mystery, the, 30, **74ff, 78**, 79, 88, 92, 94, 120
Paschal candle, 11
Paschal *triduum*, 114
patriarch, 82
Paul IV, Pope, 168
penance, sacrament of, 81, 85, 118, **129ff**
penitential fasts, 129
    rites, 130
Pentecost, 51, **72**, 83, 91
People of God, the, 27, 31
Pépin the Short, 156, 178
Peterson, E, 49n
pilgrimages, 165
Pius X, Pope, 94, 145, 171
Pius XII, 54n, 118, 136, 171
Pontifical, the, 87, 167, 169
porrectio, 135
prayer, 63,
    liturgical prayer, **110ff**
    attitude for, **115ff**
    as penance, 130
    for the dying, 132
Preface, the, **111**
Prémontré, Abbey of, 164, 165
presbyterium, 54
priesthood,
    Aaronic, 51, 52, 137, 141
    Levitical, 52
    of Christian people, 53-4
    apostolic nature of, 136-7
    of Christ, *see* Christ

Quikeborn, 172

Radbertus, Paschasius, 78
realities, earthly and divine, 67-8
reform, 102, 105, 109
reform of Roman Curia, **162-7**
Régamey, P, 16
relics, 165
religious orders, liturgy of, 132-3
Renaissance, the, 115
responsories, 108
revelation, 68-70
    biblical, 27, 28, 120, 129, 131
rites, 84, **114ff**
    Easter, 12
    of agrarian religions, 19, 63
    diversity of in the Church, **45ff**, 53, 81, 85
    sacrificial r. of Old Testament, 52
    pagan, 58, 62
    received from Christ, 63
    theology of Christian, 66, 79-83
    are mysteries, 83
    of purification, 120
    see also blessings, consecrations, dedications; liturgy, Christian liturgy; saints ;
        sacramental rites, *see* each sacrament rites of various Churches and localities, *see* Coptic, Egyptian, Byzantine etc.
ritual prescriptions, 47, 167ff
Roguet, P, 64n
rogation processions, 137
Roman Curia, reform of, **162ff**
Roman Martyrology, the, 105, **169ff**
Romano-Frankish rite, the, 122, 123, 140, 155, **158ff, 178-9**
Romano-Germanic Pontifical, the, 160
Roman Ritual, the, 36, 48, 87, 132, 137, 169

Roman rite, the, 52, 86, 94, 104, 119
  introit in, 36
  liturgy of, 46, 91, **110ff**
  Sunday liturgy of, 50, 93, 101, 103
  Paschal liturgy of, 80, 91
  Epiphany cycle in, 92
  Divine Office in, 93-4, 102, 107, **143-7**
  liturgical lectionary of, **102ff**
  singing of Gospel in, 105
  psalmody in, **105ff**
  collect in, 112
  ordination in, 118, 135
  baptism in, 127
  confirmation in, 128
  Lenten fast in, 130
  sacrament of the sick in, 131
  dedication of Churches in, 138
  historical development of, **148-173**
Rome, ancient, 20
  influence of ceremonial of on Christianity, 117, 122, 127, 134, 152
Rosary, the, 146
rubrics, 46, 102

sacrament, 58, 73, 78, **84ff**
  and liturgical mystery, **64ff**
  classical theology of, 64ff, 131
  liturgy of, 79
  of Christ, 86, 126
  of the Church, 86, 126
  see also baptism, matrimony etc.
sacrament of the sick, 43, 85, 118, 122, **131-3**
sacramental gesture, 115, **117ff**
sacramentals, 44, 48, 59, 66, **85-87**, 126
sacramentalism, 6, 64, 8off, **120ff**
sacramental order, 83ff, 87
sacramental structure of the Church, 43
sacred, the, **12ff**
St Ambrose, 109, 151, 181
St Augustine, 37, 64, 152
St Boniface, 178
St Benedict, 94, 109
St Charles Borromeo, 177
St Clement of Rome, 51
St Germanus of Paris, 178
St Gregory, 88, 104, **153ff**
St Ignatius of Antioch, 51, 98
St Irenaeus, 70
St Isidore, 65
St John Chrysostom, 134

St Justin, 101
St Paul, 71, 77, 79, 127, 184
  his concept of mystery, **6off**
St Thomas Aquinas, sacramental theology of, 64ff, 67, 73
St John's Abbey, 172
saints, veneration of, 59, 88, 112, 123
  legends of, 90
  liturgy of, *see* sanctoral cycle
salt, 127
salvation,
  history of, **7off**, 80
  mystery of, 79, 86, 91, 120
  plan of, 40, 78, 84, 111, 125
sanctoral cycle, the, **87ff**, 147, 165, 166, 168
sanctuary, service of, 51
Sarum rite, the, 179
Scripture, 85, 91, **101ff**, 107-8, 131, 136, 168, 172, *see also* revelation
Second Council of Nicæa, the, 123
sermon, the, 102
sign, concept of in theology of sacrament, 65, 84, 130, 131
sign of the Cross, the, 127
sin, 57
  Sinai, 30, 37, 47, 69, 76
singing, 36, 51, 74n, 101, **105ff**, 114, 141, 144
Society of St Gregory, the, 172
Solesmes, Abbey of, 171
sub-deacon, 105, 135
Sunday, 93
  collect of, 94
  vigil, 94, 144
  cycle, 103
  see also Roman rite, Byzantine rite etc.
symbolism, 8ff, 29, 92, 94
  and allegory, 11
  of material things in liturgy, 11, **119ff**, 126, 127
  of rites, 50, 62, **8off**, 129, 163
synagogue, liturgy of, *see* Judaism,
Syrian rite, the, 103, 123, 128, 129, 143, 150, 175
  psalmody in, 107, 108, 113
Syro-Aramean rite, **179**

Teaching of the Apostles, the, 47
Temple, the, 50, 51, 101
  Solomon's, 14, 15, 29, 31
  and Christ, 15

Temple, the—*cont.*
the Body of Christ, 27, 29, 31, 123, 139
in Old Testament, 31, 106
and Israel, 31
in St Paul, 32
temporal cycle of the Church, the, 59, 79, **88, 91**
time, 8, 23, 57, **58ff,** 75, 80, 89, 91, 94, 146
the end of, 33
Christ triumphed over, 49
theology of, 64, **69-74,** 82, 92
totalitarian regimes, political worship of, 18, 20
troparion, 108

Vernacular Society, the, 172
Vespers, 147

viaticum, 132
Visigothic Spain, rite of, 109, 156, 158, **176-7**
Vonier, Dom, 73n

water, 10, 79, 80-1, 120-1, 126, 129, 130
Western Church, the, 35, 52, 66, 82, 84, 87, 92, 107, 109, 111, 122, 128
development of liturgy in, **148ff, 175ff**
see also Roman rite, Sarum rite etc.
wine, 10, 79, **82-3, 121-2**
worship, 67, 75, 78, 82, 93
see also liturgy, Christian liturgy
worshipping community, 29, 64, 73
Word, the, 35, 68, 69, 79, 84
at work in the liturgy, 38
in history, **69ff**